Resurrection, Scripture, and Reformed Apologetics

McMaster Divinity College Press
McMaster Theological Studies Series

Defining Issues in Pentecostalism (2008)

Pentecostalism and Globalization (2009)

You Mean I Don't Have to Tithe? (2009)

Baptism (2011)

Resurrection, Scripture, and Reformed Apologetics

A Test for Consistency in Theology and Apologetic Method

Steven D. West

☙PICKWICK *Publications* · Eugene, Oregon

RESURRECTION, SCRIPTURE, AND REFORMED APOLOGETICS
A Test for Consistency in Theology and Apologetic Method

McMaster Theological Studies Series

Copyright © 2012 Steven D. West. All rights reserved. Except for brief quotations in critical publications or reviews, no part of this book may be reproduced in any manner without prior written permission from the publisher. Write: Permissions, Wipf and Stock Publishers, 199 W. 8th Ave., Suite 3, Eugene, OR 97401.

McMaster Divinity College Press
1280 Main Street West
Hamilton, Ontario, Canada
L8S 4K1

Pickwick Publications
An Imprint of Wipf and Stock Publishers
199 W. 8th Av.e, Suite 3
Eugene, OR 97401

www.wipfandstock.com

ISBN 13: 978-1-61097-847-7

Cataloguing-in-Publication data:

West, Steven D.

Resurrection, scripture, and reformed apologetics : a test for consistency in theology and apologetic method / Steven D. West.

McMaster Theological Studies Series

x + 228 pp. ; 23 cm. Includes bibliographical references and index.

ISBN 13: 978-1-61097-847-7

1. Apologetics. 2. Bible—Evidences, authority, etc. I. Title. II. Series.

BT1103 W41 2012

Manufactured in the U.S.A.

*For Charlotte and Brooklyn.
The best part of any work day
is when you come to my office
to play "working with my daddy."*

Contents

Acknowledgments / ix

1 Introduction / 1
2 Evidentialism / 7
3 Reformed Epistemology / 83
4 Presuppositionalism / 134
5 Reformed Apologetics, Theology, and the Bible / 183
6 Conclusion / 209

Bibliography / 215
Index of Names / 225

Acknowledgments

I HAVE BEEN PRIVILEGED to be guided in my studies by professors who are both competent and kind. I knew that Dr. Roger Grainger was going to be an excellent PhD dissertation supervisor when he told me that he regarded the topic for my research proposal with interest and "enthusiasm." I gratefully acknowledge his help and support.

I have learned over the past number of years that without the help of patient administrators I would be hopelessly lost in the necessary evils of formatting, submitting proper paper work, and taking care of a myriad of details. Three individuals who have deeply impressed me with their ability and cheerful patience are Keith Edwards, Deborah Michaud, and Peggy Evans. It is now my privilege to teach at Toronto Baptist Seminary where Keith and Debbie are continually helping me with office matters. Although I do not get to work with Peggy Evans on an ongoing basis, I want to acknowledge that without her help and kind attitude I simply *never* would have been capable of getting my work into an acceptable form. Thank you all for going the administrative extra mile!

I would also like to thank MacDiv, and especially Lois Dow, for accepting this work for publication, and working with me to put this research and argumentation into print. It is my hope that this book can help further understanding and discussion on the subject.

Steven West

1

Introduction

THINK OF A YOUNG person who grows up in the broadly Reformed theological tradition. When the time comes they leave their home, friends, and church to attend university in another city. Growing up they had made a profession of faith, were baptized, and were actively involved in various church ministries. They could be described as "committed" or "faithful" to the Lord. But at university they are exposed to new intellectual challenges to their faith. They meet some adherents of other religions who are kinder, gentler, and more decent than many of the members of the university Christian club. They hear powerful arguments against the existence of God, and every so often they are even met with *ad hominem* attacks, and the evidence for their faith is scorned. Although this experience does not produce a crisis of faith, the young believer does want to find intellectually acceptable answers for these challenges. When they return home for their first reading break, they stop by their pastor's office to discuss these issues.

Now, it is entirely likely that their pastor is a godly individual who has spent years preaching, teaching, administrating, visiting, counseling, and doing all the tasks required by an active ministry. It is also entirely likely that this pastor has had neither the time, interest, nor training to engage the freshest philosophical arguments against the Christian faith. Rather than pretending to be an expert, or dismissing the challenges, or rebuking the believer for their weak faith, the pastor wisely listens, encourages, and then proposes that they read some books on apologetics so that they can continue to discuss these issues as they learn.

The pastor searches for some helpful resources and recognizes that some of the authors of books on apologetics are Reformed thinkers. He orders two books. Both books arrive at the same time, and he begins to read. The first author explains that the best way to approach challenges to the faith is to rely on evidence and logic, and the type of reasoning we use in everyday life. They assert that believers need to use logical arguments to prove that God exists. Once they have established the existence of God, they can advance to historical arguments for the life, death, and resurrection of Jesus Christ. If we can prove that God exists, and that Jesus Christ was resurrected, then the teachings of Christianity are vindicated, and our faith receives intellectual affirmation. The pastor closes the book feeling quite satisfied. It is refreshing to discover that faith and reason are such close allies.

With high expectation the pastor opens the second book. It is also a book on apologetics, written by a Reformed thinker that the pastor knows and trusts theologically. This book begins by arguing that the apologetic system endorsed by the first book is a complete failure. It vigorously states that all the traditional arguments that are supposed to prove the existence of God contain significant fallacies and that no amount of historical evidence can prove that a miracle like the resurrection actually occurred. Rather than trying to build up a case for Christianity point by point, the proper apologetic method presupposes the entire Christian worldview, and then argues that without Christianity being true, nothing in life, thought, or experience can make sense. The believer is to understand the unbeliever's worldview, and then show them where their non-Christian worldview suffers from contradiction or incoherence. After finishing this particular book, the pastor is feeling far less satisfied than before; which author was right?

The whole goal of this exercise was just to help the young congregant get through university. All that the pastor desired was to find honest answers to difficult questions. Now however the pastor feels less equipped to be of assistance than before reading the books. Regrettably, the experience is about to get worse. Spending time reading articles on the internet reveals a third position called Reformed epistemology. Now, besides the subdivisions in each main position, the pastor has three apologetic systems to study, each of which lays claim to being in continuity with the Reformed tradition. Instead of discovering straightforward answers to philosophical questions, the pastor has discovered a complicated, specialized world of apologetic discourse. The net result is less certainty than ever before about the best way to defend the faith.

It can be very surprising (not to mention initially rather frustrating) to discover that there is so much diversity in Reformed apologetics, and occasionally more than a little acrimony between Reformed apologists. The three main methodologies are evidentialism, Reformed epistemology, and presuppositionalism. Each of these schools of thought has adherents who attempt to demonstrate the coherence of their apologetic, epistemology, and theology, as well as to tie themselves to the historic Reformed theological tradition.[1] In other words, there is a self-conscious desire amongst these apologists to be consistently Reformed in theology, to show that they really do stand in the historic Reformed tradition, and to prove that their philosophical arguments are compatible with their theological and doctrinal commitments.

The main argument of this book is that it is possible to identify the apologetic method that is most consistent with the historical confessional distinctives of the Reformed tradition. This can be done by examining the relationship between two exceptionally important apologetic issues. The first is the resurrection of Jesus Christ, and the second is the Bible as the Word of God.

I take the resurrection of Jesus Christ as a test case for apologetic methodologies. The historical case for the resurrection, and the location of that case in the apologist's system, is critical for an understanding of the function that evidence, logic, historical argument, and the doctrine of Scripture play in a given apologetic method. In the concreteness of the resurrection, various theoretical and philosophical strands are brought together and illustrated by a particular example. In any apologetic method, the utility of the case for the resurrection reveals a whole underlying network of worldview beliefs. As a result, it is essential to this study that the apologetic methods be set forth and critiqued as total systems. The overarching frameworks of the methodologies must be clearly perceived in order that the doctrines of the resurrection and Scripture will be seen to fit in them either coherently or dissonantly.

---

1. Classical apologetics, or evidentialism, is far more widely distributed in Christianity than just the Reformed circle. As will be seen, there is no discernible difference between Reformed and non-Reformed evidential cases for the resurrection.

Resurrection, Scripture, and Reformed Apologetics

The historicity of the resurrection of Jesus Christ from the dead has been the subject of a number of important recent publications.[2] Arguing historically for Christ's resurrection is an integral part of the evidential apologetic method, whether this argument stands as the second step after classical proofs are used to demonstrate the validity (or necessity) of a theistic universe, or whether it is the first step towards demonstrating that only theism can account for the historical data of the resurrection event. While presuppositionalists and Reformed epistemologists value historical Christian evidences, they locate historical arguments differently in their methodologies than do evidentialists, and they are far more skeptical concerning the coercive power of the historical argument. This is made clear in a published exchange between the different apologetic camps.[3]

The major apologetic questions revolving around the Bible as the Word of God are particularly acute in Reformed circles, which traditionally have affirmed *sola scriptura*, and had a high view of inspiration and inerrancy. Traditional evidential approaches attempt to move logically from the resurrection as a vindication of Jesus' teachings to Jesus' teachings as a vindication of Scripture as God's Word.[4] In this manner, defending the Bible as the Word of God is preceded by a defense of the resurrection (which may be preceded by a defense of theism apart from Christian evidences). For a variety of reasons, presuppositionalists and Reformed epistemologists reject this tactic. The decision about how to defend the doctrine of Scripture in an apologetic system is crucial. Should the apologist labor to demonstrate that theism is true, and then endeavor to demonstrate that the resurrection is a historically valid fact, and then logically try to argue from those premises to an infallible canon of Scripture? It is extremely important to understand the proper relationship that the doctrine of the resurrection and the doctrine of Scripture should sustain to each other in an apologetic methodology. The main argument of this book is that the Reformed apologetic method that is most coherently able to relate these two doctrines is the one that should be chosen by Reformed believers. We can make progress past the current impasses if we carefully analyze the topic with this focal point.

2. Davis, *Risen Indeed*; Craig, *The Son Rises*; Habermas and Licona, *Case for the Resurrection*; Wright, *Resurrection of the Son of God*.

3. Cowan, ed. *Five Views on Apologetics*.

4. Geisler, *Christian Apologetics*; Montgomery, *Where is History Going?*; Sproul, *Defending Your Faith*.

Introduction

It is readily acknowledged that not every individual in Reformed circles believes that the Bible is infallible or inerrant (I will use the terms as rough synonyms). It is also acknowledged, by those honest enough to be fair with history, that even if they disagree with a strong doctrine of inerrancy, such a strong commitment was the historical position in Protestant theology.[5] Today there are many who wish to reject this historical position on the Scriptures, but there are also many who wish to retain it. For those in the latter camp, relating their high view of Scripture coherently in their systematic theology and apologetic methodology is essential. If they want to affirm full inerrancy, they must choose a method of defending the faith that will bear the weight of that doctrinal formulation. A defense of the theological formulation of inerrancy will not be provided in this study, since it would encompass too much additional argumentation.[6] It will be assumed descriptively that there are those who wish to accept and defend inerrancy, and the apologetic methods will be tested to determine which methodology is most consistent with this theological position.

I believe that it is possible to identify the apologetic method that is most consistent with Reformed theology and philosophy, and that this will be demonstrable through a study of the relationship between the doctrines of Scripture and the resurrection in Reformed apologetic methodologies. The main issue here will be whether or not the totality of the system of defense, and that which it seeks to defend, are integrally related in a non-contradictory and logically cohesive fashion. My concern is determining which apologetic method is best suited to defending the conservative Reformed doctrinal understanding of the Scriptures as inspired and inerrant.

The next three chapters (and especially the next one) will contain a fair amount of description. It is important that the three apologetic methodologies be understood on their own terms, and the best way to do this is to pay careful attention to the actual arguments of their leading proponents. Chapter 2 will be the longest chapter, and the most descriptive, because it will set the stage for the entire book by expositing the best contemporary cases for the resurrection of Jesus Christ, as well as examining

---

5. Pinnock and Callen, *Scripture Principle*.

6. For theological treatments of Scripture that endorse such a perspective, see Carson, *Collected Writings on Scripture*; Frame, *The Doctrine of the Word of God*; Carson and Woodbridge, eds., *Scripture and Truth*; Montgomery, ed., *God's Inerrant Word*; Stonehouse and Woolley, eds., *Infallible Word*.

the evidential apologetic methodology. This double duty is necessary in order to see the practical, concrete strength of the historical case for the resurrection, as well as to see the theoretical strength evidentialists assign to this case in their wider apologetic systems. Chapters 3 and 4 will examine Reformed epistemology and presuppositionalism respectively, again with a particular focus on how they relate the resurrection to the doctrine of Scripture. The fifth chapter will contain more analysis than description, as the apologetic methods will be examined to see which offers the most cogent defense of the faith.

2

Evidentialism

INTRODUCTION

THE FIRST SECTION OF this chapter will summarize the particular historical cases for the resurrection of Jesus Christ as argued by leading contemporary Christian philosophers and apologists today. These thinkers were selected for their recognized scholarship in this area, as well as for making unique and nuanced contributions to the field. They represent the cutting edge of current Christian scholarship in favor of the historical resurrection of Jesus from the dead. In order to clearly allow the authors to have their own voices, interaction with other sources will be kept to a minimum when their particular positions are sketched. This should provide for clarity, while still making room for some limited but necessary points of clarification. After examining work on the resurrection by Richard Swinburne, N. T. Wright, and the team of Gary Habermas and Michael Licona—all of whom argue in favor of the resurrection—I will survey a case against the resurrection from the atheist philosopher Michael Martin. After these cases have been examined, the next section is concerned with a priori considerations surrounding the miraculous. If miracles cannot happen, then it naturally and clearly follows that they do not happen. Thus, depending on the nature of the case, an investigation into whether or not a miracle occurred may literally be an investigation into the impossible. Yet even if miracles are possible, there may be reasons for thinking that they are so improbable that every miracle claim should be dismissed. In other words, the historical data in favor of the resurrection may be excellent, and yet still not be strong enough to warrant belief in the resurrection, depending on how low the probability (or even possibility) of a miracle such as the resurrection occurring happens to be.

Following the discussion of a priori considerations for the miraculous, we will examine the evidential case for the inerrancy of Scripture. How do these doctrines relate, and what steps do the apologists take to defend inerrancy? After these arguments are presented, we will examine the larger apologetic system for internal cogency. This section is relatively brief, since the following two chapters will present the critiques of these approaches that come from the Reformed epistemologists and the presuppositionalists. In many ways—as will quickly become evident—segments of this chapter are largely descriptive. As the chapter develops, however, there will be a "thickening" of interaction. In other words, the descriptive element will be slowly merged into a more prescriptive analysis. For the argument of this book to succeed, it is vital for there to be a common background understanding of what the historical case for the resurrection looks like in contemporary scholarship. In order to avoid misunderstandings in critique, it is first imperative to outline what the evidence actually *is* for the resurrection.

While the section immediately following is largely summative, it is important to identify the current status of historical argumentation concerning the resurrection; after all, if the historical case is airtight, then this will have obvious implications for all apologists, not just those who operate theologically out of a Reformed position. And if the historical case is impossible to make, or is highly improbable, then this will also have obvious implications for defending the Christian faith. The first items to investigate, therefore, are the particulars of the historical argument for the resurrection of Jesus Christ.

EVIDENTIAL CASES FOR AND AGAINST THE RESURRECTION

Richard Swinburne

Swinburne has used the Bayesian probability calculus throughout his philosophical career to argue for the existence of God.[1] In *The Resurrection of God Incarnate* he turns again to the probability calculus to argue for the

---

1. For his fullest use of Bayesian formulations to prove theism, see Swinburne, *Existence of God*.

resurrection of Jesus Christ as a historical event.[2] The formalization of Swinburne's argument in mathematical notation is left to his appendix,[3] but the probabilistic approach is articulated in philosophically informal terms throughout the entire book. Swinburne argues that knowing whether or not the resurrection of Jesus Christ truly happened as a historical event requires examining both a priori and a posteriori factors. Probabilities cannot be assigned apart from particular historical data and a priori philosophical reflection.

Swinburne presents a thesis summary near the beginning of his book:

> I shall argue that, in so far as the evidence is against the claim that there is such a God, then the occurrence of such an event as the Resurrection is improbable. If the evidence suggests that there is such a God, then it will give some probability to the occurrence of such a miracle in so far as God has reason to bring about such an event. I shall argue that he does have such reason.[4]

Here Swinburne clearly articulates his position concerning the location of the argument for the resurrection in a theistic philosophical system. The probability of the resurrection is directly tied to the probability of the existence of God. If the evidence for the existence of God is high, the probability of an event like the resurrection increases, if it can be seen that God has a reason for performing an act such as a resurrection. If on background knowledge, however, God's existence is deemed improbable, then the resurrection as a historical fact becomes improbable as well. Clearly Swinburne is alerting his readers right away that he does not believe that the historicity of the resurrection can be made probable on the basis of historical considerations alone. It must be tied to other evidence for the existence of God.

This places Swinburne in one particular historical stream of apologetics. Colin Brown, in his comprehensive study on the historical development of the concept of miracle and its relationship to reason, identifies the tendency for fluctuation in what apologists thought miracles could establish:

---

2. This section is going to survey Swinburne's argument in *Resurrection of God Incarnate*.
3. Ibid., 204–16.
4. Ibid., 2.

> From time to time miracles have been seen as clear-cut proof of God's hand in history unambiguously underwriting the truth-claims of the faith. At such times apologists have taken the offensive, and have built miracles into the foundation of their apologetic systems. But at other times apologists have been pushed onto the defensive, and have appeared to some to be almost apologizing for their belief in miracles. At such times apologists have argued that miracles are credible against the background of certain beliefs about God and his purposes. When this occurs, miracles have been removed from the foundation of the edifice and have become the copestone of faith.[5]

Swinburne is in the camp of those who place miracles against background beliefs. Furthermore he is, according to the typology I will use, a classical evidentialist, rather than an *evidentialist.[6]

Does God exist? If God does exist, does he have a reason to perform an action like the resurrection? After these two questions are considered, the next question, according to Swinburne,[7] is whether or not Jesus of Nazareth would seem to be the sort of person that God would want to make the subject of the resurrection event. He labels it "a serious mistake" to examine data for the resurrection while excluding an investigation of the life and teachings of Jesus. The claim, after all, is not that any individual was raised in the first third of the first century, but rather that one particular individual, Jesus of Nazareth, was raised. Thus the resurrection event is not properly treated if it is considered in a theological or historical vacuum. The a posteriori claim is not for a more general categorization of miracle (i.e., has any individual been resurrected?), but for a particular case where the historical likelihood for the resurrection

---

5. Brown, *Miracles and the Critical Mind*, 3.

6. At times I will place the symbol * before "evidential" or "evidentialist" or cognates, to indicate that the apologetic is representative of an approach that does not start with establishing theism in order to argue for the miraculous; rather, *evidentialism begins with the historicity of the miraculous in order to argue for theism. The approach that establishes theism first will be termed classical apologetics, and the approach that starts with miracles *evidentialism. This is due to the confusion that exists sometimes in the naked word *evidentialism*, given that it can apply to both classical apologetics and *evidential apologetics depending on the context. Where differentiation is desirable, * will be inserted to indicate the narrower classification. Really *evidentialism is a subcategory of evidentialism (as is classical apologetics, even though classical and evidential are often used interchangeably).

7. Swinburne, *Resurrection of God Incarnate*, 3.

of the individual is inseparably bound together with his life before death, and not just with attempting to prove that he experienced resurrection life after death. Whether or not God would have reason to raise this particular man from the dead is a necessary way of framing the discussion for Swinburne as he develops his case.

Any attempt to reach a conclusion about the resurrection that fails to take into account all relevant background knowledge (such as the existence of the universe, scientific regularity, etc.) and merely tries to argue straightforwardly for or against the historicity of the resurrection is, according to Swinburne, "highly irrational," [8] because it leaves to the side 95 percent of the relevant information needed to form a rational opinion on whether or not the resurrection occurred.[9] This is because one cannot decide on the strength of the detailed historical evidence surrounding the resurrection without deciding on the prior odds of this being the sort of universe where a resurrection is in fact possible. Theological persuasion (or lack thereof) plays a large, though often unacknowledged, role in the evaluation of historical data.

For the present discussion, Swinburne assumes the scientific regularity of the universe and the existence of God as a priori givens for his analysis of the historical case for the resurrection. These a priori considerations are not strictly abstract or logically necessary, but are reached on the basis of argumentation. Since his book on the resurrection is much more narrowly focused in its subject matter, however, Swinburne assumes rather than argues for this theistic background, and goes on to set forth three types of evidence that are utilized in constructing a detailed historical case. They are memory beliefs, testimony joined with the principle of credulity, and physical traces.[10] Simply put, we are forced to rely on our own memories (even though we recognize they are fallible, and more apt to accurately recall some events than others); we are forced as a general principle in life to trust the testimony of others; and sometimes physical traces are discovered after empirical investigation, such as when a detective discovers fingerprints at a crime scene.[11] A theory that has an explanatory scope capable of accommodating all the relevant data,

8. Ibid.
9. Cf. Pannenberg, *Jesus—God and Man*, 73.
10. Swinburne, *Resurrection of God Incarnate*, 10–15.
11. Swinburne made the same points, albeit in briefer form, in "Evidence for the Resurrection," 192–94.

combined with the highest degree of simplicity is, all things considered, the rational choice for plausible historical reconstruction.[12] Theories suffer when they become unwieldy and complicated. If a simpler or more elegant theory has a sufficient explanatory scope, alternative theories that are unnecessarily complex, or theories with multiplied contingencies, are not to be preferred instead. Although it is not difficult to imagine a scenario in which a more complicated explanation is true and a simpler one is false, the principle of Occam's Razor is a very useful tool, and notwithstanding exceptions, simplicity is a useful criterion.

What happens at times in historical or scientific investigation, however, is that detailed evidence seems to conflict with accepted background evidence or a particular paradigm.[13] For Swinburne, "the most interesting clashes of evidence, for our purposes, occur when detailed historical evidence points to something which background evidence suggests is most unlikely to have occurred."[14] This is where the critical discussion on the probability of God's existence comes roaring in with full force. After examining the definitions of miracles and laws of nature, Swinburne notes that miracles are related to natural laws in such a way that, if natural laws exist as ultimate, they cannot be violated (i.e., miracles cannot occur), but if natural laws exist dependently (i.e., they are sustained and operationally dependent on a higher source), then miracles can occur.[15] Background knowledge and a priori considerations are not to be excluded from the discussion.

This is because, for Swinburne, one arrives at two different conclusions concerning the historicity of the resurrection depending on what one accepts as genuine background knowledge. He argues that the detailed historical evidence in favor of the resurrection is quite good, but it "is not strong enough to equal the very strong force of the background evidence—if the latter is construed only as evidence of what are the laws of nature."[16] Swinburne does not construe the evidence this way, of course; he argues that the background evidence makes the existence of God much more probable than not. Rather than providing details, he

---

12. Swinburne, *Resurrection of God Incarnate*, 15.

13. For a famous exposition of this phenomenon in relation to science, see Kuhn, *Structure of Scientific Revolutions*.

14. Swinburne, *Resurrection of God Incarnate*, 16.

15. Ibid., 25.

16. Ibid., 30.

directs his readers in a footnote to some of his previous works where he makes this case.[17] But the main point is that one's reading and analysis of the background evidence will either bear heavily on, or completely determine, one's evaluation of the possibility or impossibility of the resurrection occurring as a historical fact. Just to move the argument along, and to avoid getting bogged down, Swinburne places the probability of God's existence at as likely as not, which as a Bayesian numerical is 0.5.[18] This move leaves the question of theism open. It allows for the historical data to receive a hearing, while merely granting that God may exist (or that the odds of his existence are as likely as not).

Swinburne then proceeds to ask whether or not God would have reason to become incarnate. He believes that God does in fact have reasons for the incarnation. Three reasons are identified: "to provide a measure of reconciliation with God for a broken relationship, to identify with our suffering, and to show and teach us how to live and encourage us to do so."[19] If these are a priori reasons for God to become incarnate, then it would also seem rational to expect that God's incarnate life would have certain distinguishing characteristics. Swinburne believes that such a life would have five marks:

> If God is to become incarnate in order to fulfil all the purposes for becoming incarnate listed in Chapter 2, we would expect his life to show these five marks. His life must be, as far as we can judge, a perfect human life in which he provides healing; he must teach deep moral and theological truths (ones, in so far as we can judge, plausibly true); he must show himself to believe that he is God Incarnate; he must teach that his life provides an atonement for our sins; and he must found a church which continues his teaching and work.[20]

In order to prevent a mistake being made concerning whether or not an individual's life could plausibly be considered the life belonging

---

17. Ibid., 30–31 n. 12. The most important work he identifies is his *Existence of God*.

18. Swinburne, *Resurrection of God Incarnate*, 31.

19. Ibid., 37.

20. Ibid., 59. In my judgment these criteria seem suspiciously ad hoc or more a posteriori than a priori. Yet it would be impossible to be exposed for any significant length of time to Christian teaching about the incarnation, and after having imbibed it, to then try to reflect on what a priori reasons God would have for becoming incarnate. It could also be argued that only through the incarnation could we learn why the incarnation was necessary.

to God incarnate, Swinburne argues that it would be expected that God would authenticate such a life by the performance of a super-miracle (i.e., an event so impressive it would stand as a divine signature at the end of the life).[21] The resurrection qualifies as such a super-miracle. Swinburne maintains that it would be very unlikely for there ever to be a life that contained these five marks and also ended in a super-miracle. If it were to be found that such a life was lived, and that such a super-miracle stood as the climactic event to that life, then one could reasonably conclude that, given the background evidence, this was the life of God incarnate.[22]

To what sources can we turn in order to investigate the type of life Jesus lived? Swinburne acknowledges there are different sources: "But the fact remains that by far the most important evidence is contained in the books of the New Testament. So much is going to depend on what we judge the conventions of genre, the trustworthiness of the authors, and sources of those books to be."[23] His position is that the Gospels are clearly trying to tell history, and that Matthew and Luke, who depended on Mark's Gospel, understood Mark to be depicting historical events.[24] In the case of John's Gospel, Swinburne is happy to acknowledge that John is not always interested in historical events *per se*, and that oftentimes John uses symbolism to make a theological point. Such symbolism can be identified, however, as being markedly different from a straightforward depiction of historical facts.[25] When it comes to reading John, "John's Gospel must be used with care, but it is a historical source."[26]

Because of the way that information was transmitted in the ancient world, Swinburne concedes that it was almost inevitable for discrepancies to be introduced into the biblical accounts.[27] This does not mean, however, that such minor discrepancies are capable of overthrowing all historical credibility when it comes to the New Testament writings. Certainly many ancient historical works contain errors, but this does not lead scholars to jettison them entirely, or to banish them as being utterly

---

21. Ibid., 62.
22. Ibid., 64.
23. Ibid., 69.
24. Ibid., 73.
25. Ibid., 74.
26. Ibid., 81.
27. Ibid., 82.

unreliable. Even today it is difficult to imagine historians being willing to have their work either accepted as perfect or completely rejected. For Swinburne, the important factor is not the minor discrepancies in the Gospels, but the common consensus the writers display on the main framework of Jesus' life.[28] It is the major agreement and not the deviation on minor details that should be highlighted when it comes to weighing historical reliability.

Swinburne fleshes out his argument by examining his requirements one by one:

> The first requirement for Jesus to be God Incarnate is that the life of Jesus should have been a perfect human life—a life which we can offer instead of our own life as our reparation for sin and a life which showed us how to live—and that he should have provided deep moral teaching. The evidence for the holiness of another person's life can, of course, come only from their public behaviour. But I suggest that such evidence as there is of Jesus' public behaviour is such as one would expect if he led a perfect human life.[29]

Again, this seems perhaps a little ad hoc. It seems doubtful that if every person had to envision what a perfect human life would look like, they would describe the lifestyle and teachings of Jesus. Rather, it is possible to look back on the life of Jesus, and say that his life showed what a perfect human life would be like in that culture and time. Thus it may be more accurate to say that Jesus demonstrates—indeed, transforms—the human understanding of a perfect life. Swinburne states that Jesus' public behavior is what we should expect it to be; on the contrary, certainly even Jesus' disciples were not expecting Jesus to act as he did. Neither were the crowds, the religious leaders, or his own family.

For Swinburne this does not mean that everything Jesus did will seem morally exemplary to us, or that we will understand everything that he taught. What it does mean is that Jesus' life was surrounded by sober accounts of historical miracles, he offered deep teaching, and although there is some moral ambiguity surrounding some of the accounts of his life, such incidents are rare, and can be accounted for through logical argument, or simply chalked up to our own moral misunderstandings.[30]

28. Ibid., 76.
29. Ibid., 83.
30. Ibid., 85–95.

Judaism was not expecting the Messiah to provide a higher moral code than was being observed by the best citizens; but the early Christians taught that Jesus did in fact provide such an elevated ethical standard, and such teaching in the early church is only understandable on the basis of the historical fact that they followed what Jesus actually instructed.[31]

Swinburne goes on to argue that Jesus did make claims to deity (i.e., that he really was God incarnate), but he had to do so in implicit ways during his lifetime, since prior to the christological formulation of Chalcedon, Christ could not have simply declared that he was God without causing confusion in his listeners.[32] After his resurrection, however, there were retrospective clues that pointed to such a self-understanding. Jesus was worshiped as God and did not reject it (even, for example, when Thomas stated to him in direct vocative address "My Lord and my God" [John 20:28]). His opponents thought he blasphemed by taking divine prerogatives, and Jesus did not correct them by saying he was not worthy of such ascriptions.[33] Later, the New Testament writers shared the conviction that Jesus was God incarnate. One of the fascinating elements of this confession was that Judaism had no expectation of God becoming incarnate. (Isaiah 9:5 or Micah 5:1–2 may be taken as prophetic of God incarnate, but this was not a conscious expectation; it may have been present, but was unrecognized.) The early Christians did not see Jesus as God incarnate through the lens of an anticipated eschatological happening.[34] Swinburne thinks that Jesus did not leave as many or as powerful clues as he might have, but what he did leave was sufficient to draw the identification of Jesus of Nazareth with God incarnate.[35]

Swinburne continues by arguing that Jesus fulfilled the expected marks of God incarnate by publicly teaching that his life was an atonement for sin.[36] After citing biblical data to support this claim—including Jesus' teaching at the Last Supper—Swinburne quickly moves on to his final mark. He writes:

---

31. Ibid., 96.
32. Ibid., 98.
33. Ibid., 98–111.
34. Ibid., 115.
35. Ibid., 116.
36. Ibid., 117–26.

> My final requirement for Jesus being God Incarnate is that he should found a church which would provide God's forgiveness to repentant sinners and which would hand on his teaching, including his teaching about his own atoning work and what he implied about his divinity.[37]

The historical facts surrounding this mark are among the easiest to identify, given the existence of the church today. The church's own teaching on the doctrine of ecclesiology is that this is precisely what Jesus did, and why the church has existed through time and continues to exist today.[38]

Swinburne concludes his study of the prior historical marks of God incarnate with the following analysis: "Jesus satisfies not too badly and far better than any other figure in history the prior historical criteria for being God Incarnate, and so for being the person on whose life and teaching God would put his signature in the form of a super-miracle."[39] Having thus laid out his prior case of expectations for God incarnate, and compared them to the life of Jesus, Swinburne next turns to the posterior historical evidence.

He begins this new section in his book by asserting:

> If Jesus rose bodily from the dead and wished his Church to know about it, two things are to be expected: first, that it would seem to his Church (which meant paradigmatically the Eleven remaining from the Twelve after the betrayal of Judas) that they saw and talked to him; and secondly, that the tomb should be empty.[40]

Swinburne fleshes out this section by examining the accounts of Jesus' appearances, the evidence that the tomb was in fact empty, and rival explanatory accounts for what may have happened.

These two factors mentioned by Swinburne (i.e., the post-resurrection appearances and the empty tomb) are the hallmarks of the historical case for the resurrection. Combining the empty tomb and the resurrection appearances of Jesus is commonplace amongst apologists.[41] A third factor (i.e., the rise of the church and belief in the resurrection) can be

---

37. Ibid., 127.
38. Ibid., 127–40.
39. Ibid., 141.
40. Ibid., 145.
41. As the following sections dealing with the work of Gary Habermas and Michael Licona, as well as N. T. Wright, will show; cf. Carnely, *Structure of Resurrection Belief*, 39.

added as well.[42] The triadic arrangement is used by William Lane Craig: "The historical evidence for the resurrection of Jesus consists primarily in the evidence supporting three main facts: the empty tomb of Jesus, the appearances of Jesus to his disciples, and the origin of the Christian faith."[43] These elements are not merely the philosophical and historical lines of argumentation drawn by apologists; they are found at the beginning of the church: "The Easter traditions of primitive Christianity divide into two different strands: the traditions about appearances of the resurrected Lord, and the traditions about the discovery of Jesus' empty grave."[44]

First, Swinburne turns his attention to the accounts of Jesus' appearances. He argues that the New Testament explicitly and forcefully grounds belief in Jesus in his resurrection appearances.[45] There is no reason to dispute this claim, so the real issue is whether or not there are discrepancies or prevailing examples of counter-evidence to overturn the validity of these claims.[46] Swinburne argues that 1 Corinthians 15 provides the earliest creedal statement concerning the resurrection, and that everything known about Paul from the non-disputed Pauline corpus of epistles indicates that Paul was sincere in his beliefs. It could be argued that Paul was mistaken or deluded, but not that he was insincere. Paul attests to his faith in the resurrection creed, and he attests that this was the faith of the early pillars of the church. If Paul confessed his faith in the post-resurrection appearances, and claims that Peter, James, and others also believed that Jesus had appeared to them, then Swinburne believes Paul can be trusted to honestly and accurately convey his own beliefs on the matter, and to reliably transmit the beliefs of those he mentioned.[47] Thus it is extremely unlikely that Paul was mistaken about their beliefs, and even if he was, Paul was at least sincerely mistaken, and not duplicitous.

Minor discrepancies in the texts are not unexpected to Swinburne. The details in the texts that contain discrepancies are, however, concerning trivial or relatively unimportant details. Such minor conflicts in secondary detail do not detract from the common historical core that is the

---

42. The existence of the church carries tremendous weight in N. T. Wright's argument, as will be seen below.

43. Craig, *The Son Rises*, 45.

44. Pannenberg, *Jesus—God and Man*, 88.

45. Swinburne, *Resurrection of God Incarnate*, 146.

46. Ibid., 147.

47. Ibid., 147–48.

subject of the witnesses' joint testimony.[48] Thus the existence of minor discrepancies in the extant textual witness does not affect Swinburne's view of the posterior historical evidence for the appearances of Jesus. In principle, minor discrepancies do not impugn the account of multiple witnesses. If one witness says they heard a gunshot around 5:45, and another says it was at 6:00, the case for there having been a gunshot is strengthened (excluding complicating contingencies), rather than weakened, since they both testify to one major, memorable event, and are only differing on a secondary, less memorable, and general detail.

What strengthens the case is the fact that the first recorded appearance is to Mary Magdalene. Unless a very strong claim had been made at the earliest time, says Swinburne, the early church simply would not have given her the honor of being designated as the first individual to receive an appearance of the risen Christ.[49] Not only would this honor likely have gone to a male disciple, but there were two other reasons not to have women as prominent witnesses to the risen Christ. The first is that generally women were not considered to be reliable witnesses (which was a very culturally ingrained opinion), and the second is that several of the particular women who followed Jesus would not have been considered to be reliable witnesses, since they had had demons exorcised from them.[50] Whether or not one believes in demon possession, or in exorcism, or that Jesus exorcised demons from these women, the important element here is that such stories are part of the Gospel and church tradition. If stories were going to be fabricated, one would not posit women as witnesses, let alone women of such low morals and godliness that they were actually possessed or oppressed at one time by demonic beings.

To the post-resurrection appearances of Jesus Christ is added, in the second place, the datum that the tomb was declared to be physically empty. This indicates in the strongest of possible terms that the post-resurrection appearances were not spiritual visions, or Jesus appearing in a non-embodied state. Not only that, but it was not even Jesus appearing in a second body, while the first one remained interred. No, the claim was that Jesus' body had been crucified, and this same body had been raised and glorified by God. As a result, the tomb was empty.[51] It "beggars

48. Ibid., 148–54.
49. Ibid., 154.
50. Ibid, 151 n. 13.
51. Ibid., 160.

belief" that the disciples would not have checked the tomb as early as possible after hearing the reports that Jesus was alive, and so the empty tomb was part of their earliest belief.[52]

Swinburne also adds to his case the fact that the first Christians began to worship on Sunday, the first day of the week, although for their entire lifetimes they had been permeated by Sabbath keeping on the seventh day of the week.[53] He had previously included this point as an appendix in his contribution to *The Resurrection*, which was identified by one commentator as a very profound point.[54] The fact that Christians universally began to worship God and celebrate the Eucharist on Sunday indicates quite clearly that the foundational event of the church was understood to have occurred on a Sunday. What was this event? Without any doubt it was the resurrection, or at least the pervasive belief that the resurrection had occurred on the first day of the week.

Before turning his attention to rival theories and accounts of what happened to Jesus, Swinburne makes two more observations. The first is that the disciples were not expecting a resurrection. They did not believe the reports they first heard from the women. They had not understood the Old Testament to teach that the Messiah would die and that subsequently he would be raised from the dead.[55] As such, their resurrection belief cannot be thoughtfully considered to be a case of the disciples convincing themselves that something had happened to Jesus (namely, a resurrection) that they had eagerly been expecting.[56] The second is that Jesus did not appear to all (he did not, for example, appear to all his enemies, or Pilate, etc.). Interestingly, the fact that Jesus did not appear to important figures like Pilate, Herod, Roman senators, or Jewish rulers, but rather appeared to women, was one reason given by first-century philosophers to reject the resurrection.[57] Swinburne explains this on the basis of God a priori not being expected to make his incarnation overwhelmingly obvious. He would have been more subtle, and provided some "epistemic distance" so that human beings could freely choose what sort of life and

---

52. Ibid., 162.

53. Ibid., 163–70.

54. Wilkens, "A Summit Observed," 2. Swinburne's appendix is at the end of his article "Evidence for the Resurrection," 207–12.

55. Swinburne, *Resurrection of God Incarnate*, 170.

56. Ibid., 171.

57. Cook, "Pagan Philosophers and 1 Thessalonians," 518–19.

Evidentialism

character they wanted to lead and form.[58] Since this is how God has acted towards humanity, and since he has endowed human creatures with free will, Swinburne concludes that it would be unexpected for God to dramatically confront those who had already rejected him.[59]

This a priori reflection could, of course, be strenuously challenged by both philosophers and theologians. It is rooted in a species of libertarian freedom that is debatable on philosophical, theological, and biblical grounds. Furthermore, it is quite possible to propose other reasons why God would not make the incarnation overwhelmingly obvious (e.g., human beings could not handle any more of his unshielded glory, or it was simply in the secret purposes of God's sovereign counsel to work in his elect through subtler means than a brash display of power). This is not to say that these other examples are more compelling—or more truthful—than Swinburne's proposal; it is merely to point out that subtlety in the incarnation is not intrinsically tied to one perspective on the relationship between freedom, responsibility, and the human will.

Swinburne does not spend much space talking about the various rival accounts of what might have happened to Jesus (just over ten pages).[60] He believes that all alternatives can be expressed under five headings:

> If Jesus was not raised bodily from the tomb, and yet, as I have argued, the disciples in general believed that he was, what did happen to the body? What alternatives are there and how plausible are they? The possible alternatives can be divided exhaustively into five. I take them in order of (what I judge to be) decreasing improbability.[61]

The five theories are: 1. Jesus did not die on the Cross. 2. The body remained in the tomb. 3. The body was stolen by enemies of Jesus. 4. The body was stolen by grave-robbers. 5. The body was stolen by friends of Jesus.[62]

Ultimately, Swinburne rejects each alternative as historically suspect because they multiply complexities, and must combine unlikely events

---

58. Swinburne, *Resurrection of God Incarnate*, 35–36.
59. Ibid., 171–72.
60. Ibid., 187–98.
61. Ibid., 174.
62. Ibid., 175–84.

into an inflationary implausibility.⁶³ For example, it is possible to imagine that friends of Jesus stole the body, then lied to the disciples, and someone pretended to be Jesus, and convinced them he was alive.⁶⁴ But this multiplies hypotheses, and becomes vastly too complicated (not to mention speculative) to be a serious historical possibility. Combining theories to explain the empty tomb with theories to explain the appearances (e.g., hallucination or mass hysteria leading to mass visions) multiplies the improbability; since both sides of the conjunctive are weak, their combined force is weaker still. This rejection takes place on the basis of historical reconstruction, leaving the background knowledge of the existence of God aside. It is to be remembered, however, that one of Swinburne's main contentions is that a fully thought-out conclusion regarding the likelihood of Jesus really being historically resurrected from the dead cannot afford to exclude an a prior decision on the probability of theism.

At this point Swinburne is prepared to offer some concluding thoughts. He begins by noting: "The Resurrection of Jesus, if it occurred, would constitute a massive violation of natural laws. The coming to full bodily life again of a human dead by normal criteria in such a way as to be able to appear and disappear would clearly be a violation of natural laws which only God could bring about."⁶⁵ Given the life of Jesus, the miracles he performed, and the fact that he claimed his death would be an atonement for sins, Swinburne concludes that his resurrection would constitute God's acceptance of atonement, and vindicate Jesus' life and teachings.⁶⁶ He goes further and concludes that if God were to become incarnate, the life of Jesus is largely what we would expect, and it would be very unlikely that we would find the data concerning Jesus if God were in fact to become incarnate in someone else.⁶⁷ In conclusion, Swinburne states: "If the background evidence leaves it not too improbable that there is a God likely to act in the ways discussed, then the total evidence makes it very probable that Jesus was God Incarnate who rose from the dead."⁶⁸

---

63. Ibid., 185–86.
64. Ibid., 185.
65. Ibid., 187.
66. Ibid., 189–96.
67. Ibid., 202.
68. Ibid., 203.

Evidentialism

Thus ends Swinburne's informal argument for the probability of Jesus' resurrection from the dead. He adds an appendix entitled *Formalizing the Argument*, where he formalizes the argument into Bayesian, mathematical notation.[69] For our purposes two observations will suffice concerning the formalized argument. First, although the language of the appendix becomes numerically symbolic as opposed to using literary symbols, the thrust of the argument is the same. It is the same argument presented in two different (although overlapping) language/symbol conventions. In other words, the appendix is simply another mode of expressing the argument contained in the body of the book. Second, Bayesian probabilities are still vulnerable to the charge of subjectivity. The assigning of numerical values is an attempt to put the ephemeral feeling of a piece of evidence's strength or weight into a mathematical mode. Swinburne makes this very clear: "Now I stress again that we cannot really give exact values to these probabilities, nor to analogous probabilities in science or history... But we can conclude that these things are probable, or not very probable on the basis of other things being very probable, or not very probable or most unlikely; and that is all I am doing here."[70]

The subjectivity of the values does not make them completely vacuous, or entirely arbitrary. They are, however, inherently connected to the arguments Swinburne develops in the book. He states: "Someone who disagrees with these values will have to find fault with the arguments of Part II and III and of Chapter 3."[71] Minor variances in the assigned numerals aside, the probability calculus used in the appendix depends on the strength of the argument in the body of Swinburne's book. The formalization of the argument is just that: it is a restating of the same argument in formal terms. For what it is worth, however, Swinburne concludes that the probability for the resurrection is 0.97.

Gary Habermas and Michael Licona

Although the main source for this section will be a book that was co-authored by Gary Habermas and Michael Licona, *The Case for the Resurrection of Jesus*, Habermas will be the key thinker cited, because he has written extensively on the resurrection, publishing numerous books

---

69. Ibid., 204–14.
70. Ibid., 215.
71. Ibid.

and articles on the subject.[72] As the more prominent apologist for the resurrection, and as a leading spokesperson for an *evidential apologetic, Habermas will be referred to as an individual more frequently in this work than Licona. *The Case for the Resurrection of Jesus* is a contemporary, yet traditional, apologetic for the historicity of the resurrection. Because of this, sketching the flow of the argument will be less time consuming than it was for Swinburne's *The Resurrection of God Incarnate*. Much to his credit, Swinburne's work combines traditional arguments with a highly original presentation, and fresh insights. Habermas's work is less creative or strikingly original, but it does represent a solid—and perhaps not equaled—*evidentialist historical argument for the resurrection.

Habermas and Licona anchor the credibility of Jesus on the historicity of the resurrection event: "Such a historical test of truth is unique to Christianity. If Jesus *did not* rise from the dead, he was a false prophet and a charlatan whom no rational person should follow. Conversely, if he *did* rise from the dead, this event confirmed his radical claim."[73] The resurrection is also that which confirms the truth of God's written revelation (i.e., the Bible), and is the foundation from which an argument for the trustworthiness of the New Testament is to be made.[74] As will be seen in due course, this is exactly the opposite direction from that in which other apologetic systems move.

If the resurrection event is of such crucial importance in confirming Scripture and proving the trustworthiness of the New Testament, it is vitally important to understand the standard used to determine whether or not an event truly occurred in history. Habermas and Licona note that it is virtually impossible to prove any historical event with 100 percent certainty.

They write:

> The standards of evidence do not require that the case for something is irrefutable. Such 100 percent certainty is only possible in the rarest of circumstances. Rather, the standard requires proof beyond a reasonable doubt in criminal cases and proof that makes

---

72. Two such pertinent works are his *Resurrection of Jesus*, and a debate he published with Antony Flew, *Did Jesus Rise from the Dead?*

73. Habermas and Licona, *Case for the Resurrection*, 27; emphasis original.

74. Ibid., 28–29.

the truth of an accusation more probable than not in civil cases. If this is not understood, our criteria for proof may be unrealistic.[75]

Like Swinburne, they construe the historical case for the resurrection of Jesus Christ from the dead on probabilistic lines. The standard for historical verification is based on the preponderance of evidence, and the probability of the historical reconstruction. It is not expected, nor required, that such an investigation will yield 100 percent certainty—although this does not mean that Habermas and Licona do not feel the liberty to speak of Jesus' resurrection as "a historical certainty."[76]

In order to introduce the particulars of the argument for the resurrection of Jesus Christ, they identify five principles that historians can use when they are evaluating an alleged event of history. The five principles Habermas and Licona cite are:

1. Multiple, independent sources support historical claims.
2. Attestation by an enemy supports historical claims.
3. Embarrassing admissions support historical claims.
4. Eyewitness testimony supports historical claims.
5. Early testimony supports historical claims.[77]

These principles are fairly self-explanatory. A plurality of sources, particularly from independent parties, strengthens evidentially based claims. If your enemy makes a statement that is damaging to them and helpful to you, it is highly unlikely that the content of their statement is false. If a witness provides testimony that contains embarrassing facts about themselves, it is likely to be the truth, because they would not concoct a lie that made them look badly. Eyewitness testimony is accorded a higher degree of respect than hearsay. Lastly, testimony several years after an event is generally considered more reliable than testimony several centuries later. All of these criteria are generalizations, with counter-examples easily imagined for each point. But as generalizations they do stand as intuitively and experientially solid. As *The Case for the Resurrection of Jesus* unfolds its argument, these five criteria are employed to demonstrate the historical likelihood of Jesus' resurrection.

75. Ibid., 32.
76. Ibid., 33.
77. Ibid., 36–40.

After outlining the five principles applicable to historical investigation in general, Habermas and Licona move on to some of the historical particulars surrounding the resurrection. They term their approach the "minimal facts approach," and state, "This approach *considers only those data that are so strongly attested historically that they are granted by nearly every scholar who studies the subject, even the rather skeptical ones*" (emphasis in original).[78] For their investigation, they stress that: "We are not assuming inspiration or even general reliability of the New Testament in our case for Jesus' resurrection. In our minimal facts approach, we are only regarding the New Testament as an ancient volume of literature containing twenty-seven separate books and letters."[79]

There are five facts chosen that fit the minimal facts approach. Four of these facts are unanimously accepted by scholars who have seriously studied the resurrection, and the last one by 75 percent.[80] The first four facts are the fact of the crucifixion of Jesus Christ; the fact that the disciples believed he rose from the dead; the fact that Saul was suddenly converted; and the fact that Jesus' skeptical brother James was converted. The fifth fact is that the tomb was empty.[81] It is the empty tomb that does not command the same unanimity amongst scholars as the first four minimal facts, according to Habermas's studies.

While it is not germane to our present purposes to outline the entire web of argumentation Habermas and Licona use to support these facts, it is worthwhile to see, in a few exemplary instances, how they use the five principles of historical investigation to buttress their historical understanding of the resurrection. The best example is the fifth fact, the one that does not command universal assent. Habermas and Licona argue that the empty tomb is supported by three main lines of evidence. The first is that the disciples, fifty days after the crucifixion, were preaching the resurrection of Jesus in Jerusalem, the very city where the crucifixion had taken place. Any number of parties and individuals could have disconfirmed the resurrection claims by pointing to the tomb, if it were not in fact empty.[82] Even if Jesus had been subject to significant decay, the

---

78. Ibid., 44.
79. Ibid., 51.
80. Ibid., 70.
81. Ibid., 48–77.
82. Ibid., 70.

wounds from the crucifixion and spear, coupled with the tomb's location, would have been sufficient to demonstrate that Jesus had not been raised to life. If nothing else, the production of a body with such wounds would have undercut the Christian claims, and Christianity would not have gotten off the ground.[83]

Besides this theoretical argument (which they term "The Jerusalem Factor"), Habermas and Licona also note the existence of enemy attestation for the empty tomb. Not only is there multiple, independent attestation for the empty tomb, but some of it comes indirectly from enemies. The "only early opposing theory" offered by the enemies of Jesus was that the disciples stole the body. While the explicit charge is one of theft, this implicitly concedes the fact that the tomb was empty.[84] The extant historical evidence is that the Jewish reply to Christian claims did in fact hinge on the tomb being empty.[85] Certainly the enemies of Jesus did not believe that Jesus' disciples stole the body, but then left it in the same tomb in which he was originally buried. Charging the disciples with theft only makes sense if the body of Jesus was no longer to be found in the tomb in which he had been buried.

The principle of embarrassment is also applied to support the factuality of the empty tomb. Habermas and Licona argue that women were not legally qualified to be witnesses, and so the early church would never have invented a story that placed women as the primary and chronologically first witnesses to the empty tomb and risen Lord. If the church were to invent a story surrounding the resurrection of Jesus, it would not put women in this position, and also make the male disciples look so cowardly and confused. Thus the principle of embarrassment strengthens the contention that the empty tomb was in fact just that—empty.[86]

While Swinburne provides a short discussion on rival accounts for what happened concerning the resurrection, Habermas and Licona spend far more time analyzing rival theories than they do in presenting and supporting their positive, minimal facts approach. This indicates that they find the evidence to be both clear and persuasive, and only requiring the demonstration that rival theories are less well supported and plausible

83. Ibid.
84. Ibid., 71.
85. Pannenberg, *Jesus—God and Man*, 101.
86. Habermas and Licona, *Case for the Resurrection*, 71–74.

in order to conclude that the resurrection is as certain as a historical event can be. In particular, Habermas has such a body of thorough work in this regard that Wright, in his massive work on the resurrection, simply refers his readers to Habermas for a full response to objections to the resurrection.[87] For now it will suffice to note that, in general, Habermas identifies a recurring problem that renders rival hypotheses improbable. This problem is that rival hypotheses must multiply improbable events together in order to produce a theory that has sufficient explanatory scope. For example, in order to explain the empty tomb, it could be argued that someone other than the disciples stole the body (although there is no evidence for this). This accounts for the empty tomb by sheer guesswork, but then how are the facts that the disciples believed Jesus was alive and had appeared to them to be accounted for, as well as the conversions of James and Paul to be explained? To the theft of the body must be added hallucinations, and not just of Peter, but of Paul as well. If the probability of someone stealing the body is remote, and of hallucinations even more so, the combined probability of this theory is exceptionally low indeed.[88] All rival accounts have to implausibly explain both the empty tomb and the appearances of Jesus, and when explanations for both are added up, the probability is vanishingly small. Here again the hallmark of the resurrection argument, and the two most important pieces of data, are the empty tomb and the appearances. It is these two items that must be interpreted and cogently explained in order for any alleged historical reconstruction to stand.

After the historical investigation of the resurrection events, Habermas and Licona tie Jesus' resurrection to his claims, predictions, teachings, and life.[89] This is necessary because, although a scientist or historian can evaluate the claim "Jesus was seen alive after his death," it is also true that, "*in his capacity as a scientist or historian*, he perhaps could not draw the conclusion: 'God raised Jesus from the dead,' since he is unable to detect God's actions with the tools of his trade" (emphasis in original).[90] It is a mistake to attempt to isolate one event—the resurrection—out of the entire life of Jesus.

---

87. Wright, *Resurrection of the Son of God*, 718 n. 91.
88. Habermas and Licona, *Case for the Resurrection*, 121.
89. Ibid., 136.
90. Ibid., 135.

Evidentialism

It is also a mistake to attempt to finally evaluate the issue entirely apart from any consideration of whether or not God exists. If atheism obtains, then the resurrection did not happen. Habermas and Licona quickly discuss the problem of evil, the existence of a designer (as demonstrated by specified complexity and the wider anthropic argument), and the necessity of a first cause, following the *Kalam* cosmological argument.[91] This particular version of the cosmological argument states: "1. Whatever begins to exist has a cause. 2. The universe began to exist. 3. Therefore, the universe has a cause."[92] Other versions of the cosmological argument appeal to the existence of logically contingent and necessary beings, or dependent and independent beings (these follow Thomas Aquinas and Samuel Clarke), but the *Kalam* version argues from the premise that the universe came into temporal existence, and therefore is an effect requiring an antecedently existing cause.[93] All evidence considered, Habermas and Licona think the evidence for the existence of God is quite strong, and therefore there is no reason to reject the possibility of the miraculous.[94] There is, therefore, no a priori reason to doubt the historical case surrounding the resurrection of Jesus Christ from the dead.[95]

In summary, Habermas and Licona conclude:

> Can the historian establish that it was God who raised Jesus? The historian can conclude that Jesus rose from the dead. But the historian cannot conclude from historical inquiry alone that God raised Jesus from the dead. This is not to say that we are unjustified in concluding that God raised Jesus. It is simply to admit that historical inquiry alone cannot answer the question of the *cause* of Jesus' resurrection. It can only address whether the event occurred. Nevertheless, after looking at the data for the existence of God, Jesus' claims about himself, his prediction of the resurrection, his miracles and the fulfilled prophecy, the limits of historical inquiry do not keep us from concluding that God raised Jesus

---

91. Ibid., 172–81.

92. Craig, *Reasonable Faith*, 92.

93. Ibid., 91–125; Beck, "Thomistic Cosmological Argument"; Geivett, "The *Kalam* Cosmological Argument"; Geivett, "Two Versions of the Cosmological Argument"; Rowe, *Philosophy of Religion*, 19–36.

94. Habermas and Licona, *Case for the Resurrection*, 174–81.

95. For interesting remarks on the nature of classical and traditional evidential apologetics, in regards to the relationship between theistic proofs and historical evidence, see Craig, "Classical Apologist's Closing Remarks," 316–17.

> from the dead. This interpretation of the facts is a far better option than to subscribe to another theory that lacks any credible data.[96]

Historical inquiry can prove that Jesus was raised from the dead, and then philosophical inquiry can demonstrate that God's existence is likely. Habermas explicitly claims that the minimal facts approach is a historical as opposed to a philosophical approach.[97] For Habermas, historical inquiry proves that Jesus came back to life after he died, and philosophy can then be used to demonstrate the validity of theism.[98] However, miracles can prove the existence of God, even without further philosophical argumentation. When combined with Jesus' life and claims, it is entirely probable that God raised Jesus from the dead. It is therefore rational for the believer to accept these claims in the judgment of Habermas and Licona.[99]

In the relationship of the resurrection to Scripture, Habermas and Licona have already been cited as stating that the resurrection is the foundation for the trustworthiness of the New Testament. They take great care to distance this apologetic from the authority or inerrancy of Scripture, writing:

> We have presented evidence for Jesus' resurrection using a "minimal facts" approach, which considers only those data that are so strongly attested historically that even the majority of nonbelieving scholars accept them as facts. We have not appealed to or even suggested the inspiration or inerrancy of the Bible in order to support our case. Therefore, one cannot object to Jesus' resurrection simply because he or she rejects that the Bible is divinely inspired.[100]

Later, they state: "Therefore, one cannot object to Jesus' resurrection because he rejects the Bible, since in our argument nothing hinges on the trustworthiness of the Bible."[101] This point receives great stress in their book. The apologetic of Habermas and Licona does not require the inerrancy, inspiration, or even general reliability of the Scriptures.

---

96. Habermas and Licona, *Case for the Resurrection*, 183. Emphasis in the original.
97. Habermas, "Evidential Apologist's Closing Remarks," 342.
98. Habermas, "Evidential Apologetics," 98 n. 20.
99. Habermas and Licona, *Case for the Resurrection*, 183–84.
100. Ibid., 75.
101. Ibid., 149.

N. T. Wright

Wright's large volume on the resurrection, *The Resurrection of the Son of God*, is vast in scope and painstaking in depth. It canvasses historical, theological, philosophical, and exegetical details in order to present a comprehensive analysis of the meaning of the resurrection of Jesus and its historicity as a space-time event. While it may seem unjust to examine Wright's work in a short compass, the basic steps in his argument are quite simple. It is in providing background material and in defending his steps that Wright's work grows in volume. The argument lends itself, however, to succinct articulation.

One of the first issues Wright tackles is the definition of "historical" or "history." Such definitions are critical in discussions of whether or not the resurrection of Jesus Christ is a "historical" event. Wright identifies five distinct ways in which the words "history" or "historical" are used. First, history is an event, even if it was unobserved, unrecorded, and unlikely to ever be known with precision. Wright suggests that the death of the last pterodactyl is such an event—it surely happened, but when, where, and other precise details are not likely to ever be known.[102] Yet such an event did take place, and in this first sense of "history" it qualifies as a historical event.

The second meaning of "history" is similar, but more subjective. It entails significance, rather than just obtaining. While every event is "historical" in the first sense, not every event or person is "historic." In order to qualify as "history" in this second sense, there must be a perception of momentousness, significance, or importance: in other words, the event or person must be extremely consequential in order to justifiably be described as part of history in this second, more narrow sense.[103]

A third way in which the word "history" is used is in the sense of a demonstrable or provable event. Wright notes that this view is somewhat more controversial. It is more restrictive, and only allows the word "history" to be applied to an event which can be proven to have occurred. Thus all events that may have happened but cannot be demonstrated to have happened are disqualified from being termed "historical" in this sense.[104]

---

102. Wright, *Resurrection of the Son of God*, 12.
103. Ibid., 13.
104. Ibid.

Fourth, there is a sense in which "history" refers to events that are recorded (or could be recorded), or passed along through oral reports. Wright calls this *writing-about-events-in-the-past* (emphasis in original).[105]

Last, Wright argues there is a coming together of points three and four that is often found in discussions of Jesus. Here the meaning is what post-Enlightenment, or modern historians can say about an event or topic. Wright says:

> In this sense, "historical" means not only that which can be demonstrated and written, but that which can be demonstrated and written *within the post-Enlightenment worldview*. This is what people have often had in mind when they have rejected "the historical Jesus" (which hereby, of course, comes to mean "the Jesus that fits the Procrustean bed of a reductionistic worldview") in favour of the "the Christ of faith."[106]

This last category is very perceptive, and emerges in both implicit and explicit ways in discussions of the resurrection (by both believers and skeptics), as will be seen in later analysis.

In developing his argument for the resurrection, Wright turns to an examination of the non-Jewish views on the resurrection that were commonplace in pre-Christian—and contemporaneous with Christian—beliefs. Wright convincingly demonstrates the truth of his thesis that "Christianity was born into a world where its central claim was known to be false . . . outside Judaism, nobody believed in resurrection."[107] After making this claim he examines the philosophical and religious claims of the Greco-Roman world, and finds them to deny and utterly dismiss the idea of a physical resurrection after death.[108] There was absolutely no support for the doctrine of a resurrection in non-Jewish thought, and plenty of direct opposition to the very idea.

Before moving into his examination of Jewish thinking concerning resurrection, Wright sets out the direction he will be moving in: when Christians claimed that Jesus was resurrected, they were claiming that

---

105. Ibid.

106. Ibid. Emphasis original.

107. Ibid., 35. For an excellent article that argues for the same position, see Habermas, "Resurrection Claims in Non-Christian Religions."

108. Wright, *Resurrection of the Son of God*, 32–84.

what had happened to him had never happened to anyone else; the whole pagan world thought that such a claim was ridiculous and impossible; and while the Jewish world largely did accept the idea of resurrection, they looked for it only at the very end of the age.[109] Not every group in Judaism believed in an end-time resurrection, but the dominant demographic of the Jewish population and devoutly religious did, and such a view was well established in both canonical and non-canonical Jewish writings. Resurrection was definitely embedded in the Tanak and beyond, but it was always something that was clearly held to have not yet happened. It would not happen to one individual; it would happen to all the righteous (at a minimum), simultaneously when the new age began and the old epoch passed away.[110]

Although already noted, it is crucial to grasp the surpassing significance of the fact that nobody in the non-Jewish world gave the idea of resurrection any credence whatsoever, and nobody in the Jewish world expected a resurrection to happen ahead of the end time.[111] One of the corollary points that Wright draws from this—which he identifies as one of his central arguments—is that it is astonishing that, given that the early Christians engaged pagan thinkers and were tapped into Jewish traditions, there did not develop a spectrum of beliefs in early Christianity concerning the resurrection.[112] The united witness of the early Christian church was that a resurrection had indeed taken place, and yet it had happened only to one man. Such a view was completely opposed to Gentile thought, and completely unexpected in Jewish thought. Yet, despite its improbability, this was the united and central teaching of the Christian church. Wright spends a very large number of pages examining the canonical and non-canonical Christian writings (focusing, naturally, on the canonical), and painstakingly supports the claim that the Christian church held to the physical resurrection of Jesus Christ, and that he was a suffering and victorious Messiah.[113] This argumentation is persuasive, but beyond the scope of the present descriptive sketch of Wright's argument for the historicity of the resurrection.

109. Ibid., 83.
110. Ibid., 85–206.
111. Ibid., 205–6.
112. Ibid., 209.
113. Ibid., 209–682.

Moving into his concluding section, Wright presents his argument in seven steps. I will summarize them:

1. Christian belief in the resurrection could not have spontaneously emerged from its antecedent Jewish milieu.

2–4. The empty tomb and the appearances of Jesus—only when joined together—can provide a rationale for the emergence of the belief in the resurrection. Unless a person died, disappeared, and then reappeared, the previous understanding of resurrection was too entrenched and ingrained to be modified.

5. Other explanations offered for the production of this belief fail to have the same degree of explanatory power.

6. Therefore, it is "historically highly probable" that Jesus' tomb was empty, and the disciples encountered him alive again.

7. The last and most important question remaining then, is whether or not any other explanation besides the one that the disciples provided can explain why Christianity universally and firmly believed that Jesus Christ was crucified, buried, and resurrected on the third day.[114]

Wright goes on to observe that, in the common-sense use of the concept of *probability* that is used by historians (which is different from the technical use in philosophy) the resurrection is the most probable explanation for the reality of this belief existing in the Christian church.[115]

Furthermore, Wright argues that the resurrection is not merely a sufficient condition for the arising of this belief, but a necessary component of any sufficient condition for the belief's arising.[116] In his estimation, only the data of the empty tomb and the appearances of the risen Christ could be sufficient and necessary for the emergence of this belief.[117] He goes on to state, "In terms of the kind of proof which historians normally accept, the case we have presented, that the tomb-plus-appearances combination is what generated early Christian belief, is as watertight as one is

---

114. Ibid., 686–87.
115. Ibid., 687 n. 3.
116. Ibid., 688–705.
117. Ibid., 706.

likely to find."[118] Abduction, or inference to the best explanation, is what historians rely on, and the available data is best explained by the resurrection.[119] Wright notes that the Enlightenment ideal was to let historical facts rather than dogma and authority establish the truth, and if this is followed faithfully without appealing to methodological naturalism's a priori notions about what can or cannot happen, then the resurrection stands as the conclusion most agreeable to the methods and tools of the historian. Positively, the resurrection accounts for the data, and negatively, all other attempts at explanation have failed.[120]

There are two other items that Wright adduces in support of the resurrection of Jesus that are more subtle but nevertheless quite significant. He notes that the change from worshipping on the Sabbath to the first day of the week is critical.[121] Sabbath keeping was a major component of the first believers' worldview, and the only thing that could account for the change from gathering on the Sabbath to gathering on Sunday was that something monumental had occurred historically on the first day of the week.[122] The second item has been mentioned numerous times, Wright points out, but has not been fully appreciated: women—the first witnesses to the empty tomb—were not acceptable as legal witnesses. These two items, although not coercive in isolation, do lend some significant circumstantial weight to the case for the resurrection of the Son of God.[123]

Wright's approach to the Scriptures in regard to the historical case for the resurrection is as follows. In regard to the Gospel accounts, Wright says: "I suggest, in fact, that the stories must be regarded as early, certainly well before Paul; and that, when placed side by side, they tell a tale which, despite the multiple surface inconsistencies, succeeds in hanging together. To put it crudely, the fact that they cannot agree over how many women, or angels, were at the tomb, or even on the location of the appearances, does not mean that nothing happened."[124]

---

118. Ibid., 707.
119. Ibid., 716–17.
120. Ibid., 717.
121. Ibid., 579–80.
122. Ibid., 580.
123. Ibid., 607.
124. Ibid., 614.

If there are inconsistencies, though, this does not mean for Wright that the post-Enlightenment critics (i.e., critics who hold that traditional sources of authority and sacred writings including the Bible can contain errors and must be judged according to the standards of human reason and evidence) are always accurate in their arguments about how many inconsistencies there really are. Even if it is granted that the Bible may contain errors, this does not mean that every alleged error is genuine. Instead, Wright understands some of the inconsistencies to be perfectly natural and acceptable:

> The last two features—the appearance to Peter, and the single-day framework—alert us to something which a first-century writer would have taken for granted but which post-Enlightenment critics sometimes forget. In the ancient world, someone who was intending to tell people what actually happened did not feel obliged (any more than a good journalist, or indeed a real practising historian would today) to mention every single feature of every single incident. Peter went to the tomb; "some of our number" went to the tomb. If I say "the bishop went to the party" and if somebody else says "the bishop and his two daughters went to the party," we have not contradicted one another.[125]

Nevertheless, Wright does not think that harmonization in details is possible. For example, the event of Peter's denial (how many cock crows, how many times did he deny knowing Jesus) cannot be harmonized. But, claims Wright, this is not because the event was invented, but rather because it truly happened. If the event was fabricated, such minor discrepancies would be ironed out. Variation in detail is evidence against the hypothesis that the story was fabricated, because one mark of collusion where people get together to get their story straight is wooden repetition in minor details.[126]

As a thought experiment, one does wonder if those opposed to the Christian faith would not gladly argue for collusion among the apostles if there were no discrepancies (prima facie or otherwise) in the accounts. It does seem within the realm of logical possibility that, if every detail was identical in all the accounts, this would be taken as a reason for dismissing the historical independence and validity of the narratives. One nineteenth-century lawyer expresses the judicial opinion that minor

125. Ibid., 648.
126. Ibid., 649.

discrepancies in court are generally taken as evidence that the witnesses are not in collusion; they are not taken as evidence that the major event described did not in fact take place.[127]

Clearly for Wright the historical case for the resurrection of Jesus Christ does not turn on the inerrancy or infallibility of Scripture. By focusing on the historical core of the New Testament witness, and by offering a philosophical condition for the phenomenon of the appearance, growth, and existence of the church, Wright concludes that not only is the resurrection a sufficient explanation, it is the only explanation for all the relevant data: "My claim is stronger: that the bodily resurrection of Jesus provides a *necessary* condition for these things; in other words, no other explanation could or would do. All the efforts to find alternative explanations fail, and they were bound to do so" (emphasis in original).[128] In Wright's estimation, the biblical record of such events may not be perfect, but this does not undercut the historical and logical validity of the conclusion that the resurrection alone is the necessary and sufficient condition for explaining the historical phenomena.

Michael Martin

Martin has been a prominent defender of positive disbelief in the existence of God. His *Atheism: A Philosophical Justification* is a widely regarded and rigorous defense of the philosophical merits of atheism, and the demerits of theism. He has, with Ricki Monnier, edited two anthologies respectively entitled *The Impossibility of God* and *The Improbability of God*. Thus, Martin brings an extensive and specialized philosophical background to the question of the resurrection, and he does not examine it in an intellectual vacuum. By way of contrast to Swinburne, Habermas and Licona, and Wright, Martin's evaluation of the historicity of the resurrection will be helpful for seeing how the putative fact of the resurrection can be viewed by someone who forcefully denies the existence of God.

Martin begins his essay on the resurrection by tying it into the whole of the Christian worldview (Martin uses "Christian worldview" in its broadest sense):

---

127. Morrison, *Proofs of Christ's Resurrection*. For current lawyers' perspectives, see Montgomery, "The Jury Returns," 325, 339 n. 21.

128. Wright, *Resurrection of the Son of God*, 717.

> I argued in chapter 16 [of *Atheism, Morality, and Meaning*, the volume in which his essay on the resurrection is found] that there is no plausible theory of the atonement. Yet without one the Christian worldview makes no sense and the incarnation, death, and resurrection of Jesus are all pointless. But now let us suppose for the sake of argument that a plausible theory of the atonement is available. Unless there is good reason to suppose that the resurrection occurred, life in the Christian worldview would still be without meaning. Indeed, the truth of the resurrection is pivotal to both the Christian worldview and the meaning of a Christian life. In this chapter I will argue, however, that there is no good evidence that Jesus arose from the dead; consequently, that there is no reason to suppose that life has meaning in a Christian worldview.[129]

Martin states here that there is no good reason to believe that the resurrection occurred, and it is this claim that he sets out to defend.

The first argument that he offers is as follows:

> 1. A miracle claim is initially improbable relative to our background knowledge.
>
> 2. If a claim is initially improbable relative to our background knowledge and the evidence for it is not strong, then it should be disbelieved.
>
> 3. The resurrection of Jesus is a miracle claim.
>
> 4. The evidence for the resurrection is not strong.
>
> 5. Therefore, the resurrection of Jesus should be disbelieved.[130]

As with the Christian scholars canvassed above, Martin believes background evidence plays an important role in the argument, but this time in the opposite direction. But why should premise (1) be accepted? Martin says that, "traditionally, a miracle has been defined as a violation of a law of nature caused by the intervention of God."[131] Granting the truth of theism, Martin argues, does not make miracles probable, only possible. God may decide never to use miracles at all, and he may decide that there would be too many negative effects—for example, confusion, misleading people, and detrimentally impeding science, since science

---

129. Martin, *Atheism, Morality and Meaning*, 291.
130. Ibid., 293.
131. Ibid.

Evidentialism

deals with regularities of laws.[132] This position is similar to that of Overall, who argues that the existence of a miracle would actually count *against* the existence of the Christian God.[133] Since a benevolent God would want human beings to know and learn, an interference with natural law would be confusing and detrimental to his purposes. Thus, a miracle would actually be a reason to deny God's existence.

This objection to the miraculous seems extraordinarily thin. It is far too reductionistic. Perhaps God has multifaceted purposes, most of which require natural regularity, and others that require special interferences with nature to demonstrate his power, presence, glory, etc. It is also, of course, possible that God would interact in history in a special way to simply help his people. Regardless of the particular reasons God may have for performing miracles, it does seem a serious stretch to say that a miracle would be evidence against God, or that a miracle would seriously destroy scientific investigation.

For argument's sake, however, Martin agrees with Swinburne that given theism, miracles are possible, but he denies that this helps make any particular case of an alleged miracle probable.[134] There still needs to be a movement from what is theoretically possible to what is concretely probable. In fact, the vast majority of claims to miracles are rejected by many religious believers themselves—even those who believe in the miraculous.[135] Furthermore, it is highly doubtful that all religious believers who accept the possibility of miracles occurring ascribe the exact same degree of probability to every single reported miracle they have ever heard. Thus, even for the religious, any singular claim for a miracle is likely to be regarded with low probability.

Yet Martin recognizes that the claim that Jesus was resurrected from the dead is not an ordinary miracle claim. It is a particular claim, and it is possible that God had a special purpose in bringing it about. Martin argues, however, that even if one concedes to Swinburne that God had a purpose for atonement and incarnation, it is highly unlikely that God would become incarnate in first-century Palestine in the person of Jesus.[136]

---

132. Ibid.
133. Overall, "Miracles as Evidence against the Existence of God."
134. Martin, *Atheism, Morality and Meaning*, 294.
135. Ibid., 295.
136. Ibid., 296.

Why would he become incarnate in this one person, in that one place, at that one time? As Martin phrases the question, "Indeed, given the innumerable alternatives at God's disposal it would seem a priori unlikely that the incarnation and the resurrection would have taken place where and when they allegedly did."[137] The more specific a claim, the more unlikely it is initially; the more general, the more likely. For example, it is more likely that we can predict that a certain individual will contract a cold in the next decade, and less likely that we can predict the particular future day on which they will contract a cold.[138] Even if it is likely that a redeeming event would take place on Earth, it is initially improbable that it took place at a particular time with a particular person.[139]

This last point is true, but trivial. If God became incarnate, it would be highly improbable that any one person, selected randomly, would be the incarnate God. But if God were to become incarnate, surely at least *one* person would be the incarnate God! And if one person were to be God incarnate, they would have to be born at *one* time, in *one* location. Also, if God became incarnate, surely, as Swinburne argues (see above), there would be evidence for it. The Christian testimony is not a speculative guess as to who God will incarnate himself as; it is that he came and revealed himself. It is enormously improbable that, beginning at conception, any one individual is going to be God incarnate. Yet, looking back on a life with certain marks, and sealed with a super-miracle (as Swinburne puts it), is a quite different epistemic position than merely looking for blank statistical probabilities with no accidental data whatsoever. Thus Martin is, strictly speaking, correct that it is initially improbable that any one person is going to be God incarnate, but this can be quite easily overcome by a posteriori evidence. It is enormously improbable to identify the one particular individual who will randomly pick the winning lottery ticket ahead of time—it is not as hard to identify them after the draw.[140] Furthermore, there is the question of Messianic prediction and the implications of foreknowledge in biblical prophecy—a question beyond the delimitations of this current work. More will be said about antecedent probability in the next section.

137. Ibid.
138. Ibid., 297.
139. Ibid., 298.
140. For dissimilarities between initial improbabilities and lottery winning (with special reference to David Hume), see Schlesinger, "Miracles and Probabilities," 222–23.

Martin does add, however, that redemption could occur without a resurrection at all, and thus a resurrection is a priori highly unlikely.[141] An analogous point is made by Houlden, who argues that Christians believed Jesus was the Savior on grounds other than the resurrection, making the resurrection unessential for Christian belief in Jesus as savior.[142] Evidence for this is taken from the book of Hebrews, where the resurrection is not mentioned, but Jesus is still presented as the ascended high priest.[143] It could, of course, be argued in response to Houlden's understanding of the theology of Hebrews that the ascension is the focal point, and the resurrection is simply assumed in the background without being mentioned—perhaps because it was taken for granted by the readers.[144] Nevertheless, Martin does not provide a convincing alternative understanding of how the Christian God could provide redemption without an atonement and resurrection.

Moving on from probability, Martin turns to address the historical evidence for the resurrection. He cites Crossan and Ludemann as authorities on the unreliability of the New Testament accounts of the resurrection.[145] Martin maintains that it is unlikely Jesus was ever buried. Furthermore, he says that the empty tomb would have been venerated by Jesus' followers, and appeals to "New Testament scholars [who] agree."[146] In his endnote to support this claim, Martin only appeals to the majority of the Jesus Seminar.[147] It seems doubtful to me that most biblical scholars

141. Martin, *Atheism, Morality and Meaning*, 299.

142. Houlden, "The Resurrection and Christianity," 205.

143. Ibid., 200.

144. A similar debate exists concerning whether or not the physical resurrection was important to the apostle Paul. For the position that the physical resurrection was irrelevant to Paul, see Bostock, "Osiris and the Resurrection of Christ," 271; Lindars, "The Resurrection and the Empty Tomb," 118. For rather obvious and convincing reasons as to why Paul did not mention the empty tomb, while still believing that Christ physically rose from the dead, see Pannenberg, *Jesus—God and Man*, 100; Wright, *Resurrection of the Son of God*, 321; Davis, *Risen Indeed*, 75–78.

145. Martin, *Atheism, Morality and Meaning*, 301. Crossan's conclusions on the historical life of Jesus and his authentic sayings lean heavily on the material in the *Gospel of Thomas*. For a balanced and sober critique of Crossan's use of this text, see Quarles, "Use of the *Gospel of Thomas*," 535–36. Quarles concludes that Crossan is far too premature in adducing conclusions from the *Gospel of Thomas*, and that the text itself is simply not accepted as being a primary, independent witness.

146. Martin, *Atheism, Morality and Meaning*, 301.

147. Ibid., 315 n. 17.

would find the Jesus Seminar the most reliable and authoritative organization for supporting claims. In fact, the historian Maurice Casey, who is not a Christian, states that the Jesus Seminar is missing the best critical scholars in America, and most of their Fellows are "not in any reasonable sense authorities at all."[148] Still, the Jesus Seminar determines their position on an averaged majority vote, which is statistically poorly designed, and which also has led to bizarre conclusions.[149] Does this reflect a bias in Martin, or is he perhaps not aware of the status of the Jesus Seminar in serious biblical scholarship? Perhaps Martin is unaware of the fact that "As several scholars have pointed out, the seminar is not representative of biblical scholarship generally, and its conclusions are driven by unwarranted presuppositions."[150]

In response to Christian apologists who maintain that, had the empty tomb story been invented years after the fact, it would have been met with the response that the location of the tomb was currently unknown, Martin says: "However, for all we know, this is precisely what critics did maintain. Zealous disciples are not always persuaded by arguments or by strong negative evidence."[151] Yet here, clearly, "for all we know" is a crucial phrase. There is not a shred of positive evidence that this was claimed: it is a naked appeal to an argument from silence. Although there will be further discussion below on Martin's use of arguments from silence, it seems that he allows himself the luxury of relying on them, while denying his opponents the same latitude.

Martin quickly disposes of the apologetic significance of the women as witnesses, by suggesting women could be witnesses if there were no men available, and suggests that the women may have been at the tomb not as witnesses but with another function[152] (he suggests that this other function may involve parallels to Egyptian mythology and the role of women with Osiris).[153] As far as preaching the resurrection in Jerusalem fifty days after the burial, Martin again states that Jesus may not have been buried in the first place, and that the Jewish world was not interested in

---

148. Casey, *Jesus of Nazareth*, 20.
149. Ibid., 21.
150. Carson and Moo, *Introduction to the New Testament*, 121.
151. Martin, *Atheism, Morality and Meaning*, 301.
152. Ibid.
153. Ibid., 316 n. 22.

Evidentialism

Christian teachings at this time. Furthermore, even after fifty days Jesus' body would not have been identifiable.[154]

The Argument from Veneration is articulated by Martin to argue—not presume—that the tomb was not empty. He states the argument in the following way:

1. If the empty tomb stories are true, the location of the tomb was known.

2. If the location of the tomb was known, it is likely that Christians would have venerated the tomb shortly after Jesus' resurrection.

3. Christians did not venerate the tomb shortly after Jesus' resurrection.

4. It is not likely that the empty tomb stories are true.[155]

An alternative understanding of the lack of veneration surrounding the empty tomb is supplied by Craig. He argues that tombs were only considered holy because of the interment of a holy person. It was the person, not the tomb, who was venerated. If Jesus' body had been in the tomb, Craig maintains, *then* it would have been venerated; the fact that it was not considered holy was because Jesus' holy body was no longer there.[156] This argument seems at least as likely as Martin's, and so nothing much can be made of the lack of veneration at the tomb for either side.

Other considerations aside, it is at this point that Martin runs (at the minimum) into a deep inconsistency with his historical methodology. This Argument from Veneration rests on silence. That there is no direct evidence that the early disciples met at the tomb is no evidence that they may not have done so. Recall Martin's statement that the enemies of Jesus may have responded that the tomb was empty, but we just don't have the evidence for it. Why can't Christians say, in response to his argument from veneration, that the early Christians might have met at the tomb, we just don't have the evidence for it? Martin's case at this point needs to be clarified by an analysis of the uses of arguments from silence; for Martin, they only seem capable of running his way.

Next, Martin turns to a staple in the apologetic for the resurrection: the conduct of the disciples. Perhaps one of the more memorable ways of

---

154. Ibid., 302.
155. Ibid.
156. Craig, *The Son Rises*, 84.

expressing the Christian argument comes from Peter Kreeft. If the disciples simply invented the story of the Christian message, what did they get for it? As Kreeft says, they were:

> mocked, hated, sneered and jeered at, exiled, deprived of property and reputation and rights, imprisoned, whipped, tortured, clubbed to a pulp, beheaded, crucified, boiled in oil, sawed in pieces, fed to lions, and cut to ribbons by gladiators. If the miracle of the Resurrection did not really happen, then an even more incredible miracle happened: twelve Jewish fishermen invented the world's biggest lie for no reason at all and died for it with joy, as did millions of others.[157]

Less dramatic, but to the same point, is the observation of Gerald O'Collins that: "After a brief ministry in which he lacked the worldly resources available to other religious founders, Jesus died a shameful and scandalous death. Then, despite the crucifixion, the disciples began to propagate Christianity dynamically in the name of the one who had failed so disgracefully."[158] Yes, it must be conceded that people will die for what they mistakenly believe is truth, but it is considerably more difficult to believe that all of the original disciples would endure such treatment and then die for what they all knew was a lie they had concocted together. In response to this traditional Christian argument, Martin simply argues that the age was one of credulity and charlatans, and that people were easily and frequently falling into all sorts of ridiculous beliefs. Since the New Testament was written decades after all the eyewitnesses were old or dead, there is no reason to think the teachings could be controlled.[159] This reasoning implicitly assumes rather than argues for an extremely late dating of manuscripts, with an extreme range that is highly doubtful. Martin draws a parallel between early Christians and cults today; negative evidence did not deter their growth.[160]

The Gospels have many parallels with the growth and development of legends, according to Martin.[161] Pagan and Jewish sources do not confirm the details of the resurrection, and the later Christian writings show

---

157. Kreeft, *Fundamentals of the Faith*, 67–68.
158. O'Collins, *Jesus Risen*, 99.
159. Martin, *Atheism, Morality and Meaning*, 303–4.
160. Ibid., 304.
161. Ibid., 304–6.

development and more details than the earlier ones.¹⁶² Not only this, but Martin states that there were many resurrection myths previous to Christianity.¹⁶³ The early Christians were creative, so there are new elements, but they are not fully original. The Gospel accounts are not understated as people think; it is just that other sources are more overstated. Combining legends with hallucinations can explain the appearances.¹⁶⁴ Martin believes that group hallucinations can account for the appearances, and this even without normal triggers being present. Behind this, there was a belief that a resurrection could occur for one person (cf. Mark 6:14), and there was a background of resurrection and life after death myths.¹⁶⁵

Despite Martin's assertions, in my judgment, Wright has convincingly demonstrated that this claim is false (see previous section). Regarding antecedents to the Christian belief in the resurrection, C. F. D. Moule forcefully expresses the findings of his research:

> . . . but I have been able to discover none which suggests the entry upon *eternal* life by an *individual, before* the wind-up of history: and it's *this* that one has to account for. Clearly the NT shows no reflection of any belief that Jesus had been *revived*, back to the old mortal life; the (various) endings of the story, in the different Gospels and the Acts, all indicate (in their different ways) that it was believed to be the absolute life of the new age; and yet, entered upon by an *individual*, ahead of time, instead of by *all* the righteous, out *beyond* history. I can see nothing that would naturally lead to this, in any antecedent set of beliefs.¹⁶⁶

The evidence for the resurrection that is grounded on the rise of Christianity is quickly dismissed. Martin asserts that it is possible that: "Early Christians believed deeply but falsely that the resurrection had occurred. They *thought* that the disciples saw the risen Jesus and they interpreted their beliefs theologically at least partly in terms of the myths and legends of their times."¹⁶⁷

162. Ibid., 305.
163. Ibid., 306.
164. Ibid., 307.
165. Ibid., 307–8.
166. Moule and Cupitt, "The Resurrection: A Disagreement," 508–9. Emphasis in original.
167. Martin, *Atheism, Morality and Meaning*, 308.

Lastly, Martin sets out three more lines of reasoning for doubting the resurrection. The first is that the Gospel accounts have many details that cannot be harmonized, not just a few minor ones,[168] although at this point Martin is not as harsh as others.[169] The second is that there is no independent confirmation in other sources for the Gospel accounts, and the third is that the eyewitnesses in such traumatic situations tend to be highly unreliable.[170]

In conclusion, Martin believes that he has supported his case, and that belief in the resurrection (and hence Christianity) is unreasonable. Even if the resurrection seems to be the best explanation in comparison to other specific explanations, this does not mean that it can be rationally accepted.[171] For Martin, even if he (or others) cannot supply a better specific alternative explanation, this does not mean that the resurrection should be accepted. The atheist might only be able to supply a vague scenario that lacks details—perhaps we could say evidence—but for Martin this should still be accepted instead of what Christians propose.[172] Thus Martin would presumably not be troubled by Wolfhart Pannenberg's report that: "It has been said rightly that the legends created by excessive criticism have been less credible than the biblical reports themselves."[173] Martin also goes against the grain of how scientists and historians choose hypotheses: "Scientists and historians rarely consider the merits of hypotheses in isolation. Usually scientists assess the ratio of probabilities among competing hypotheses. It is rational of scientists to hold onto a theory or a hypothesis, however improbable by itself, as long as no better, more probable, alternative is available."[174] In Martin's final analysis, the initially low probability of the resurrection is not overcome by the historical data for the resurrection event.

---

168. Ibid., 309–11.
169. For a harsh tone, see Howe, "On the Resurrection."
170. Martin, *Atheism, Morality and Meaning*, 311–12.
171. Ibid., 312–13.
172. Ibid., 313.
173. Pannenberg, "Response to the Debate," 134.
174. Tucker, "Miracles," 385.

A PRIORI CONSIDERATIONS

As is seen in the preceding discussion, the investigation into the resurrection event does not terminate completely on historical considerations alone. Philosophical issues emerge concerning initial probability and background evidence. Rather than simply asking if a miracle occurred, a further question that needs to be addressed is whether or not a miracle is even possible. Beyond this, if a miracle is logically possible, is it also possible that the miracle could be identified as such? How do probability and evidence relate for miracle claims? The point of departure for this section will be—as it often is in this discussion today—the work of David Hume. Concerning Hume's discussion of miracles, George Mavrodes comments: "Section X of David Hume's *An Enquiry concerning Human Understanding* is probably the most celebrated and most influential discussion of miracles in Western philosophical literature."[175] Not all the discussion has been positive, of course. In the estimation of Antony Flew, "The Section 'Of Miracles' has probably provoked more polemic than anything else which Hume ever wrote."[176] Francis Beckwith agrees that it is "indisputable" that Hume's section on miracles is the most talked about in current philosophical discussions, even though most of Hume's arguments are not original.[177] Nevertheless, Hume is undeniably the champion of this style of argumentation, and it is his work that serves as the point of departure for the discussion. This is such a feature of contemporary discourse that it is as difficult to see future studies of probability and miracles ignoring Hume as it is to see future studies on epistemology ignoring Kant.

In the more than two centuries since Hume's life and work, his work has been discussed so often that there are now common ways of parsing it. Yet despite this fact, there is still no common agreement on its overall

---

175. Mavrodes, "David Hume and the Probability of Miracles," 167.

176. Flew, *Hume's Philosophy of Belief*, 171.

177. Beckwith, *David Hume's Argument against Miracles*, 23. For many readers, since the contemporary discussion tends to begin with Hume, it is natural to believe that his formulations and arguments are completely original. One of the benefits of Brown's study *Miracles and the Critical Mind* is that when he discusses Hume the reader has already been exposed to examples of similar arguments in their pre-Humean formulations. So when Brown makes the case that Hume's arguments are far from original (p. 79), the reader has already seen the historical antecedents.

cogency or success.[178] The debate rages around Hume and prior probabilities; the fact that it is still a contemporary discussion obviously demonstrates that there is still substantial disagreement among scholars.[179] The main issue is whether or not any one particular, purportedly miraculous, event could ever enjoy a high enough probability to warrant acceptance as a genuine miracle, given the complete human experience for non-miraculous natural uniformity and regularity in natural/scientific law.

In the main, the contours of Hume's argument are well known by those who study the philosophical concept of miracles generally, and the historical evidential case for the resurrection particularly. Hume lays down his famous dictum concerning probability and certainty that: "A wise man, therefore, proportions his belief to the evidence."[180] At this point, it is difficult to see anything objectionable in Hume's rule. All he has stated is a commonsense idea that governs the strength of belief. If there is plenty of solid evidence for X, and little good evidence against X, then one has the epistemic right to hold X with a high degree of certitude. There are other instances, of course, where the evidence for or against Y may seem nearly equal (but let it be assumed that the evidence against Y is marginally stronger). In this case, the wise person will not believe but this belief will be held more tentatively than in the case of believing X. The wise person holds to X, and the wise person does not hold to Y; but he or she holds to them with varying degrees of conviction, in proportion to the evidence for each respective position.

It is in the application of this principle to the concept of miracles that Hume becomes controversial. As he develops his discussion, he defines miracles and then immediately rejects the possibility of ever accepting the report of one. Hume writes: "A miracle is a violation of the laws of nature; and as a firm and unalterable experience has established these laws, the proof against a miracle, from the very nature of the fact, is as entire as any argument from experience can possibly be imagined."[181] In other words, there is full evidence for the existence of natural laws. They are recognized as natural laws because in human experience they are never violated. Given Hume's definition that a miracle is a violation of the laws

---

178. On opposite extremes are Earman, *Hume's Abject Failure*, and Fogelin, *A Defense of Hume on Miracles*.

179. Owen, "Hume *versus* Price," 196–97.

180. Hume, *Enquiry*, 80.

181. Ibid., 83.

of nature, coupled with his dictum about a wise man proportioning belief to the evidence, the conclusion Hume adduces is that the evidence for the non-violation of the law will always be greater than the evidence for the violation of the law. This is because the law is only recognized as such because of the unalterable experience of those who describe and recognize the law. To claim a miracle is to claim the violation of something unalterable; therefore, the evidence against the claim is always greater than the evidence for it. In fact, for Hume, even to claim that a miracle occurred is by definition to disprove it—since the claim is really that something that does not happen happened. Hume expresses this point the following way: "There must, therefore, be a uniform experience against every miraculous event, otherwise the event would not merit that appellation [i.e., miracle]."[182]

Here, it almost appears (and perhaps is the case) that Hume is arguing that a claim for a miracle is self-refuting, or even bordering on being self-referentially incoherent. I am not claiming that he is actually arguing this, at least not in a very narrow, logical sense. But in a broader sense, in real life experience, he does seem to be saying that by definition a miracle cannot be accepted as such. How, then, could a miracle ever be demonstrated to have existence? Theoretically, these natural laws may be violated, but practically, human beings could never believe that they had been. Thus in the abstract Hume's concept of miracles is not fully self-refuting, but in human experience, a claim for the miraculous is self-destructive in a wider sense, because to claim a miracle is to appeal to background laws that destroy the cogency and credibility of the claim.

In a celebrated passage, Hume draws his conclusion against the possibility of accepting a miracle:

> The plain consequence is (and it is a general maxim worthy of our attention), "That no testimony is sufficient to establish a miracle, unless the testimony be of such a kind, that its falsehood would be more miraculous, than the fact, which it endeavours to establish. And even in that case there is a mutual destruction of arguments, and the superior only gives us an assurance suitable to that degree of force, which remains, after deducting the inferior." When any one tells me, that he saw a dead man restored to life, I immediately consider with myself, whether it be more probable, that this person should either deceive or be deceived, or that the fact, which he

---

182. Ibid., 83.

relates, should really have happened. I weigh one miracle against the other; and according to the superiority, which I discover, I pronounce my decision, and always reject the greater miracle. If the falsehood of his testimony would be more miraculous, than the event which he relates; then, and not till then, can he pretend to command my belief or opinion.[183]

Tongue-in-cheek, Hume says he will accept the account of a miracle only if it would be a greater miracle for the one telling him about the miracle to be wrong! In proportion to the firm and unalterable human experience for the regularity of the laws of nature, however, it will always be a lesser miracle that the testimony be wrong than that the laws of nature be violated, and so Hume will always reject the claim that a miraculous event has occurred.

Although Hume goes on to provide some reasons for doubting testimony about miracles, it is his theoretical work as outlined above that is critical. It is generally agreed by supporters and opponents alike that Hume's reasons for rejecting testimony regarding the miraculous are unconvincing. Hume argues that there are not enough qualified men in history who have argued together for a miraculous event; that people love reports of miracles for illicit excitement, even though they have never experienced anything like that which is reported; that reports of miracles "are observed to chiefly abound among ignorant and barbarous nations"; and that the competing miracle claims in other religions serve to undercut and defeat all religious systems, since they are all mutually contradictory.[184] Concerning this last point, Michael Martin says, "Here Hume was clearly wrong, and I know of no way of revising Hume's argument that is in keeping with its spirit."[185] It has been further recognized, now that religious inclusivism and religious pluralism are recognized positions regarding different world religions, that miracle claims in different religions do not necessarily have to be seen as bearing competing weight. In fact, depending on one's position, miracles in different religions may serve to provide some measure of divine authentication for each religion. This point is made both by a scholar who generally disagrees with Hume,[186]

---

183. Ibid., 83.
184. Hume, "Of Miracles," 494–96.
185. Martin, *Atheism: A Philosophical Justification*, 201.
186. Houston, *Reported Miracles*, 203–4.

and one who generally agrees with him.[187] Now, it may also be argued that Hume was ultimately right about miracle claims in other religions (i.e., that religious pluralism is false and so putative miracles really do undercut each other and are mutually contradictory), but Hume simply does not recognize even the broad logical possibility that miracle claims in different religions do not have to be in full competition with one another, or that they may even be mutually reinforcing.

From a slightly different angle, this position may lend extra strength to Sorensen's contention that:

> Complete devastation of the argument from miracles requires the following kind of scepticism: reports of miracles are never, even collectively, sufficient evidence to merit a wise man's belief that at least one miracle took place. However, one cannot establish this kind of scepticism merely by showing that the correctness of any report of a miracle is improbable. One must show that the low probabilities of the individual testimonies do not add up in such a way as to make probable "There is at least one miracle."[188]

Here Sorensen's main contention is that Hume was wrong to set natural law against each individual report of a miracle; he would have to set natural law against the *collective* testimony for the miraculous in order to rule out miracles from ever happening. If pluralism—or something like it—did in fact obtain, then miracle reports in different religions could very well serve a mutually reinforcing rather than a mutually weakening function.

Even if Hume is incorrect in his narrower reasoning when it comes to rejecting the testimony about miracles, if his wider, more theoretical work is correct then it is still epistemically irresponsible to ever accept the report of a miracle. This would, obviously, have a tremendous impact on accepting the testimony about the resurrection of Jesus Christ—which is certainly a claim for the occurrence of a very great miracle indeed. What, then, does the resurrection apologist have by way of a response to Hume (and contemporary Humeans)? If Hume is right, then the evidential arguments canvassed in the preceding sections are not only insufficient, they are literally a waste of time: no matter how strong they are, they will never be stronger than the unalterable experience against them, and thus

---

187. Mackie, *Miracle of Theism*, 15.
188. Sorensen, "Hume's Scepticism," 60.

any wise person will reject them as insufficient. The evidential arguments, if one follows Hume strictly enough, are really rejected before they begin; the details of the argument are utterly irrelevant because the conclusion that a miracle has not occurred is necessary. As Mackie says, "Hume's case against miracles is an epistemological argument: it does not try to show that miracles never do happen or never could happen, but only that we never have good reasons for believing that they have happened."[189]

There are serious problems with Hume's a priori argument, recognized by atheists and theists alike. In fact, some very serious criticism comes from Michael Martin, whom we discussed above for his argument against the historicity of the resurrection. Martin notes that for a miracle claim to pass Hume's test and be accepted, it needs to be demonstrated that the purported event E actually took place, and also that E violates a natural law. Put into an outline format, Martin provides an example of this reasoning, from the law of nature, which can be designated L*:

(L*) No person has been brought back to life

(L*) has been confirmed by the deaths of billons of people; the evidence is overwhelming.

Now consider the hypothesis (H*):

(H*) Some people have been brought back to life.[190]

Hume's argument is that we cannot have good evidence for H*, because it violates L*, for which there is tremendous evidence. In Martin's evaluation, "There is much that is wrong with this argument."[191] For example, much of our knowledge of what happens, or what natural laws are, does not come from our own experience, but from testimony. Furthermore, in human testimony, there are reports of miracles, and even reports that people have come back to life.[192] As one nineteenth-century essayist noted concerning Hume's assertion that history is completely uniform in its testimony of experience against miracles: "But in what history

---

189. Mackie, *Miracle of Theism*, 19.
190. Martin, *Atheism: A Philosophical Justification*, 195.
191. Ibid.
192. Ibid., 196.

Evidentialism

is any such experience written? History in its *letter*, is full of events which contradict Nature's uniformity, of interruptions, marvels, miracles."[193]

There is a further justificatory problem with Hume's claims, with no substantiating evidence, that the whole testimony of the human race is against a resurrection: the problem is *how could he know this*? Mavrodes considers the sample of deaths that Hume has personally experienced, and suggests that Hume may have been acquainted with forty or one hundred dead people immediately after their death. If there were to be one (or several) resurrections in history, it would be extremely unlikely that Hume would personally witness one. Yet from his personal sample— which is too small to be statistically significant—he jumps to there being *no* examples in the history of the world. For such a strong, universal conclusion, he offers no evidence.[194] This is simply an unwarranted extrapolation far beyond the data.[195] Furthermore, Hume's claim that the whole of human experience is against resurrection is not even true.[196] If nothing less, the whole debate about the resurrection of Jesus exists because there *is* a claim that someone has experienced a resurrection! Thus the question of miracles cannot be decided purely on a priori grounds as simple as the ones Hume sets forth. His position on testimony is practically incapable of falsification.

There is also a vicious circularity in Hume's case. C. S. Lewis astutely observes that, in one respect, Hume's logic and conclusion is inescapable:

> Now of course we must agree with Hume that if there is absolutely "uniform experience" against miracles, if in other words they never happened, why then they never have. Unfortunately we know that all the reports of them are to be uniform only if we know that all the reports of them are false. And we can know all the reports to be false only if we know already that miracles have never occurred. In fact, we are arguing in a circle.[197]

Lewis moves on to show how the circularity is hidden by Hume's phrasing:

---

193. Jackson, *Philosophy of Natural Theology*, 258; emphasis in the original.
194. Mavrodes, "David Hume and the Probability of Miracles," 176–80.
195. Newman, "Miracles and the Historicity of the Easter Week Narratives," 277.
196. Mavrodes, "David Hume and the Probability of Miracles," 180.
197. Lewis, *Miracles*, 162.

> The question, "Do miracles occur?" and the question, "Is the course of Nature absolutely uniform?" are the same question asked in two different ways. Hume, by sleight of hand, treats them as two different questions. He first answers "Yes," to the question whether Nature is absolutely uniform; and then uses this "Yes" as a ground for answering "No," to the question, "Do miracles occur?" The single real question which he set out to answer is never discussed at all. He gets the answer to one form of the question by assuming the answer to another form of the same question.[198]

Besides the circularity of Hume's position, there is a critical oversight in his argumentation. He focuses exclusively on the testimony of others to a miraculous event. But, as was seen in the evidential survey of resurrection apologetics, there are other species of evidence that go beyond mere testimony. As Swinburne points out, there can be physical traces left behind at a crime scene.[199] There are also personal memory beliefs that count as evidence.[200] Beyond this, Hume does not provide guidance for what one should do if one observes a miracle for oneself. What if a miraculous event occurs in a way that is properly basic, such as an immediate sensory experience? What would Hume say, for example, if he himself saw someone walking on water?[201] What does one do when one is the eyewitness of the event, and not just the one who is hearing the testimony? While Hume does not directly address this question (he probably thought it quite impossible for a wise person to end up in such a situation), it is likely that Hume would counsel that the evidence of the senses and their reliability must be weighed.[202]

Perhaps the most powerful objection that Hume has against miracles is the inability of the observer to know with certainty the cause of the event, and that the event was indeed a genuine instance of a violation of the laws of nature. Our formulations of natural laws are supposed to be descriptive, so they are fluid and capable of expansion. How could an observer of a "miracle" know that they had not simply witnessed an unexplained event, or an uncaused event, or an event that simply represented

---

198. Ibid., 164.

199. Swinburne, *Resurrection of God Incarnate*, 10–15. See also J. A. Cover, "Miracles and Christian Theism," 356–57.

200. Swinburne, *Concept of Miracle*, 34–35.

201. Ibid, 35.

202. Mackie, *Miracle of Theism*, 28.

a further expansion of a known law (or perhaps even the discovery of a previously undiscovered law)? Events are not brute facts. Every event is overlaid with interpretation. A strange occurrence may strike a believer as a miracle, and the believer may attribute its cause to God, whereas an unbeliever may reject the miraculous and attribute the miracle to an anomalous but naturally explicable event.[203]

After supplying a hypothetical example of an extremely well evidenced, unexplained event, Hume writes: "It is evident, that our present philosophers, instead of doubting the fact, ought to receive it as certain, and ought to search for the causes whence it might be derived."[204] In other words, a seemingly inexplicable event should not be dismissed out of hand, but rather a naturalistic causal relationship should be assumed to exist, and then sought out. Hume's point has been expressed in the following way: "The key to Hume's argument is his belief that one cannot affirm both that an occurrence is a violation of a natural law and that the relevant law is genuine (adequate)."[205] Mackie refers to this as Hume's fork, and argues that it is a very powerful disjunction: if the law is genuine, then it outweighs the testimony, and if the testimony outweighs the law, then the law is not genuine, or something unexplained transpired.[206] Although Hume did not specify this disjunction, and although his presentation of these points seems confused (bordering on contradictory), he likely would have endorsed Mackie's rendering of it as truly in keeping with the spirit of his argument.[207]

Anomalies are not identical with miracles, and lack of explanatory power today does not mean that a scientific or natural law has truly been violated in the sense required by Hume for a genuine miracle to have occurred: tomorrow, a better understanding of scientific laws may make what is ostensibly miraculous today perfectly understandable in terms of natural law. So the challenge is not simply the a priori objection against miracles; even if evidence for an incredible event is accepted, how can the conclusion be drawn that this event is in fact a violation of natural law by a supernatural being?

---

203. Owen, "Hume *versus* Price," 201.
204. Hume, *Enquiry*, 92.
205. Basinger, "Christian Theism and the Concept of Miracle," 139.
206. Mackie, *Miracle of Theism*, 26.
207. Houston, *Reported Miracles*, 63.

Amidst the tedium of philosophical dispute, a believer may be forgiven for *prima facie* thinking this is a desperate dodge, a stubborn digging-in rather than a willingness to face an unacceptable conclusion. Yet after further consideration, this point grows in both seriousness and cogency. Scientific knowledge is advancing tremendously. Light is now known in specified conditions to act like both a wave and a particle, something that was once thought contradictory according to the reigning conventional wisdom. Statistically observed phenomena, when seen repeatedly, move from the status of scientific theories to scientific laws (this is not meant as a technical description). But there is always a level of corrigibility about the formulations of scientific laws. Anomalies can accrue that can be ignored, fit into an expanded or modified law, cause the creation of a new law, or cause the rejection of the old law ("law" in this sentence can be replaced with "theory" for a weaker read). Swinburne's position is that if a certain instance can be repeated, the law should be modified; but if the instance is non-repeatable, it can be affirmed as well as the law. This means that, theoretically, a recognized law can be modified depending on actual events, or it can also be held intact and recognized as having been violated in a particular instance.[208]

For the resurrection, the question needs to be asked as to whether or not one person coming back to life from the dead can be explained by absolutely nothing other than an immediate act of God. Is it possible that a human corpse could simply—against admittedly high statistical improbabilities—"undo" death? Could cells regain cellular function, and the body's systems spontaneously work individually and collectively to power the human being back into a state of life?

Swinburne argues that if a certain event transpires that we know is virtually physically impossible, we are at least in a position to logically claim that it is a miracle.[209] In fact, it is only the conjunction of the regularity of natural law with the violation of a natural law that allows for the possibility of identifying an instance of a miracle; we must have a good grasp of what is naturally possible before we could be in a position to identify something as being super-natural.[210] It is only an immoveable commitment to atheism that would make it impossible for an individual

---

208. Swinburne, *Concept of Miracle*, 29–32.
209. Ibid., 32.
210. Collins, *Science and Faith*, 248; see also Flew, *God and Philosophy*, 148.

Evidentialism

to ascribe a physically impossible event (in the sense that nothing could account for it in anything known and understood by science) to an act of God.

While it seems fair for an individual to at least be willing to accept the validity of recognizing a miracle, the concept is still more difficult to uphold when it comes to convincing a skeptic. According to Basinger:

> I shall conclude that, although the Christian theist can successfully circumvent the standard Humean epistemological barrier, he can stipulate no objective criterion for the identification of a miraculous occurrence, even if we grant that the Christian God exists and that the Canon accurately describes how this being relates to our physical universe. In short, I shall conclude that "miracle" must necessarily remain a subjective concept for the orthodox Christian theist.[211]

Basinger ties this position to the fact that our current knowledge of science and nature is so finite it must always be understood as provisional. Causation in the universe may be so complex and complicated that what is currently scientifically inexplicable (or understood to be physically impossible), may yet one day no longer be inexplicable.[212] This limited human knowledge and massive causal complexity makes the category of miracle far more subjective than is often realized.[213] While subjectivity may not be what the apologist is driving for, it does cut both ways. Schlesinger highlights the distinction: "It is important to point out that we should grant Hume only that it is unreasonable for a non-theist to accept miracle stories as credible. For a theist, on the other hand, it is quite rational to pay credence to such stories."[214]

Interpretation will take place within the confines of a worldview. In some worldviews, miracles may not possibly occur, and in others they may not possibly be recognized. But in the Christian worldview, miracles are a distinct possibility, and they are recognizable (even if an unbeliever will not find them veridical or the evidence for them persuasive). Even if the Christian holds to miracles provisionally, and even if completely objective criteria for their identification cannot be articulated, a Christian may still

---

211. Basinger, "Christian Theism and the Concept of Miracle," 137.

212. Ibid., 140.

213. Ibid., 149.

214 Schlesinger, "Miracles and Probabilities," 226; cf. Woods, "Evidential Value," 30; Polkinghorne, *Exploring Reality*, 87–88.

have warrant for interpreting a particular event as a miracle. While it may be that a dead man came back to life in purely natural terms through a sheer statistical anomaly, the believer is rational to hold the odds of God causing the event as far more probable than its having naturally occurred. While there is some difficulty attendant in deciding what a miracle is or is not, it does seem fair to say with Beckwith, "it is also reasonable to infer that a miracle came about by the power of a rational non-human cause (i.e., a god), on the basis of the miracle's purpose, timing, existential significance, religious context, and human impossibility."[215]

If the historical evidence for God were zero, and the logical possibility of God were zero, then it would be rational—no matter how statistically improbable—to accept a naturalistic explanation for any event. But is this really the probability of God's existence? It seems that in the final analysis Houston is right to argue that Hume's argument rests on implicit atheism; it simply does not succeed if theism obtains.[216] Flew also agrees: "We have already urged that the critical historian has to assess all testimony—and of course all other evidence too—in the light of everything he knows—or believes that he knows—about all the regularities which obtain in the world."[217] If the historian believes in theism (or even Christianity particularly), then the historian will use that worldview in their decision-making regarding the likelihood of a miraculous event.[218] Thus, for the historian, philosopher, or non-specialist, the question of theism is enormously important for the weighing and accepting of miracle claims. This is true not only for non-technical thinking, but also for rigorous, self-consciously logical analysis.[219]

---

215. Beckwith, *David Hume's Argument against Miracles*, 64.

216. Houston, *Reported Miracles*, 143–44.

217. Flew, *Hume's Philosophy of Belief*, 196.

218. There has been much made—good and ill—of Flew's recent movement from atheism to an acceptance of generic theism, or deism. Flew, in response to Wright's argument for the resurrection, has stated that once omnipotence is granted, only what is logically impossible is excluded: See Flew, *There Is a God*, 213. In other words, once theism obtains, the evidence for a resurrection is on a very different footing than if theism does not obtain. Here Flew is being consistent: in an earlier debate with Habermas, he had stated that a resurrection would be naturally impossible, but possible supernaturally (ibid., 64). He had also written in a letter that: "Certainly given some beliefs about God, the occurrence of the resurrection does become enormously more likely" (ibid., 39).

219. For a mathematical model using Bayes's Theorem, where the authors conclude that the Theorem will yield different results for believers and non-believers, see Dawid and Gilles, "Bayesian Analysis."

Furthermore, even if it could be demonstrated that there was a sheer statistical fluke, and the dead man returning to life could be explained in terms of a natural process, this does not rule out the superintending plan and power of God. Material or scientific explanations are not coextensive with personal, intentional explanations. In fact, they are very different, even though both can be used to explain the same phenomenon.[220] Scientific law and personal agency operate at different explanatory levels. To reject one explanatory level because of another one is to commit the reductive fallacy. This is well illustrated by John Haught when he provides the example of roasting marshmallows over a campfire. At one explanatory level, the marshmallows are roasted because an intentional agent wants them. At another level, the roasting can be explained by chemical composition and interaction. It is wrong to deny personal intentionality, and it is wrong to deny chemical activity; they should not be set over and against each other. In fact, both are true; the genuine ultimate explanation is layered and multifaceted.[221]

There is a running debate about supernatural causation as an acceptable avenue for scientific and historical investigation, which was the topic of a representative exchange that took place as a Forum in the journal *History and Theory: Studies in the Philosophy of History*.[222] Forland argues that history *qua* history must presuppose methodological naturalism for causal explanation, whereas Gregory argues that such a presupposition is illegitimate in terms of the discipline itself. Gregory writes: "despite widespread opinion to the contrary, the belief that science and religion are necessarily incompatible does not derive from the methods or findings of the natural sciences themselves."[223] Further on, he states: "Inescapably, what lies behind questions about the *possibility* of miracles are questions about the reality and nature of God. No empirical investigation can rule out their possibility."[224] Gregory's first point is critical: according to the methods of science, methodological naturalism is not proven to be necessary, nor is it sacrosanct. There is nothing in science (or historical method) *qua* science (or historical method) that forbids the existence or

---

220. Swinburne, *Concept of Miracle*, 53–55.

221. Haught, *Is Nature Enough*, 16.

222. Forland, "God, Science, and Historical Explanation"; Forland, "Historiography without God"; Gregory, "No Room for God."

223. Gregory, "No Room for God," 499.

224. Ibid., 511.

activity of a supernatural being as the best possible causal, explanatory hypothesis for a given state of affairs. William Lane Craig expresses the same tension the following way:

> The real problem comes when we inquire concerning the *cause* of the resurrection. According to the above methodology, the historian *qua* historian could conclude that the best explanation of the facts is that "Jesus rose from the dead"; but he could not conclude, "God raised Jesus from the dead." But what I wish to suggest for the reader's consideration is that the historian, "in his off-hours," to paraphrase Bertrand Russell, that is, the historian as a human being, may indeed rightly infer from the evidence that God has acted here in history.[225]

Craig also wonders: "If it is the case that the evidence can only be plausibly explained by the historical fact of the resurrection of Jesus, why are we debarred from that conclusion?"[226] He goes on to state his conclusions very strongly:

> But furthermore, the methodological principle that prohibits any historian from adducing a supernatural cause for an event in history seems to be either arbitrary or based on bad science or philosophy. For as long as the existence of God is even possible, an event's being caused by God cannot be ruled out. To be sure, the historian ought first, as a methodological principle, to seek natural causes; but when no natural cause can be found that plausibly accounts for the data and a supernatural hypothesis presents itself as part of the historical context in which the event occurred, then the rational alternative would seem to be to choose the supernatural explanation. Naturalism has had nearly 2,000 years to explain the resurrection of Jesus and has failed to do so. The rational man can hardly now be blamed if he infers that at the tomb of Jesus on that early Easter morning a divine miracle has occurred.[227]

Kirsopp Lake (who comes to the opposite conclusion from Craig concerning the historicity of the resurrection), presents the historian's task as triadic: "The first task of the historical inquirer is to collect the pieces of evidence; the second is to discuss the trustworthiness and meaning of each separate piece; and the third is to reconstruct the events to

---

225. Craig, *Assessing the New Testament Evidence*, 419.
226. Ibid., 418.
227. Ibid., 420.

which the evidence relates."²²⁸ Using these criteria, there does not seem to be any logical compulsion to forbid the historian from reaching a supernatural conclusion concerning the cause of an event.

What is very apparent is that philosophical presuppositions are not absent in either the historian's practice or theory, and this has a tremendous bearing on theology. Perhaps there is no better example of this than that supplied in the life and work of Ernst Troeltsch, whose primary concern was with the relationship between history and theology.²²⁹ For Troeltsch, the historical method was controlling, and: "he made a strong demand that the historical method be applied to theology in full seriousness and without reservations."²³⁰ Troeltsch identified three axioms for the historical method: "Here we are concerned principally with three essential aspects: the habituation on principle to historical criticism; the importance of analogy; and the mutual interrelation of all historical developments."²³¹ Harrisville and Sundberg clarify: "The first axiom requires acclimatization in historical criticism (the principle of criticism); the second, knowledge of the significance of analogy (the principle of analogy); and the third, knowledge of the correlation occurring among all historical events (the principle of correlation)."²³²

Precisely what Troeltsch meant by his second axiom, the principle of analogy, is not altogether clear to all scholars.²³³ Although she acknowledges the lack of perspicuity in his discussion, Sarah Coakley is sure, however, that it is a mistake to interpret Troeltsch as ruling out miracles in an a priori manner, as Pannenberg has interpreted him.²³⁴ Troeltsch explains the principle of analogy as follows:

> The second basic postulate of the historical method is that the instrumentality that makes historical criticism possible is the employment of analogy. Analogous occurrences that we observe both without and within ourselves furnish us with the key to historical criticism. The illusions, distortions, deceptions, myths, and partisanship we see with our own eyes enable us to recognize similar

228. Lake, *Historical Evidence*, 6.
229. Harrisville and Sundberg, *Bible in Modern Culture*, 160.
230. Yasukata, *Ernst Troeltsch*, 165.
231. Troeltsch, "Historical and Dogmatic Method," 13.
232. Harrisville and Sundberg, *Bible in Modern Culture*, 165.
233. Coakley, *Christ without Absolutes*, 65.
234. Ibid., 24 n. 34.

> features in the materials of tradition. Agreement with normal, customary, or at least frequently attested happenings and conditions as we experience them is the criterion of probability for all events that historical criticism can recognize as having actually or possibly happened. The observation of analogies between similar events in the past provides the possibility of imputing probability to them and of interpreting what is unkown [sic] about the one by reference to what is known about the other.[235]

This view is comfortably Humean. It is easy to see how Troeltsch can be construed as ruling out miracles a priori in this passage, especially given his language about analogy allowing us to recognize what might even "possibly" happen. Nevertheless, whether it is fully a priori, or a softer position that demands understanding strange events through the lens of familiar ones,[236] the principle is still extremely strongly worded. Troeltsch acknowledges that at one level every event is absolutely and individually unique, but he also insists that every event shares a common core that relates it to other historical events.[237] If there is any doubt about the status of this principle concerning the miraculous, Troeltsch states unequivocally that even the resurrection of Jesus must face this axiom.[238] He is aware that confessional orthodoxy will suffer as a result: "Give the historical method an inch and it will take a mile. From a strictly orthodox standpoint, therefore, it seems to bear a certain similarity to the devil."[239] In contrast to the secular historical method, Troeltsch faults the historical method used by dogmatic believers because: "It claims an authority that is dogmatic rather than historical, intrinsic rather than based on comparison, immutable rather than sharing the conditions of historical existence."[240]

Not all theologian-historians accepted Troeltsch's strong interpretation of his principle of analogy, or agreed with the conclusions that he believed it entailed, as a comparison of his views with those of Pannenberg reveal. This does not mean, however, that the principle of analogy had to be either accepted or rejected in total as Troeltsch understood it. As

---

235. Troeltsch, "Historical and Dogmatic Method," 13–14.
236. Coakley, *Christ without Absolutes*, 24 n. 34.
237. Troeltsch, "Historical and Dogmatic Method," 14.
238. Ibid.
239. Ibid., 16.
240. Ibid., 22.

Alister McGrath points out in his discussion of the historical method of Pannenberg and Troeltsch: "Pannenberg is too good a historian to suggest that the principle of analogy should be abandoned; it is, after all, a proven and useful tool of historical research. Yet, Pannenberg insists, that is all that it is: It is a working tool, and cannot be allowed to define a fixed view of reality."[241] Pannenberg argues that Troeltsch's presuppositions have made it impossible for him to see the "once-for-all revelation" of God acting in particular historical events.[242] The principle of analogy is a good general rule, but a bad absolute law. A priori, or at least functionally, it makes it virtually impossible for anyone to ever recognize an event as God performing a miracle (which is highly problematic if God actually does perform miracles in history). At a minimum, the implications for the historian recognizing the resurrection are clear.

This result is especially troubling for Pannenberg, given his own contribution to the relationship between history and the Christian faith. Pannenberg argues that history must not be studied in atomistic pieces, but must be seen as a coherent whole.[243] It is the overall structure of history that provides individual events with interpretive intelligibility. The entailment of this position is that "only on the presupposition of a universal-historical horizon can one meaningfully raise the question as to whether God has revealed himself at one or another place in history. The central question for debate between history and theology arises here: how is the conception of a unity of history possible?"[244]

Pannenberg insists that "the unity of history has its ground in something transcending history."[245] What is this ground? The ground is the transcendent work of God in Jesus Christ, which is nonetheless a historical work. For Pannenberg, the unity (and therefore coherence) of history is found in the resurrection of Jesus Christ. History has not yet reached its conclusion, but its end is found in Jesus.[246] In fact, rather than seeing history as an unfolding forward process, it should be viewed as a backward chain, where events link backwards with previous events.[247] In other

---

241. McGrath, *Christian Theology*, 334.
242. Pannenberg, *Basic Questions in Theology*, 1:57.
243. Ibid., 66–67.
244. Ibid., 68.
245. Ibid., 74.
246. Ibid., 77.
247. Ibid., 75.

words: "The fact that events throw light on earlier occurrences and so establish repeatedly in a new way connections backward lays the foundation for the continuity of history."[248] There are epiphanic moments in life that shed light on previous experiences. There are breakthrough events that allow for reinterpreting past life events with more clarity. The future provides the hermeneutical key to accurately reading the past.

The goal and end of history is the revelation of the glory of God, revealed in Jesus. Pannenberg states:

> Only at the end of all things can God be revealed in his divinity, that is, as the one who works all things, who has power over everything. Only because in Jesus' resurrection the end of all things, which for us has not yet happened, has already occurred can it be said of Jesus that the ultimate already is present in him, and so also that God himself, his glory, has made its appearance in Jesus in a way that cannot be surpassed. Only because the end of the world is already present in Jesus' resurrection is God himself revealed in him.[249]

An excellent, succinct summary of Pannenberg's historical-theological position is provided by McGrath:

> Pannenberg's argument takes the following form. History, in all its totality, can only be understood when it is viewed from its endpoint. This point alone provides the perspective from which the historical process can be seen completely, and thus be properly understood. However, where Marx argued that the social sciences, by predicting the goal of history to be the hegemony of socialism, provided the key to the interpretation of history, Pannenberg declared that this was provided only in Jesus Christ. The end of history is disclosed proleptically in the history of Jesus Christ. In other words, the end of history, which has yet to take place, has been disclosed in advance of the event in the person and work of Christ.[250]

For Troeltsch, the historical method was the enemy of orthodoxy, and virtually ruled out the possibility of ever accepting a purported miracle as having genuinely occurred. For Pannenberg, the resurrection of Jesus is the anchor and foundation of history itself.

---

248. Pannenberg, *Toward a Theology of Nature*, 83.
249. Pannenberg, *Jesus—God and Man*, 69.
250. McGrath, *Christian Theology*, 333.

A consensus will not be reached by arguing about proper historical methodology in isolation from wider philosophical concerns. The issue of the possibility of a miracle, and the recognition of such an event (albeit even if only subjectively) ultimately turns on metaphysical, worldview thinking. And the methodology for defending and establishing a theistic order is what divides classical apologists from *evidential apologists. How does one move from an anomalous event to the conclusion that such an event was a direct act of God? It seems that a miracle can only be properly identified as such if this is a theistic universe. Here Swinburne seems to be on the right track in *The Resurrection of God Incarnate*. The evidence for the resurrection needs to include the background evidence for theism. Why can a historian conclude that an event was caused by God? Because they may take the background evidence for God as good, highly probable, or even certain. Thus supernatural causal explanation is not necessarily ruled out beforehand by logic or evidence. Concluding that a supernatural being is the cause of a strange event that violates an accepted law of nature—and is thus corrigibly termed a miracle—is rational if, and only if, theism is a live option.

Classical apologists argue that there needs to be a demonstration of theism prior to any event being classified as a miracle. R. C. Sproul clearly expresses the point: "We are not suggesting that one can argue from the miracle reports of the Bible to the existence of God. Before an action can be deemed a miracle or an event that only God could cause, the existence of a God capable of such action would have to be established."[251] Norman Geisler, in his critique of evidentialism, expands on the classical understanding of the relationship between theism and evidentialism:

> First, facts and events have ultimate meaning only within and by virtue of the context of the world view in which they are conceived. Hence, it is a vicious circle to argue that a given fact (say, the resuscitation of Christ's body) is evidence of a certain truth claim (say, Christ's claim to be God), *unless it can be established that the event comes in the context of a theistic universe.* For it makes no sense to claim to be the Son of *God* and to evidence it by an act of *God* (miracle) unless there is a God who can have a Son and who can act in a special way in the natural world. But in this case the mere fact of the resurrection cannot be used to establish the truth that there is a God. For the resurrection cannot even be a miracle un-

---

251. Sproul, *Defending Your Faith*, 170.

less there already is a God. Many overzealous and hasty Christian apologists rush hastily into their historical and evidential apologetics without first properly doing their theistic homework.[252]

For strict classical apologists, then, the demonstration of theism is both logically prior to—and in fact necessary for—the identification of an event as a miracle. By definition, a miracle requires the activity of a supernatural being, and so a supernatural being must exist in order for a miracle to be analytically coherent. Classical apologetics moves from philosophical arguments for theism to an investigation of potential miracles, the latter now being a live historical possibility given the establishment of the former.

In summary, the best way to distinguish between classical apologists and *evidentialists is by asking whether or not miracles by themselves can lead to a theistic conclusion, even if theistic arguments have not established that this is a theistic universe.[253] So for *evidentialists the historical data for an event like the resurrection may demand a supernatural agent or power for a cogent explanation. If it is naturally impossible, an appeal to a supernatural being is in order. An apologist may even look at the historical data and decide to at least pursue theism as a "promising hypothesis."[254] Historical data—at least theoretically—may be the only argument the *evidentialist apologist needs to establish theism.

There is, of course, a wide debate about the strength of the conclusions that can be drawn from theistic arguments. Craig identifies the probabilistic aspect that can be found even in classical apologetics, and refers to the function of theistic argumentation and historical evidences in his own work:

> The methodology of classical apologetics was first to present arguments for theism, which aimed to show that God's existence is at least more probable than not, and then to present Christian evidences, probabilistically construed, for God's revelation in Christ. This is the method I have adopted in my own work. By means of the *kalam* cosmological argument, I have endeavored to show that a Personal Creator of all the universe exists. By means of the his-

---

252. Geisler, *Christian Apologetics*, 95–95, emphasis in original.
253. Habermas, "Evidential Apologetics," 98 n. 20.
254. Houston, *Reported Miracles*, 149.

torical evidence for the resurrection of Jesus, I have tried to show that God has revealed himself in Christ.[255]

So theism may be granted a probabilistic numeral of more than 0.5 but still far less than 1.0, and then the historical case can be pursued.

Now, the Ligonier apologists (i.e., the team of Sproul, Gerstner and Lindsley) will have nothing to do with a probability of less than 1.0 when it comes to their own arguments. In their own estimation of their formulation of theistic arguments, their conclusions are completely certain. They write:

> In conclusion, we have endeavored to update the traditional theistic arguments, trying to show that when properly formulated they are *compelling certainties* and not merely suggestive possibilities. It is at this point that we have attempted to answer the objections of historic opponents, such as Immanuel Kant. It is also at this point that we have tried to tighten the statements of contemporary advocates such as Montgomery, Pinnock, Schaeffer, Geisler, and others.[256]

FROM RESURRECTION TO SCRIPTURE

Having noted the difference between classical and *evidential apologists, and having recorded the dispute concerning how strong the conclusions of theistic arguments are, it is time to move past these issues and examine how the apologists in these broad schools relate the doctrines of the resurrection and Scripture. Again, for our current purposes, the particular doctrine of Scripture in view affirms full inspiration and plenary inerrancy. Whether or not the resurrection has been argued for on historical data alone, or theistic arguments were employed antecedently, once the

---

255. Craig, "Classical Apologetics," 48–49.

256. Sproul, Gerstner, and Lindsley, *Classical Apologetics*, 136, emphasis added. Geisler in *Christian Apologetics* (p. 258) argues for the position that theism is "undeniable," with "undeniable premises that lead inescapably to the existence of [God]." Not all Christian philosophers concur, of course. For a team of scholars who make the case that theism cannot be absolutely certain, and therefore must be probabilistic, see Peterson et al., *Reason and Religious Belief*. Swinburne's many writings rely on Bayesian probabilities for theism, and as such eschew absolute certainty for theistic argumentation. For a balanced view of reason, religion, and probability from an atheistic perspective, see Rowe, *Philosophy of Religion*. In the end, much of the disagreement rests on whether one believes there is a single, coercive argument for theism, or whether the case must be built in a cumulative fashion, resting on principles of abduction.

resurrection is granted, how does this relate to the doctrine of Scripture? In apologetic methodology, what movement is there from the meaning of the resurrection to the defense of the Scriptures as the inspired, inerrant Word of God?

Before proceeding any further, it is worth noting that not all Christian apologists are concerned with this step, owing to the fact that they do not hold to the plenary inspiration and inerrancy of the Scriptures. As was pointed out in the relevant sections above, Swinburne and Wright simply accept errors and discrepancies in the canonical witness. They are neither scandalized by them nor even surprised. In fact, they argue that the presence of minor discrepancies is to be expected, and in some ways the presence of such flaws strengthens rather than detracts from the historical reliability of the sources, because they tend to weaken the thesis that the disciples and early eyewitnesses were in collusion. Since errors in the biblical record are accepted in their case for the resurrection, this precludes a defense of inerrancy later on. Although (logically speaking) they could appeal to inerrancy in the original autographs, while recognizing errors in the extant manuscripts, neither does this.

But what avenues are open for those apologists who defend plenary biblical inerrancy? Habermas and Licona, cited above, mention that their argument for the resurrection does not turn on inerrancy, or even the general reliability of the Bible. They do not, however, actually concede that the Scriptures are errant. Unlike Swinburne or Wright, then, Habermas and Licona are at least in a position to move to a defense of biblical inerrancy without being charged with wielding an inconsistent apologetic. In fact, Habermas and Licona do state that they believe the Bible is trustworthy and reliable.[257] They also indicate that the historical resurrection is the right place to begin for making a case for the Bible's trustworthiness.[258] They do not, however, pursue the issue, and actually purposefully leave it to the side, because they want to examine the historical data for the resurrection alone without engaging issues of scriptural inspiration.

Some authors, however, have gone on to flesh out the argument, and attempted to demonstrate how to move from miracles—particularly the resurrection as the great miracle—to the conclusion that the Bible is the plenarily inspired Word of God. For the sake of working with a

---

257. Habermas and Licona, *Case for the Resurrection*, 44.
258. Ibid., 28.

manageable sample, the main apologists cited will be delimited to Geisler, Montgomery, and the Ligoniers, with particular attention paid to the Ligoniers, since they are Reformed theologians as well as apologists.

The Ligoniers outline the case they intend to make in six points:

1. It is virtually granted that the Bible (not assumed to be inspired) contains generally reliable history.
2. The Bible records miracles as part of its generally reliable history.
3. These miracles authenticate the Bible's messengers and their message.
4. Therefore, the Bible message ought to be received as divine.
5. The Bible message includes the doctrine of its own inspiration.
6. Therefore, the Bible is more than a generally reliable record. It is a divinely inspired record.[259]

While admitting that the Bible needs to be defended as generally reliable history, the Ligoniers simply refer the reader to two books that defend that position, one by James Martin and another by F. F. Bruce.[260] Then they argue that the Scriptures are not just to be taken existentially, but as real history. It will, for the sake of argument, be assumed at this point that the Bible can be accepted as generally reliable history. While this would in fact need to be argued for, it will be conceded as a starting point—the question is whether or not the subsequent steps and deductions are legitimate.

The argument proceeds in the following way: In the real historical record of the Bible, there are claims for real historical miracles. Since the Bible is generally reliable in historical matters, it is generally reliable in its record of historical miracles. And it is to be expected, argue the Ligoniers, that if God sent messengers at all, he would provide them with credentials, such as being accompanied by miracles.[261] Thus, "From an *uninspired* Bible we are arguing for miracles, and from miracles we are arguing for an *inspired* Bible."[262] Miracles must come after natural theol-

---

259. Sproul, Gerstner, and Lindsley, *Classical Apologetics*, 141.
260. Ibid., 142.
261. Ibid., 144.
262. Ibid.; emphasis in original.

ogy has established the existence of God—unless God exists, Jesus cannot be God's Son, and unless God exists, the Bible cannot be God's Word.[263]

The next step in this case is to argue that, since the Bible contains miracles the message of the Bible is authenticated as coming from God, and whatever comes from God must be perfect (i.e., without error). Miracles are the best evidence for the power of God: "If infinite natural power is the ultimate argument for the existence of God, infinite supernatural power (miracle) is the ultimate argument for the revelation of God."[264] They conclude:

> Miracle without truth is spurious. That is, we accept miracles in harmony with known truth as the proof of Scripture as a revelation of God. Now we have thus proved that the Bible is the Word of God on this formula: Natural revelation plus miracle plus claimed revelation proves revelation. The Bible is established and its teaching is therefore to be accepted. This would include its teaching about miracles. That is, if the Bible says that the miracles themselves prove that the miracle-worker is a messenger of God, then (quite apart from the natural theology of the worker) we may accept the fact on authority that miracles per se authenticate an authority. The doer is a messenger of *God* and not of anyone else. This the Bible does in fact teach.[265]

For the Ligoniers there is no playing of *inspiration* against *inerrancy*. They fully affirm biblical inerrancy, and rejoice that others do as well.[266] So for the Ligoniers, their argument does not just allow them to settle for a vague, amorphous brand of general inspiration; they conclude that the Bible is completely without error.

A similar, but fuller argument is offered by Geisler. Note the similarities between his argument and the one offered by the Ligoniers:

> The evidence that the Bible is the written Word of God is anchored in the authority of Jesus Christ. The basic argument in support of this runs as follows: (1) the New Testament documents are historically reliable (Chapter 16); (2) these documents accurately present Christ as claiming to be God Incarnate and proving it by fulfilled messianic prophecy, by a sinless and miraculous life, and

---

263. Ibid., 148–49.
264. Ibid., 157.
265. Ibid., 159, emphasis in original.
266. Ibid., 286.

by predicting and accomplishing his resurrection from the dead (Chapter 17); (3) whatever Christ (who is God) teaches is true; (4) Christ taught that the Old Testament is the written Word of God and promised that his disciples would write the New Testament (Chapter 18); (5) therefore, it is true on the confirmed authority of Jesus Christ that the Bible is the written Word of God.[267]

Geisler's supporting argumentation is much more thorough than the Ligoniers', but the main contours are the same. Natural theology has first proved the existence of God, making God's activity logically possible. The Bible, on the canons of historiographical principles, is reliable. These reliable documents contain teachings of Jesus about the Scriptures, and Jesus' authority is demonstrated by miracles, particularly the resurrection. Geisler seems more aware than the Ligoniers that Jesus' attitude towards the Old Testament canon does not impinge much on the Book of Romans—so Geisler notes the preauthorization Jesus granted to his followers to write the New Testament. It is somewhat surprising that more apologists do not seem to understand that, even if they are right that Jesus endorsed the entire Old Testament canon as inspired and inerrant, this does not equal an endorsement of the New Testament canon, or epistles like the Book of Romans! The appeal is then to preauthorization, where the Spirit will guide the disciples into all truth (John 14:26). Arguments are in short supply, however, proving that this verse must be fulfilled in an inerrant New Testament canon. Nevertheless, the argument runs that God exists, and Jesus is confirmed as his Son—a Son who speaks with full authority, and who uses that authority to claim that the Bible is the inspired and inerrant Word of God. Even though Geisler does not use the phrase "inspired and inerrant" in this immediate context, the concept is clearly embedded in his thinking. In another place, Geisler and Nix state quite clearly: "*The whole Bible is inerrant.* Still another deduction to be drawn from inspiration is the fact that the Bible is inerrant (errorless)."[268] For Geisler, the inspiration of Scripture logically requires full inerrancy.

When it comes to establishing the Bible's inspiration, the *evidentialist John Warwick Montgomery and the classical apologists make the same general moves. Montgomery—in what will surely look familiar at this stage—summarizes his argument this way:

---

267. Ibid., 353.
268. Geisler and Nix, *General Introduction*, 53, emphasis in original.

> On the basis of accepted principles of textual and historical analysis, the Gospel records are found to be trustworthy historical documents—primary source evidence for the life of Christ
>
> 1. In these records Jesus exercises divine prerogatives and claims to be God in human flesh. He rests His claims on His forthcoming resurrection.
>
> 2. In all four Gospels, Christ's bodily resurrection is described in minute detail; Christ's resurrection evidences His deity.
>
> 3. The fact of the resurrection cannot be discounted on a priori, philosophical grounds; miracles are impossible only if one so defines them—but such definition rules out proper historical investigation.
>
> 4. If Christ is God, then He speaks the truth concerning the absolute divine authority of the Old Testament and of the soon-to-be-written, apostolic New Testament; concerning His death for the sins of the world; and concerning the nature of man and of history.
>
> 5. It follows from the preceding that all biblical assertions bearing on philosophy of history are to be regarded as revealed truth, and that all human attempts at historical interpretation are to be judged for truth value on the basis of harmony with scriptural revelation.[269]

Perhaps the major difference between Montgomery and the Ligoniers is that Montgomery does not concern himself with miracles in general, but with the resurrection in particular. Thus he moves to the most important miracle of all, and the one that reveals the most about Jesus Christ. If the resurrection happened, then Jesus speaks the truth, and since Jesus claims inspiration for the Scriptures, then inspired is what they are. Note that, like Geisler, Montgomery also looks ahead to the completion of the New Testament canon, and justifies accepting the post-Jesus canonical writings on the basis of Jesus' prophecy that they also would be inspired.

Montgomery is an excellent example of this style of argumentation, not only because he is a well known representative of *evidentialism, but also because he is a staunch defender of biblical inspiration and plenary inerrancy. He argues that to claim that the Bible is inspired but not iner-

---

269. Montgomery, *Where Is History Going*, 34–35.

rant is both theologically meaningless and analytically meaningless.[270] He bluntly states that a "non-inerrant inspired Scripture" is nonsensical.[271] To argue, as some do, that the Bible is inerrant in terms of theology but not in terms of history or science is rejected by Montgomery as utterly arbitrary, and question-begging: if the history recorded in the Bible is wrong, how can one prove the theology of the Bible is correct, once the truth claims are removed from any kind of verifiable or testable experience?[272]

That there are alleged errors in the Bible is accepted by Montgomery. But the way to approach such errors is dependent on what the Bible actually is. According to Montgomery: "To know how to treat biblical passages containing apparent errors or contradictions, we must determine what kind of book the Bible is."[273] To settle this question Montgomery looks at the attitude Jesus took towards the Scriptures, and concludes that Jesus taught that the Bible was completely accurate down to every word. Therefore, the Christian adopts the attitude of the Lord Jesus Christ, and approaches alleged problem passages with the understanding of Jesus that the Bible is inerrant, and so there must be a non-contradictory resolution to the textual difficulties.[274] In another book Montgomery writes: "The doctrine of biblical inerrancy derives from the attitude of Scripture towards itself, and in particular the attitude of Christ toward Scripture . . . the total trust Jesus and the apostles displayed toward Scripture entails a precise and controlled hermeneutic . . . They did not regard Scripture as erroneous or self-contradictory; neither can we. They took its miracles and prophecies as literal fact; so must we."[275]

From this general sketch several commonalities in the arguments can be identified. Regardless of whether or not the apologist believes that miracles function in an *evidential sense, or that theism needs to be established before the question of the miraculous can even be rationally discussed, there is a similar style of argument from miracle (particularly the resurrection) to the full inspiration of the Scriptures. The movement runs from accepting the Bible as a collection of historical documents, to

---

270. Montgomery, *Suicide of Christian Theology*, 334–39.
271. Ibid., 334.
272. Ibid., 337.
273. Ibid., 358.
274. Ibid.
275. Montgomery, *Faith Founded on Fact*, 223.

judging them to be trustworthy (at least generally). Since the Bible records miracles (particularly the resurrection), these miracles are to be received as veridical because the source in which they are reported is basically reliable. Jesus, as the resurrected one, is clearly the spokesperson for God. Inductively studying the Scriptures, we discover that Jesus claims to *be* God. He also endorses a view of the Scriptures that is—to employ an anachronism—that they are fully inspired and inerrant, down to the smallest details and words. Thus the follower of Jesus should likewise adopt this same position regarding the Scriptures, and accept them as fully inspired and inerrant.

In this model, then, the relationship between the doctrine of Scripture and the doctrine of the resurrection is explicated in terms of the general reliability of the former, the reality of the latter, and then the latter providing a divine authorization for the teachings of the former down to the last iota. The doctrine of Scripture is provisional and inchoate in the system previous to establishing the doctrine of the resurrection. It can be accepted as uninspired (but reliable and trustworthy—which may require argument) at the beginning. From the hypothesis that the uninspired—albeit reliable—record contains reports of miracles, the conclusion is drawn that the miracle accounts are true. Miraculous powers provide credentials to the messengers, which divinely authorize their teachings. For Jesus Christ, the super-miracle, the resurrection, confirms his teachings, which include his self-confession of deity, and the inerrancy of the biblical canon. This model places the doctrine of the resurrection before the final doctrine of Scripture.

There is an oscillation between inductive and deductive reasoning in this argument. Inductively, the Bible is seen to make claims about its own inspiration and authority. Jesus is heard to make claims about the full inspiration of the Scriptures, and he is divinely authorized and credentialed by his miracles, with the resurrection being the most important one. From this inductive data is drawn the deductive conclusion that all Scripture is in fact inerrant. Jesus does not quote every verse in the Old Testament Scriptures and say that it is inerrant. Rather, he provides the general view that all Scripture is inspired, which becomes the premise for making the deduction that every word is divinely inspired, and therefore inerrant.

Evidentialism

INTERNAL ANALYSIS OF APOLOGETIC COGENCY

A preliminary note should be sounded regarding evidence for the resurrection and Reformed apologetic method. It is quite clear that one does not need to be of strict Reformed theological convictions in order to accept this apologetic approach. Montgomery is an ordained Lutheran minister (as well as lawyer and professor). Craig, Habermas, Geisler, Wright, and Swinburne are not Reformed theologians. But the Ligonier apologists—Sproul, Gerstner, and Lindsley—are evangelical Reformed writers. Of the three, Gerstner is perhaps the most recognized scholar, while Sproul has dozens of popular level books written out of Calvinistic convictions. The style of argumentation examined in this chapter is not exclusive to, nor excluding of, Reformed thought. If someone is a classical apologist, or an *evidentialist, this does not betray anything about their particular theological views on Calvinistic thinking. Such historical evidences and philosophical arguments are broadly generic, capable of crossing wide segments of Christian schools of thought.

Another preliminary point that should be made is that this section will be somewhat truncated. In the next two chapters the criticisms of these arguments from the Reformed epistemologists and the presuppositionalists will be examined. In order to avoid too much redundancy, not every point of criticism will surface here. This is an internal check for cogency, but part of the later critiques that are leveled against these arguments will deal with their internal difficulties as well. So in order to avoid unnecessary repetition, this part will only suggest certain avenues for critique, without being exhaustive in terms of the depth of the critique, or in terms of the number of issues discussed.

The first area to highlight involves epistemology. In an audio lecture on contemporary apologetics, John Warwick Montgomery explains that in real life people change their thinking on the basis of evidence: the apologist is just trying to get them to think about God and the resurrection with the same kind of reasoning they use in ordinary life.[276] Montgomery's point may go some way to explain why simple, evidentially based books by authors like Josh McDowell and Lee Strobel enjoy such widespread popularity (at least in North America, and at least amongst Christians).[277] The conclusions of the books are based on purported facts

---

276. Montgomery, "Contemporary Apologetics Lecture 3."

277. McDowell, *New Evidence*; Strobel, *Case for Christ*. In a previous generation Morison's *Who Moved the Stone?* advanced a very similar method, and was very popular.

and evidence, and the argument is that on the basis of normal reasoning, believers can fully support their faith, and skeptics should accept the reliability of the Bible and the resurrection of Jesus (which means, of course, that they should accept Christianity as true, and convert). While much more than this could be said about C. S. Lewis's classic *Mere Christianity*, it also presents simple arguments and evidence, while answering objections to the faith in a very plain, commonsense, and normal way. Besides Lewis's undeniable gifting as an author for lucid, memorable, and understandable prose, it is also the content of the book that makes it so enduring in certain Christian circles.

This type of reasoning involves both induction and deduction, and is most closely analogous to the reasoning used in courts of law to render judicial verdicts.[278] The appeal is to normal, everyday reasoning, and the canons of regular judgment that average humans use in arriving at conclusions all the time. But what if the reasoning average humans use every day involves natural materialistic causality, or skeptical doubt, or a species of soft postmodern relativism? (The word *soft* here is meant to exclude the more viral forms of postmodernism where nothing can be known and everything is completely relative. Soft postmodernism in this context would mean that individuals have room for a large dose of relativity in their thinking, and that they are perfectly content to have loose ends in this universe and unexplained or unexplainable phenomena that they are not in an interpretive position to fully explain or understand.) In practice, what if the thinker is simply predisposed to skepticism given ancient reports of the miraculous? John Howard Sobel, near the end of an article dealing with Bayesian probability and Hume states: "It was I suppose clear from the start *that*—though it may now be somewhat clearer *why*—if anyone were to tell you that a man had died and come back to life you had better not believe him."[279] Thus for Sobel, even before working on the Bayesian calculus, he knew that it was clear that dead men do not come back to life. How many people in their regular thinking and everyday reasoning would simply hold to something similar? In other words, how many people are regular Humeans, even if they have never read Hume? How many people—in their everyday lives—are confronted by miracles that they have to regularly think about in regular, everyday ways?

278. Montgomery, "The Jury Returns"; cf. Beckwith, *David Hume's Argument against Miracles*.

279. Sobel, "On the Evidence of Testimony," 186; emphasis in original.

Evidentialism

Now, one possible response to this is that regular Humean thinkers need to be challenged to extend their thinking beyond preconceived atheistic presuppositions. They need to back up the reasonableness of their principles that exclude God and the supernatural. Here is where the apologists need to do their work, and present all the arguments and evidence for the resurrection, the reliability of the Scriptures, etc. Then they need to argue that the logic of the case is such that the only rational—or at a minimum the most rational—conclusion is that God raised Jesus from the dead. Even if a miracle is quite unexpected, or even if the possibility has never been seriously entertained, the apologist must insist that the miracle not simply be dismissed if there is good evidence for it.[280]

What is ultimately at issue here is the justification of the epistemological structures used in everyday reasoning. Are we justified in using these structures to conclude that the resurrection, and hence Christianity itself, is true? Perhaps it is not overstating the matter to say that the effectiveness of this apologetic method will vary depending on the epistemic self-consciousness of the individual. An argument could certainly be made that people in their everyday reasoning are completely unaware of technical epistemology. (Without anybody having conducted a statistical analysis, it seems obvious that the vast majority of people alive today have never taken a course in philosophy or epistemology). A deeper case would require a successful defense of the "regular thinking" of the average person in everyday matters. Yet, it is also worth noting that the same debates exist amongst professional philosophers and scholars. Nothing in this paragraph is meant to indicate in any way that evidentialists of all stripes are unaware of epistemology. Of course there are professional epistemologists who accept the tenets of evidentialism. The defense of evidentialism takes place at all levels of philosophical rigor. For example, one team of epistemologists writes:

> We advocate evidentialism in epistemology. What we call evidentialism is the view that the epistemic justification of a belief is determined by the quality of the believer's evidence for the belief. Disbelief and suspension of judgment also can be epistemically justified. The doxastic attitude that a person is justified in having is the one that fits the person's evidence. More precisely:

---

280. Pinnock, *Set Forth Your Case*, 89.

> EJ [Epistemic Justification] Doxastic attitude *D* toward proposition *p* is epistemically justified for S at time *t* if and only if having *D* toward *p* fits the evidence S has at *t*.
>
> We do not offer EJ as an analysis. Rather it serves to indicate the kind of notion of justification that we take to be characteristically epistemic—a notion that makes justification turn entirely on evidence.[281]

Clearly evidentially based epistemology is not simply for uninformed individuals on the street. Much more will be said about evidentialism in apologetics and evidentialism in epistemology later on, but for now it needs to be noted that it is important to avoid the fallacy of equivocation with these terms. As will be made even clearer further on, the word "evidentialism" is used in different contexts to communicate different concepts, and the epistemic or apologetic context can freight the word with quite different meanings.

The reader should have noticed in the citations in this chapter that professional scholars employ Bayes's Theorem and achieve completely opposite results. Some contend that regular reasoning completely precludes the supernatural as a causal agent; others contend that regular reasoning completely forces the unbiased thinker to conclude that Jesus came back to life, and that the only explanation for this fact is the immediate activity of God. Thus it is not simply a matter of expecting everyone who has studied epistemology to reach the same conclusion. Nevertheless, the philosopher at some level will have to defend their warrants; they will have to justify their beliefs, and the criteria used in that justification.

One possible beginning point is with the simple rules of logic. Sproul writes that the apologist needs to assume: "1) the law of noncontradiction; 2) the law of causality; 3) the basic (although not perfect) reliability of sense perception; and 4) the analogical use of language."[282] The main importance of these assumptions is that all thought and communication requires them; they must be invoked in order to be denied. All denials of these laws, write the Ligoniers, are *"forced and temporary."*[283] As will be

---

281. Feldman and Conee, "Evidentialism," 310.

282. Sproul, *Defending Your Faith*, 30. The first three of these assumptions in this set are the same as those explicated by Sproul, Gerstner, and Lindsley in *Classical Apologetics*, 72.

283. Sproul, Gersner, and Lindsley, *Classical Apologetics*, 72; the same words and italics are found in Sproul's *Defending Your Faith*, 69.

seen in the next chapters, not everyone agrees with this approach, but it is one attempt to back up evidential thinking with rational justification.

The second main area to highlight involves the application of logic, and the inferences that are made among these apologists when they attempt to move from miracles to their doctrinal formulations of inerrancy. Again, more will be said about this in the next two chapters, but there are contentions about both the premises and the conclusions in some of these arguments. For the time being, I will mention only one such issue.

As I cited above, Sproul, Gerstner and Lindsley have as their first point that "It is virtually granted that the Bible (not assumed to be inspired) contains generally reliable history." From this starting point they set forth a chain of reasoning that ends in the conclusion that the Bible is divinely inspired. It must be said, regardless of the validity of their reasoning, that this premise is simply and utterly unsound. It is *not* virtually granted that the Bible contains generally reliable history. Such a statement is simply a howler. For example, the conservative, evangelical team of D. A. Carson and Douglas Moo, in their *Introduction to the New Testament*, write concerning the problem of history in the Synoptic Gospels:

> A major barrier to the enterprise has always been the many places in which the Gospels appear to contradict themselves over historical details. The most troublesome texts have been the subject of many harmonizing interpretations, ranging from the ridiculous to the convincing. Our whole approach to this matter will depend greatly on what we think of the evangelists' accuracy generally. The more we are impressed by their accuracy—as the authors of this volume are—the further we will search for a satisfactory explanations. Nevertheless, there are some places where fully satisfactory answers simply are not available.[284]

About the historical reliability of Acts, Carson and Moo write:

> Acts is the New Testament book that most nearly resembles historical narration, and it is the only source for most of what it narrates. Scholars have therefore *long debated its historical accuracy*, some doubting whether we can learn much at all of "what really happened" from Acts, others insisting that Acts deserves to be considered as a serious and generally reliable historical source. *The same division of opinion is evident in contemporary scholarship.*[285]

---

284. Carson and Moo, *Introduction to the New Testament*, 122–23.
285. Ibid., 312; cf. Brown, *Introduction to the New Testament*, 319–22.

Now, this is not to say that the Synoptic Gospels and the Book of Acts are not reliable, or even inerrant—Carson and Moo hold the texts to be fully inspired and inerrant. But what this perspective does do, rightly, is present the real state of the question of the New Testament's reliability. This of course says nothing of the Old Testament, which has far less manuscript evidence, and much less archaeological evidence to verify its content. When it comes to biblical history, even in the better attested New Testament era, there is a division of opinion in scholarship, both historically and presently. To begin, as the Ligoniers do, with saying that their position on the Bible's general reliability is "virtually granted" is to begin with something that is plainly false. It may not be false to say that the Bible contains generally reliable history—but it is completely false to say that this is virtually granted. This mistake is not made by all apologists in this chapter, but it is a flagrant example of a poor premise to use at the beginning of one's argument.

Even if one removes the egregiously false phrase "virtually granted," the general reliability of the Bible is still on precarious ground. For many scholars, the Bible contains so many errors that they have become limited inerrantists—holding the position that the Bible is inerrant in matters of theology, but errs in matters of history and science.[286] Their position—regardless of whether or not it is true—is another item that needs to be considered by those who hold to the general reliability of the Scriptures. Why, if the Bible is so generally reliable, have some scholars concluded that the concept of inerrancy cannot be applied to the biblical record? Again, it may be the limited inerrantists who hold to a false position, but there needs to be a great deal of work done to demonstrate that the Bible is generally reliable.

Anticipating a further discussion in Chapter 3, another difficulty is that a tremendous amount of what the Bible says simply cannot be vindicated historically by correlative sources. This does not imply falsity or fictitiousness, but it is simply a recognition that there are many people, places, and events in the Bible that find no corroboration in extant extra-biblical records. Furthermore, the Old Testament writers must also have been prophets: they record secret motives, thoughts, words spoken in bedrooms, and even the thoughts and speech of God in heaven. Such writing requires omniscience.[287] The Old Testament historical writings

---

286. Brown, *Introduction to the New Testament*, 31.
287. Waltke, *Old Testament Theology*, 59–60.

are far more than a chronicle of names, dates, and places (many of which cannot be verified from extra-biblical sources). They involve words, motives, thoughts, and the drama of heaven. How can such categories be vindicated by normal historical methodology? It must also be remembered that the Bible does not contain just historical material, or even just propositions. The Scriptures are full of questions, poems, proverbs, emotional expressions, prophecies, etc. In what sense are the Psalms or Song of Songs to be taken as generally reliable history? This line of objection will be picked up in the next two chapters, where the issue of event versus interpretation and significance will be discussed. If events are not brute facts, and require interpretation at any level, then there is a two-dimensional aspect to understanding history, and these two dimensions are not coextensive. It is theoretically quite possible to record an event accurately, while completely misinterpreting it, ascribing the wrong motives to an individual involved, misunderstanding its importance, etc. Even if the Bible were exceptionally and verifiably accurate at the level of event, this does not logically entail exceptional (or even reliable) accuracy at the level of significance and interpretation.

Consider the following thought experiment: what would be the response if a young writer were to write a biography of Tolstoy, containing a conversation Tolstoy had with a friend (which was never recorded anywhere else, and which the author had not overheard), and the words Tolstoy thought (if Tolstoy never shared them), and how God spoke to the angels about something Tolstoy did? Is it not the case that, no matter how accurate the names, dates, and places were, the biography would not be accepted as generally reliable? And what would an appeal to the general reliability of other aspects of the biography contribute to the acceptance of these special parts? There is a category confusion that takes place here. It is simply invalid to make the category leap from "normal" history—even if undisputed—to the writing of history that requires an omniscient perspective. Or, to illustrate the link between event and significance, what if a historian perfectly recorded the events of the Battle of the Bulge, and then proceeded to interpret the event as bearing the meaning that Hitler's forces lost the battle because Allah fought for the Allies? How many non-adherents to Islam would conclude that, because the historian impeccably recorded the events, this interpretation must be accurate as well? How many Muslims would accept this argument, for that matter, on the basis of the argument that the rest of the book contained general historical reliability?

In brief, this discussion has suggested, but not thoroughly pursued, some types of logical difficulties that involve the apologetic relationship between the resurrection and the inerrancy of Scripture. In one example, a premise in the argument is seen to be wildly unsound. In another example, there is a challenge to a premise based on that premise's internal coherence. Accepting the Bible as generally reliable history is problematic on the definitional level; much of the Bible's "history" requires inspiration in order to be acceptable, since it covers an area far beyond the reach of materially verifiable historical praxis. The internal logic of the premise represents a confusion of both logical and historical categories. Since much more will be said by way of critique in the next two chapters, we can leave these weaknesses for now. They are representative, however, of some of the difficulties embedded in these lines of reasoning.

CONCLUSION

This chapter has set the foundation for the rest of the study. It has worked through the wide contours of the evidence for the resurrection, and objections that have been raised against it. Both a posteriori and a priori factors have been considered. Without anything approaching exhaustive detail, it has been suggested that the arguments require a further defense at the epistemological level in order to justify assumptions, and that there are some obvious difficulties in both validity and soundness in some of the premises advanced by some of the representative apologists. Fuller critiques will be brought to bear in the subsequent chapters.

The apologist who is defending the conservative Reformed faith needs to defend the resurrection, and also needs to defend the full inerrancy of the Bible. So far, from the cursory examination given to the evidence for the resurrection, and the attempted movement to the inerrancy of Scripture, the arguments contained in this chapter are not watertight. They are definitely not logically coercive. It remains to be seen whether or not there is a better apologetic method on the horizon, or whether these arguments are the best defense of the Reformed position available.

3

Reformed Epistemology

INTRODUCTION

Worldwide discussions concerning Reformed epistemology take place more in the academic guild than in church level apologetics. Many of the issues deal with the finer points of epistemological theories, and as such the arguments are presented and rebutted in international journals of philosophy and other academic publications. While it will be beyond our scope to examine all the arguments and counterarguments involving Reformed epistemology, these debates will be identified when they are of relevant concern. This chapter will be significantly shorter than the last one, since the last one had the dual job of laying a necessary background framework for the rest of our discussion, as well as examining the evidential apologetic methodology. No such dual purpose exists for the present chapter; it is more narrowly focused on the nature and method of Reformed epistemology.

POSITIVE AND NEGATIVE EPISTEMOLOGICAL CONSIDERATIONS

While the next section will engage in a more specific manner the relationship between evidentialist cases for the resurrection and Reformed epistemology, in order to understand Reformed epistemology it is necessary to set it in contrast to Enlightenment evidential epistemology. More specifically, it is necessary to understand the self-conscious opposition to, and rejection of, classical foundationalism by the Reformed epistemologists.

At the heart of the matter the disagreement is more philosophical and epistemic than theological. The reasons provided for rejecting classical foundationalism pave the way for a new vantage point of understanding the epistemic criteria for proper basicality and doxastic practices (i.e., belief forming practices, or the method by which we come to form and hold beliefs). While the fundamental debate is pitched in the epistemological and philosophical sphere, the purposes of the Reformed epistemologists are to explicitly connect the entailments of their epistemic views with responsible belief in God.

Foundationalism

One of the major contentions of Reformed epistemology is that the standards for the epistemic justification of knowledge found in classical foundationalism are too stringent. They hold that not only do these standards make proving the existence of God impossible, but they make every philosophical argument of consequence impossible to prove as well.[1] Nevertheless, for the last three centuries—the time after John Locke—evidentialism has had the distinction of being the most widely accepted theory for knowledge, probability, and epistemic justification in belief acceptance. When applied to theistic discussion, evidentialism, "is the view that belief in God is rationally justifiable or acceptable only if there is good evidence for it, where good evidence would be arguments from other propositions one knows."[2] In this context, the "other propositions one knows" would constitute knowledge by passing the standards of classical foundationalism. This view of theistic discussion is not found in the minority of philosophers, but is rather what has undergirded philosophical discussions of theism in the Western world. As Nicholas Wolterstorff writes: "Scarcely anything has been more characteristic of the modern Western intellectual than the conviction that unless one has good reasons for one's theistic beliefs, one ought to give them up. In the dialogue between belief and unbelief, belief is assumed guilty until it proves its innocence by evidence."[3]

Classical (or strong) foundationalism provides three categories of epistemic states that allow a belief to be held in a way that is considered

---

1. Plantinga, *Warranted Christian Belief*, 69–70.
2. Ibid., 70; see also Langtry, "Properly Unargued Belief in God," 129.
3. Wolterstorff, "Migration of Theistic Arguments," 38, emphasis in original.

justified with full certainty. The first is that the belief is self-evidently true (like analytic truth as later articulated by the logical positivists); the second is that the belief is incorrigible (such that the individual who has the belief in question cannot be in error); and the third is that it is evident to the senses (perceptual states such as believing one sees the color red).[4] What these three criteria share in common is that they are accepted on the basis of their own coercive truth. As such, they are not accepted on the basis of arguments, or from deductions from another core of beliefs. These types of beliefs form the foundation for other beliefs, so they are considered to be properly basic or foundational.

The evidentialist John Locke believed that the existence of God could be one of the most certain beliefs deduced from this foundationalism.[5] Basic beliefs, and their entailments, were to be rationally accepted. Locke laid down some general rules that could be applied to building a structure of knowledge on the foundation provided by basic beliefs. First, a proposition had to be formulated on a particular subject. Second, evidence was to be collected that both supported the proposition and its negation, and the evidence in question had to be factual. When this was finished, the logical force of the overall case was to be evaluated. After this, finally, when the evidence for the proposition had been weighed, a belief could be held with the firmness of conviction allowed by the proportionality of the total evidence.[6] Unless a belief was foundational or met the requirements of this evidential exercise, and unless the one who held the belief did so with a confidence that matched the logical probability of the case, the holding of the belief in question (or the level of conviction in which it was held) was considered to be unjustified.

Reformed epistemologists argue that this "doxastic ideal" does not correspond to our epistemic realities, and so jettison not regular doxastic practices, but the ideal itself.[7] In fact, one of the most promising qualities of the Reformed epistemologists is that they are willing to question the reasoning behind accepting the epistemic standards of classical foundationalism. This questioning has led to two interesting insights. The first insight is that classical foundationalism fails to correspond to how human

---

4. Wood, *Epistemology*, 85–86.
5. Noted by Plantinga, *Warranted Christian Belief*, 77.
6. Wolterstorff, "Epistemology of Religion," 311.
7. Ibid., 312–15.

beings actually form their beliefs.[8] It has distorted doxastic practice into something unnatural, and placed epistemology in the position of a judge, instead of using epistemological studies to clarify how it is that humans make judgments on beliefs, and how these beliefs come to be held in a warranted manner.[9] There is a sense in which classical foundationalism was too prescriptive without paying enough attention to descriptive realities.

The second insight that strikes against classical foundationalism is that it is self-referentially incoherent. Just as the verification principle of the logical positivists failed its own standard, so the three criteria for basic beliefs of the classical foundationalists fail to meet their own standards of basicality. It is not self-evidently or analytically true that analytically true beliefs are properly basic. Although $1 + 1 = 2$ may lay claim to being self-evident, or bachelors being unmarried is analytically inescapable, surely the proposition analytic truths are properly basic is quite a different belief than the other propositions that fit in those categories. Are these foundational standards perceptually based? Surely nobody argues that it is a perceptual experience that qualifies perceptual experiences as being properly basic. We are not in perceptual states where our immediate perception is of one of the three tenets of classical foundationalism. Pain states may be incorrigible, but beliefs about foundational beliefs are not incorrigible; that is why they are debated and discussed so vigorously. There is built into the very subject of discussion concerning classical foundationalism the possibility of the system being wrong, or corrigible (so it is not then incorrigible). In essence, then, classical foundationalism insists that beliefs must be built on a foundation that, on the basis of its own reasoning, rejects its own foundational blocks as non-foundational. Since all other beliefs are to be built on this foundation, and all other beliefs are judged on their relationship to this foundation, classical foundationalism actually has no foundation at all. It insists that all beliefs be built on a foundation that collapses under the weight of its own standards. As Plantinga notes, since the foundational beliefs in classical foundationalism are not basic, they require an argument from other beliefs in order to establish them, but no such argument has ever been constructed.[10] Thus classical foundationalism succumbs to making inferential beliefs the foundation

---

8. Clark, *Return to Reason*, 158.
9. Wolterstorff, "Epistemology of Religion," 318.
10. Plantinga, *Warranted Christian Belief*, 94–95.

for its proposed structural accounting of knowledge, while denying that inferential beliefs can be foundational. This is simply a classic example of self-referential incoherence.

Reformed epistemologists do not abandon foundationalism, however. They reject classical or strong foundationalism with those three central tenets, but their structure of knowledge is still built on top of foundational beliefs. In place of strong foundationalism they recommend a more modest foundationalism. As William Alston points out:

> There is also the modest foundationalism I favor, according to which there are fallible and corrigible foundations, beliefs that possess prima facie justification from experience, but where this justification is subject to being overridden by sufficient indications to the contrary. Note that this modest foundationalism is committed to the possibility, and the reality, of mutual epistemic support.[11]

Plantinga also holds that beliefs can be held in a basic, non-inferential way, but also that these beliefs can be rejected as defeaters and contrary evidence accumulate.[12] Still, at the bottom level, foundational beliefs are basic, and they are non-inferential. Inferential and evidential beliefs are grounded in these basic beliefs, and are ultimately supported by them. Reformed epistemology does not seek to replace foundationalistic epistemic theory with a non-foundational coherence theory or the like, but rather modifies and broadens the base of the thinker's epistemic foundation. It is only the stringent species of foundationalism in its classical manifestation that is rejected; foundational, basic beliefs are still deemed necessary in order for genuine knowledge to obtain.

The Reformed epistemologists seek a broader foundational base that will include more types of properly basic beliefs, so that epistemological theory and actual knowledge are seen to fit together in a congruous relationship. They contend that in real life, human beings are justified or warranted in accepting their memory beliefs, the real existence of the past (e.g., the world is older than five minutes, and did not just spring into existence with traces of breakfast in our stomachs), and the existence

---

11. Alston, *Perceiving God*, 300.
12. Plantinga, *Warranted Christian Belief*, 343–44.

of other minds.[13] Plantinga's groundbreaking work in *God and Other Minds* sought to demonstrate that belief in God is analogous to believing in the existence of other minds. There are good arguments for believing in their existence, and good arguments against believing in their existence. If a belief in other minds can be justified, then it is also possible that a belief in the existence of God can be justified as well, on roughly the same grounds.

Justification is a very highly debated and ambiguous concept in epistemology.[14] Alston denies that justified belief is necessary for knowledge.[15] His understanding is that:

> Justification is an evaluative status; to be justified is to be in an evaluatively favorable position. For one to be epistemically justified in holding a belief, as opposed to prudentially or morally justified, is for it to be a good thing, from the epistemic point of view, for one to believe that p ... We may think of the epistemic point of view as defined by the aim at maximizing the number of one's true beliefs and minimizing the number of one's false beliefs.[16]

Justification is also a matter of degree.[17] Plantinga notes that to be in a state of justification (no matter what the context) is to be in a state of innocence or blamelessness.[18] Epistemologically, for classical foundationalists like Locke: "your assent to p is justified only if the degree of your assent to p is proportional to the degree to which p is probable with respect to what is certain for you. If you believe in some other way, then you are going contrary to your epistemic obligations; you are guilty; you are flouting epistemic duty."[19]

Locke's understanding has been at the heart of the West's "justificationist" epistemological tradition for centuries; a tradition that Plantinga finds misguided.[20] In Plantinga's perspective, for an individual to fulfill their epistemic duties they must try to believe important truths, and

---

13. Plantinga, *God and Other Minds*; Plantinga and Wolterstorff, eds. *Faith and Rationality*; Clark, *Return to Reason*.
14. Alston, *Beyond "Justification,"* 11–21.
15. Alston, *Perceiving God*, 285.
16. Ibid., 72, emphasis in original.
17. Ibid.
18. Plantinga, *Warranted Christian Belief*, 87.
19. Ibid.
20. Ibid., 88.

disbelieve important falsehoods.[21] For a Christian, if they do not find objections to Christianity compelling, they are of course to be considered justified on this accounting: even insane beliefs are justified on this account, if the thinking subject has done their best to believe only the truth.[22] They may be wrong, deluded, or their cognitive faculties may be a mess, but it is clear that the person who has done their personal best has not violated their epistemic duties.[23]

In more recent work, Alston has come to understand the epistemic justification of a belief in the following way: "coherence of a belief with a sufficiently coherent system of belief or a belief's being formed by the exercise of an intellectual virtue or a belief's being formed by the proper functioning of a cognitive faculty."[24] He holds that justification is too broad to be narrowed to one fundamental principle, and that it must be seen as: "an irreducible plurality of positive epistemic statuses—epistemic desiderata—of beliefs, each of which defines a distinctive dimension of epistemic evaluation."[25] To this end, Alston presents and defends a whole list of desirable epistemic desiderata in this book, and then argues that: "[truth conducive] desiderata are the most important ones for our cognitive activity, which has as its basic aim a high preponderance of true over false beliefs about matters of interest and importance to us."[26] Fundamentally, then, Alston has not changed his understanding of epistemic justification from his earlier work. Both he and Plantinga have very similar understandings of what justification does and does not entail. As will be seen, however, their more positive cases for basic beliefs are not identical, even though they are in many ways mutually complementary.

While the general contentions of the Reformed epistemologists are similar enough to allow them to be grouped together, their individual presentations and developments represent unique contributions to the field. The two leading writers are Alston and Plantinga. Alston's epistemic arguments have concerned immediate experiential religious data, and socially acceptable doxastic practices. Plantinga has developed his own

---

21. Ibid., 99–100.
22. Ibid., 100–103.
23. Ibid., 103.
24. Alston, *Beyond "Justification,"* 28; emphasis in original.
25. Ibid., 47.
26. Ibid., 229; emphasis in original.

version of warrant as the property that confers justification on beliefs, and has argued that such a construal of warrant allows for Christian belief to be warranted and accepted on a non-inferential, properly basic basis. Their uniquely specialized programs make individual analysis preferable to continuing a general treatment of Reformed epistemology where both Alston's and Plantinga's views are examined at the same time. Thus the next two subsections will be devoted to the positive cases Alston and Plantinga attempt to make for being epistemologically responsible, and accepting as rational a direct, non-inferential experience of God.

William Alston

In *Perceiving God: The Epistemology of Religious Experience*, Alston writes: "The chief aim of this book is to defend the view that putative direct awareness of God can provide justification for certain kinds of beliefs about God."[27] He aims to isolate common elements in Christian mystical experience in order to have a generally agreed-upon, working understanding of what a direct experience of God in the Christian tradition is like. After some lengthy quotations from Christian mystics, he identifies three common elements: "Let's note some salient features of these accounts. (A) They report an experiential awareness of God. (B) The awareness is direct. (C) The awareness is reported to be of God." [28]

Alston acknowledges that the subject may not be able to accurately describe or parse the experience, but he does not believe that this counts against the reality of the phenomenon. He writes:

> Our sources clearly suppose that there is a distinctive phenomenal content to their perceptions of God, that God is present to them in ways that impart a distinctive character to their experience. And their inability to enumerate these qualia no more prevents them from perceiving God through being aware of the qualia than the inability of one of us to analyze a rural scene into its constituent basic qualia prevents us from perceiving that scene.[29]

Perception and description can be related in a variety of ways, but they are not identical, nor is the subject's ability to perceive something contingent on their ability to describe it. It will also not do, according to

---

27. Aliston, *Perceiving God*, 9.
28. Ibid., 14; emphasis original.
29. Ibid., 54.

Alston, to make an a priori judgment about what can be presented to us in a non-sensory, immediate manner, since it is only by experience that we can learn what will be presented to our experience.[30]

In order to be able to justify his beliefs, Alston says, "I will . . . take the position that in order for me to justifiably believe that p it is necessary not only that I have an adequate ground but that my belief be based on that ground, be held because of it."[31] Justification must be based on the ground provided, the ground the individual really uses to anchor their belief, and not on possible grounds, or even genuine grounds that exist but of which the individual is unaware, or could become aware of if they more deeply considered their belief.[32] The ground must be adequate, and the belief in question must actually be rooted in that ground, or else the individual is not in fact justified in holding their belief. They might hold a legitimate belief that is capable of justification on other grounds, but if those other grounds are not the actual grounds for the individual's belief, the individual fails to be epistemically justified.

The larger position that Alston accepts for epistemic justification is externalism rather than internalism, although he does provide a fairly balanced and integrated perspective between the two. His main problem with epistemic internalism is that the posited consciousness of grounds leads to an infinite regress of required supporting reasons for beliefs, and it also can be used to justify beliefs that are not in fact true.[33] On internalism one must have grounds to believe that one's grounds are adequate; but this keeps pushing the question back one more level, and thus sets up the infinite regression of grounding every belief on a deeper antecedent ground. There are elements of internalist thought in his externalism, however. Alston writes: "I balance my externalist perspective on the adequacy of grounds with an internalist perspective on the existence of grounds, requiring of a 'justifying ground' that it be the sort of thing that is typically recognizable by the subject just on reflection."[34]

A large part of Alston's project involves drawing an analogy between the reliability of beliefs that are grounded on sense perception, and the

---

30. Ibid., 59.
31. Ibid., 74; emphasis original.
32. Ibid., 85 n. 22.
33. Ibid., 75.
34. Ibid.; emphasis original.

epistemic status of Christian mystical perceptual doxastic practice (CMP). It is impossible to test sense perception without falling into circularity; that which is being tested must be used in the testing.[35] This is the reality of the human experience, and cannot be otherwise. In order for it to be rational to hold sense perception as reliable, sense perception must be reliable for the test to be reliable. Thus epistemic circularity is inescapable for justifying the reliability of our senses.[36]

The main question is one of reliability. Alston wants to know if certain ways of forming beliefs are reliable. He writes: "So, in a nutshell, a doxastic practice is reliable provided it would yield mostly true beliefs in a sufficiently large and varied run of employment in situations of the sorts we typically encounter."[37] As mentioned above, Alston is aware that such a determination will involve epistemic and procedural circularity, but there is nothing that can be done to eliminate this totally. It can be mitigated somewhat, however, if the frame of reference is not the external world, but the interior phenomenological experience of our sense perception itself. In other words, the reliability of sense perception can be tested not on the basis of whether or not predictions about what we will sense are veridical in the external, objective world, but rather on the basis of what we will sense given a hypothesis or set of circumstances.[38] The predictive success of sense perception is based on how reliably we can predict what will happen to our senses, or what we will perceive, given certain circumstances.[39] It is best tested by the hypothetico-deductive method.

Alston argues that there is no better reason to accept the reliability of sense perception than the accuracy of our predictions concerning what our perceptive experiences in the future are likely to be. On the basis of an inference to the best explanation, this predictive success is most congenially explained by the fact that our sense perception is actually reliable. His clearest and most succinct expression of this understanding is found when he writes: "The claim under discussion here is that SP [sense perception] is reliable, and the argument for that claim is that our success in predicting sense experience on the basis of SP and associated

---

35. Ibid., 107.
36. Ibid., 108.
37. Ibid., 104–5; emphasis original.
38. Ibid., 136.
39. Ibid., 137.

practices is best explained by supposing SP and the associated practices to be reliable."[40] Granted this is circular, and granted it is the same sort of argument that skeptics used to deny the possibility of knowledge, Alston firmly believes nevertheless that in real life we are not able to withhold belief or embrace skepticism, and so must use and accept the results of SP, granted their reliability in predictive success.[41]

Another major area that Alston examines in order to provide a foundation for his justification of religious experience involves doxastic practices. Alston writes: "My theory of doxastic practices is firmly realistic, recognizing a single reality that is what it is, regardless of how we think or talk about it. The doxastic practice is a source of criteria of justification and rationality; it does not determine truth or reality. In other words, for me doxastic practices are crucial epistemologically, not metaphysically."[42] This is an extremely important point, and one that will come up again in this discussion on Reformed epistemology. Alston is saying that the doxastic practices must be justifiable epistemologically, even if they are not in contact with metaphysical reality. Being rationally justified in holding a certain belief is no guarantee that the belief being held is true.

Basic doxastic practices are formed when we are still pre-critical, well before we are capable of reflection.[43] Beliefs are formed long before we are able to understand that we are even forming beliefs, let alone inquire as to how and why we are forming and holding certain beliefs in certain ways. As we mature, however, we should come to be more self-conscious epistemologically. When a certain doxastic practice has persisted in an individual over time, this is evidence in favor of its being epistemically reliable. When a doxastic practice has persisted through generations, however, this is very strong evidence that it should be taken seriously.[44] While certain unreliable doxastic practices exist for a time, they gradually are phased out as more reliable belief-forming procedures are identified. Such is the case with magic and omens.[45] Of critical importance here is that Alston is arguing that a socially established doxastic practice is to

40. Ibid., 141.
41. Ibid., 150.
42. Ibid., 165 n. 37.
43. Ibid., 169.
44. Ibid., 170.
45. Ibid., 172.

be taken seriously. Before moving into his next major section, he writes: "That is the final conclusion I want to take from this chapter for use in the rest of the book—for any established doxastic practice it is rational to suppose that it is reliable, and hence rational to suppose that its doxastic outputs are prima facie justified."[46]

These contentions set the stage for Alston's justification of Christian mystical perceptual doxastic practice. He writes: "My main thesis of this chapter, and indeed in the whole book, is that CMP is rationally engaged in since it is a socially established doxastic practice that is not demonstrably unreliable or otherwise disqualified for rational acceptance."[47] Much the same point is described further on: "The basic contention is that it is prima facie rational to engage in CMP, not because it is analogous to SP in one or another respect, but because it is a socially established doxastic practice; and that it is unqualifiedly rational to engage in it, as we shall argue in the next chapter, because we lack sufficient reason for regarding it as unreliable or otherwise disqualified for rational participation."[48]

The Christian community has long held that non-sensory, experiential perceptions of God can produce immediate beliefs about what the believer is experiencing. Taking this into consideration, the Christian community or society has its own socially accepted doxastic practice. The reliability of this doxastic practice has not been demonstrated to be poor, and as such the Christian community has the right (i.e., they are rational, or epistemologically justified) in accepting beliefs that are formed on the basis of Christian mystical perceptual doxastic practice. It is irrelevant that not every individual in the world has had these experiences, or even that not every Christian has had them. What counts is that the Christian social community accepts—and has for centuries—this particular set of doxastic practices, which lends a prima facie validity to the generated beliefs.

Alston is quick to admit that CMP seems to generate more inconsistencies than SP (i.e., sense perception).[49] SP is more globally distributed, and its reliability can be rationally considered very high. This does not mean, however, that SP is perfectly reliable, as Alston correctly notes:

---

46. Ibid., 183; emphasis original.
47. Ibid., 194.
48. Ibid., 223.
49. Ibid., 238.

> Certainly SP displays a modicum of inconsistency in its results. Witnesses to a crime or an automobile accident not infrequently contradict each other. Not even Descartes' chosen sources will escape the stigma. Rational intuition can be found to be wholly at one with itself only by carefully editing its deliverances so as to filter out one member of each contradictory pair. If we include in the pool every case of something's seeming self-evident to someone, it is notorious that we will wind up with a number of such pairs.[50]

For human beings, sense perception and even rational intuition do not provide perfectly reliable conclusions. So the fact that CMP does not attain a perfect standard does not mean that it is therefore unreliable. Alston believes that CMP should be assigned a lower score in terms of reliability than SP, but does not believe that this makes CMP irrational to engage in.[51] There is even a place for modifying religious beliefs on the basis of doxastic practices that are more firmly established.[52]

As will be discussed after the section on Plantinga, Alston is committed only to the prima facie rationality of accepting beliefs generated by CMP. This means that other evidence, or putative defeaters, can come into play and make it irrational to hold a belief that at one time could have been held rationally. Defeaters or contrary evidence can make it impossible for a believer to hold religious beliefs with rational justification. Alston thinks that religious diversity and the competing beliefs generated by different religious mystical doxastic practices are the most difficult challenge to his proposal.[53] Such defeaters will be examined below; for now, it is important to stress that the rational justification of beliefs grounded in CMP is only prima facie and, at the minimum, potentially subject to being overwhelmed and defeated.

Alvin Plantinga

Alston identifies Plantinga's view of proper basicality as "a close cousin"[54] of his own position that was outlined above. Plantinga's view has de-

---

50. Ibid., 235.
51. Ibid., 238.
52. Ibid., 239. The example Alston uses is of believing that the earth is only 6,000 years old, and he maintains this should be rejected in place of the much more widely established doxastic practice of accepting the deliverances of sound science.
53. Ibid., 255.
54. Ibid., 195.

veloped considerably from its early beginnings.⁵⁵ His project has been to demonstrate the epistemic validity of accepting not only theism, but Christian theism. Thus the culminating book in his warrant trilogy applies his notion of warrant to Christian belief.⁵⁶ For Plantinga warrant is that which, if present in sufficient quantity, changes mere true belief into knowledge.⁵⁷ He furthermore expounds his notion of warrant in terms of proper function. This will be examined below. Whether or not one agrees with his technical epistemology, or his application of that epistemology to forming and holding Christian beliefs, advocates and opponents alike recognize that Plantinga's work is a tour de force in contemporary philosophy of religion, and more specifically in religious epistemology.

His contention in *Warranted Christian Belief* is that de jure and de facto objections exist towards Christianity, and the former ultimately hinge on the latter.⁵⁸ Plantinga identifies de jure objections as roughly a species of objections that argues: "Christian belief, whether or not true, is at any rate unjustifiable, or rationally unjustified, or irrational, or not intellectually respectable, or contrary to sound morality, or without sufficient evidence, or in some other way rationally unacceptable, not up to snuff from an intellectual point of view."⁵⁹ If, however, Christian belief is true, on Plantinga's model of warrant, he argues that such beliefs can enjoy the status of warranted belief, which is intellectually acceptable.⁶⁰ It is illegitimate, then, to argue that even if Christianity is true the Christian believer could not possibly know that it is true, or be justified in holding their beliefs.

It would be beyond the scope of this book to examine minutely every aspect of Plantinga's concept of warrant. Although it can be subjected to many technical objections, in its essence it is fairly simple to understand. Plantinga provides a succinct summary of his position: "Put in a nutshell, then, a belief has warrant for a person S only if that belief is produced in S by cognitive faculties functioning properly (subject to no

---

55. Plantinga and Wolterstorff, eds., *Faith and Rationality*; Plantinga, *Warrant: The Current Debate*; Plantinga, *Warrant and Proper Function*; Plantinga, *Warranted Christian Belief*.

56. Plantinga, *Warranted Christian Belief*.

57. Plantinga and Tooley, *Knowledge of God*, 9.

58. Plantinga, *Warranted Christian Belief*, xiii.

59. Ibid., ix.

60. Ibid., xiii.

dysfunction) in a cognitive environment that is appropriate for S's kind of cognitive faculties, according to a design plan that is successfully aimed at truth."[61] This summary includes several distinct but mutually reinforcing and dependent strands.

The first is that the belief that is produced is produced by cognitive faculties. There is little objectionable at that point. What is important is that the cognitive faculties in question must be in a condition where they are functioning properly. Dysfunctional cognitive faculties may produce all kinds of beliefs, some of which may be true and some of which may be false, but the beliefs produced by dysfunctional cognitive faculties cannot be trusted. They cannot enjoy the status of being warranted.

Since the cognitive faculties of the one forming and holding a belief must be functioning properly, it is imperative that the faculties be designed to function in a certain way.[62] (The model will be assuming normative, mature cognitive development, apart from infants, the mentally infirm, or those suffering from brain injury or illness.) In order for the concepts of "function" and "dysfunction" to be meaningful, there must be "a way in which a thing is supposed to work."[63] If any organ or faculty in the body is not working the way that it is supposed to, we recognize that there is a problem, or a dysfunction. This is because we recognize that there is a particular way the organ or faculty is supposed to function; when it is working properly, it does certain things, and when it is dysfunctional, it fails to do these things or does other things that are harmful. Involved here is the idea of "purpose," that there is a certain purpose for this organ or faculty, and if it does not achieve its purpose, it is dysfunctional.[64] More will be said about function and the knowledge of God (following Paul in Romans 1) in Chapter 5.

There is another condition that is essential to proper function. The faculty must also be located in an environment where it can achieve its purpose. For a human body, the lungs function properly when they (to oversimplify things) breathe. As long as the lungs are in an environment like the one in which humans live, they can properly fulfill their purpose. However, if a human being sticks their head under water, their lungs may

---

61. Ibid., 156.
62. Ibid., 154.
63. Ibid.; emphasis original.
64. Ibid., 154–55.

still be in good working order, but they will not successfully breathe.[65] Proper function can only take place in an environment that is conducive to the successful accomplishment of what the faculty or organ is supposed to do.

Plantinga differentiates between a maxienvironment and a minienvironment, the former being composed of instances of the latter. He argues that our cognitive faculties may be designed to function properly in the general maxienvironment, but given particular circumstances, they may be subject to malfunction in a minienvironment.[66] Thus for Plantinga: "A belief B produced by an exercise E of cognitive powers has warrant sufficient for knowledge only if MBE (the minienvironment with respect to B and E) is favorable to E."[67] Our cognitive faculties must have the necessary calibration to be able to properly form true beliefs in a given minienvironment, or else our beliefs are not warranted.[68]

Cognitive faculties, then, must be functioning in a certain way, and be in an environment that is conducive to the production of true beliefs. They must be functioning in accord with a design plan, and this design plan must not only be aimed at producing true beliefs, it must be successfully aimed at their production.[69] There are many things that are designed to function in a certain way, but that malfunction and never successfully do that which they were intended to do. It is critical, then, that the design plan be successful, but also that the telos of the design plan be the production of true beliefs. If the intention of the design plan is that human cognitive faculties will provide comfort, or promote survival, then they may or may not produce true beliefs.[70] Even if they do produce true beliefs, these beliefs will be byproducts; the intended purpose would lie in another direction. Existential comfort can be produced by either believing the truth or believing a lie: if the design plan aims at comforting, then even if the beliefs produced are true, they are accidentally (i.e. non-necessarily) true. If more comfort could be produced through deception

---

65. Ibid., 155.
66. Ibid., 158.
67. Ibid., 159.
68. Ibid., 159–61.
69. Ibid., 155–56.
70. Ibid., 155.

and false belief, the cognitive faculties would function to produce such false beliefs if comfort, not truth, was the aim of the design plan.

Where the positive conditions obtain, Plantinga holds that the beliefs produced can enjoy (at least potentially) the status of being warranted. While some objections to this general account will be examined in due course, the main interest of this discussion lies in Plantinga's next phase, when he applies this model of warranted belief to Christianity. It is worth remembering, however, that even if Plantinga's second step fails (i.e., the way in which he applies this model to Christian belief), it does not mean that his model of warrant fails as a result. The model and its application to Christian belief are two distinctively different positions, and require separate arguments. If his general account of warranted belief fails, then of course it follows that his application of it to Christianity will fail as well, but the same logic does not hold for the reverse direction if the application fails.

Plantinga endeavors to produce a model of Christian belief that enjoys warrant. He understands that: "to give a model of a proposition or state of affairs S is to show how it could be that S is true or actual."[71] The model that he works with is a combination of thought that he sees in common with Thomas Aquinas and John Calvin. This "Aquinas/Calvin" or "A/C model" involves belief in theism, while the "extended A/C model" involves more ramified Christian belief.[72] Any objection to the validity of the epistemic model, according to Plantinga, will be a de facto objection to Christianity, rather than a de jure objection against the possibility of theistic knowledge.[73]

The non-extended form of the A/C model begins with a commonality shared by Aquinas and Calvin. Specifically: "Thomas Aquinas and John Calvin concur on the claim that there is a kind of natural knowledge of God (and anything on which Calvin and Aquinas are in accord is something to which we had better pay careful attention)."[74] The faculty that produces this natural knowledge of God is called the sensus divinitatis, and Plantinga defines it in the following way: "The sensus divinitatis is a disposition or set of dispositions to form theistic beliefs in various

---

71. Ibid., 169; emphasis original.
72. Ibid., 168.
73. Ibid., 169.
74. Ibid., 170.

circumstances, in response to the sorts of conditions or stimuli that trigger the working of this sense of divinity."[75] This faculty was designed by God to produce theistic beliefs in human beings when they are in certain situations and circumstances. It is a natural part of our noetic equipment or cognitive faculties, and is designed to function properly in the environment that God also designed to be conducive to the production of true beliefs about him. It is at this juncture that the connection between Plantinga's understanding of warranted belief and his application of it to theistic belief formation becomes very clear. As part of human cognitive faculties, the sensus divinitatis can properly function in an appropriate environment to produce warranted theistic beliefs.

How these beliefs are formed through the sensus divinitatis is an extremely crucial component of Plantinga's argument. He argues, in full consistency with his views on classical vs. modest (i.e., less stringent) foundationalism, and the criteria for proper basicality, that theistic beliefs are basic. The sensus divinitatis does not cogitate on the propositions of a logical syllogism, and then inexorably deduce a theistic conclusion. On the contrary, the theistic beliefs that are formed are not formed on the basis of premises at all, nor are they conclusions of arguments. They are produced immediately. For example, one may gaze at the starry heavens, and find the belief in the existence of God simply present in a way that is compelling to accept. In this case, the believer does not examine the stars, consider them, and upon reflection reach the conclusion that God created them—the believer simply finds theistic belief present.[76] Belief in God, in this case, is not based on other beliefs, and so is rightly considered to be basic on the tenets of foundationalism.

Basic beliefs can be overridden or defeated by other beliefs, or by the accumulation of convincing evidence to the contrary. Beliefs may arise in a basic way, but this does not mean that they are properly basic. Since the sensus divinitatis produces beliefs (in this model), the believer is able to hold their beliefs as properly basic, if they still hold them after considering contrary evidence. There is no reason to think that the believer is failing to believe justifiably, or is failing to perform an epistemic duty if they do not find their beliefs overwhelmed by further evidence, and so they are within their epistemic rights to consider their theistic beliefs

---

75. Ibid., 172.
76. Ibid., 175.

Reformed Epistemology

properly basic.[77] Furthermore, in this model God is the designer of the cognitive faculties and the environment (both maxi and mini), so there is every reason to accept the beliefs produced by the sensus divinitatis as properly basic.[78]

Here again the distinction and critical importance of de jure and de facto objections is clear. If the model is true, then the belief can enjoy the status of being sufficiently warranted to count as knowledge. If God does not exist, however, then the model cannot be true, and the beliefs cannot be warranted. The design plan, sensus divinitatis (and other cognitive faculties), and environment are all different if atheism is true. In fact, the sensus divinitatis would not even exist, since there would be no divinely designed faculty that functioned to produce a sense of the divine, or theistic belief. If theism is true, on the other hand, then it is at least logically possible that this model is also true, and so theistic belief can be epistemically justified. The metaphysical question of the existence of God cannot be separated from the epistemological question concerning whether believing in him is warranted.[79]

Having presented and defended his view of warranted belief and the A/C model, Plantinga turns to consider the extended version of the A/C model, which includes particular Christian beliefs, from a Reformed perspective.[80] Unlike the non-extended A/C model, where theistic belief arises out of original equipment in our noetic faculties, the beliefs that arise in the extended model are supernaturally bequeathed.[81] Plantinga writes:

> These beliefs do not come to the Christian just by way of memory, perception, reason, testimony, the sensus divinitatis, or any other of the cognitive faculties with which we human beings were originally created; they come instead by the work of the Holy Spirit, who gets us to accept, causes us to believe, these great truths of the gospel. These beliefs don't come just by way of the normal operation of our natural faculties; they are a supernatural gift. Still, the Christian who has received this gift of faith will of course be justified (in the basic sense of the term) in believing as he does; there

77. Ibid., 178.
78. Ibid., 179.
79. Ibid., 190.
80. Ibid., 200.
81. Ibid., 245.

> will be nothing contrary to epistemic or other duty in so believing (indeed, once he has accepted the gift, it may not be within his power to withhold belief).[82]

To come to believe in the central propositions of Christianity requires the interaction of epistemic agents. There is an encounter of wills and minds. The Holy Spirit gives the gift to the individual, and the individual accepts it in faith. Rather than having belief rise directly from a faculty, this is a belief-producing process.[83] Faith is not merely accepting the truths of the gospel intellectually, but it is personally accepting them and committing oneself to them.[84]

The Holy Spirit does not work in a vacuum. He uses the Scriptures, which contain the great things of the gospel. Plantinga explains: "What is really involved in a believer's coming to accept the great things of the gospel, therefore, are three things: Scripture (the divine teaching), the internal invitation or instigation of the Holy Spirit, and faith, the human belief that results."[85] In this triad the Spirit witnesses internally to the individual that the basic content of the biblical teaching (the "great things of the gospel") is true, and when the believer accepts this testimony by faith, personal belief in Christian doctrine results. For Plantinga, the Scriptures are the testimony of God, and it is the work of the Holy Spirit that enables us to see this.[86]

Faith is to be understood not as irrational, or unjustified belief, but as knowledge. Faith is a "belief-producing process"[87] that results in genuine knowledge. God has designed the process of faith to produce the effect of certain rational beliefs. Following the earlier model of warranted belief, the process of belief-formation through faith satisfies the criterion of being based on a design plan that is successfully aimed at truth, and the process takes place in an environment conducive to its proper function.[88] Thus the beliefs produced are produced in a reliable way, by a process that confers warrant to beliefs.

82. Ibid., 245–46.
83. Ibid., 246.
84. Ibid., 247.
85. Ibid., 249–50.
86. Ibid., 252.
87. Ibid., 256.
88. Ibid., 257.

When it comes to the Scripture, through the witness of the Holy Spirit the believer is enabled to accept that the Scripture is self-authenticating.[89] This does not mean that if someone doubts the trustworthiness or authority of the Scriptures they can read 2 Tim 3:16, "All Scripture is God-breathed and is useful for teaching, rebuking, correcting and training in righteousness" (NIV), and walk away fully convinced that the Scripture is the Word of God.[90] On the basis of the extended A/C model, however, the Scripture is self-authenticating in that by the internal instigation of the Holy Spirit, and the believer's commitment in faith, no other evidence is necessary for rationally believing in what the Scriptures teach. Accepting the teachings of the Scriptures takes place in a properly basic way.[91] Plantinga's position on this issue will be examined more fully and rigorously in the section on Reformed epistemology and Scripture.

Objections to Alston and Plantinga

While there would be advantages methodologically to engaging objections to Alston and Plantinga in separate sections, many of the objections urged against Reformed epistemology are general enough to encompass the thought of both. Where an objection or challenge is specifically leveled against only one of these thinkers, it will be made clear in the following discussion. On balance, however, most objections to Reformed epistemology are wide enough to cover both Alston and Plantinga. It is granted that large books could be written on the finer points of either one's work, but such analyses are beyond the scope and focus of this present work.

In order to engage a manageable number of objections, and also those that are most relevant, this section will be limited to an examination of three overarching objections against Reformed epistemology. The first species of objection is that belief in God is not properly basic in the way that other basic, foundational beliefs are. The second is that Reformed epistemology allows for virtually any strange belief to pass its test of proper basicality. The third is that religious pluralism or diversity represents a defeater to Christian belief being warranted on non-evidential lines. Any one of these objections, if sustained, could be quite damaging to Reformed epistemology, but all three together are formidable indeed.

---

89. Ibid., 259–60.
90. Ibid., 261.
91. Ibid., 261–66.

First, then, is the question of whether or not belief in God is correctly identified by the Reformed epistemologists as being properly basic. Mark McLeod believes that neither Alston nor Plantinga is successful in showing that theistic belief can be properly basic in the way that other foundational beliefs are, but he believes Reformed epistemology may be potentially formulated in a manner that removes this deficiency.[92] From another perspective, Robert Pargetter is agnostic concerning the potential for Reformed epistemology to demonstrate that theistic belief is properly basic:

> The problem with such an account of the rationality of belief in God is that it involves views about rationality, and epistemology generally, which are far from being generally accepted and non-controversial. So without some development of the notion of proper basicality, especially where basic beliefs are grounded in experience, it is difficult to assess whether belief in God can reasonably be construed as a properly basic belief.[93]

But even if a more modest foundationalism is accepted, and theism is proved to be properly basic, Julie Gowen does not see this as being a sufficiently strong foundation from which to build doctrinal beliefs.[94] Her concern is that the structure of religious beliefs being erected on the epistemological foundation identified in Reformed epistemology is too heavy to be supported by this foundation.

The move from basic theistic belief to Christian doctrine is, of course, attempted by Plantinga in *Warranted Christian Belief*. In its historical progression, Reformed epistemology in its early stages defended the rationality of holding to theistic belief generally, before addressing more specifically Christian doctrine. Perhaps, to stretch the epistemological image, the foundation of theism had to be firmly laid before the structure of Christian doctrine could be built. While doubtless not everyone has found Plantinga's attempt in this regard to be satisfying, it is at least an effort to demonstrate that the foundation is of sufficient strength to uphold more particular doctrinal beliefs.

Others are not hesitant about the future of Reformed epistemology's arguments; they are convinced that theistic belief can never be properly

---

92 McLeod, *Rationality and Theistic Belief*, 9–10.
93. Pargetter, "Experience, Proper Basicality and Belief in God," 141.
94. Gowen, "Foundationalism," 403.

basic. For example, John Zeis does not believe that foundational beliefs can ever be overridden, and as such any belief that is only prima facie justified is not, and indeed cannot, be properly foundational.[95] Stewart Goetz likewise believes that theism cannot be basic, since it represents an inference from a more basic belief.[96] In order to individuate God, there needs to be a prior concept of what God is like, to which the experience can be made to refer.[97] The understanding of an experience of God, then, is logically dependent on the logical inference that identifies the object of the experience as God.

That there are crucial disanalogies between immediate beliefs and theistic beliefs has been argued by Richard Grigg.[98] In the case of memory beliefs, he maintains that one can remember having had breakfast that morning, but crucially this memory is subject to evidential confirmation. If there is one less egg in the carton, and dirty dishes in the sink, this serves to confirm the validity of the memory belief.[99] In response to critics, Grigg notes that even though these tests rely on memories (and are therefore circular), they do at least provide for some external checks.[100] For Grigg, normal evidential confirmation for memory beliefs makes the analogy with basic theistic beliefs unconvincing. It is important that neither God nor theistic belief-forming mechanisms are subject to empirical testing and validation.[101]

Furthermore, Grigg argues that there is a psychological disposition in some people that makes them desire theism to be true. This separates theistic belief from basic perceptual beliefs. Grigg writes: "That is, there is obvious psychological benefit, at least for some people, in believing in God; many persons want to believe in God. But it can hardly be said that we ordinarily have this kind of bias in favor of the belief that we see a tree, that we had breakfast this morning, or that another person is angry."[102] As

---

95. Zeis, "Critique of Plantinga's Theological Foundationalism," 187. For another example of a scholar not willing to give up so easily on classical foundationalism, see Fumerton, "Plantinga, Warrant, and Christian Belief," 343.

96. Goetz, "Belief in God," 475.

97. Ibid., 479–81.

98. Grigg, "Theism and Proper Basicality," 126.

99. Ibid.

100. Grigg, "Crucial Disanalogies," 390–96.

101. Ibid., 396.

102. Grigg, "Theism and Proper Basicality," 126; emphasis in original.

far as the world being older than five minutes, Grigg argues that he does not desire for this to be true, he simply presupposes it.[103] All things being equal, it is difficult to think that an individual out for a walk has an image of a tree presented to their visual field because they have a deep-rooted desire to perceive a tree regardless of whether one is actually there or not. The human desire for God to exist, and the desire many people have for experiencing God or the supernatural, is in Grigg's estimation a crucial point of disanalogy.

More narrowly, there are also objections to Alston's analogy between sense perception (SP) and mystical perceptual doxastic practice (MP). Norman Kretzmann clearly expresses this objection:

> For instance, where SP presents a universal, constant abundance of perceptual inputs, MP's inputs seem relatively rare, scattered, intermittent, and few; where SP's outputs exhibit consistency across cultural divisions, MP's don't . . . But perhaps the most salient difference from the standpoint of practical rationality as we have seen that concept employed in this investigation is the fact that while we cannot rationally reject or suspend judgement on most sense-perceptual experience, even devout theists often conscientiously reject or suspend judgement on putative mystical perceptions. And since it is the absence of "alternatives that commend themselves to reflection as superior" that Alston offers as the linchpin of the practical rationality of acting as if SP is reliable, it looks as if he cannot argue along the same line for the practical rationality of acting as if MP is reliable.[104]

Beyond this, it is recognized that for beliefs generated by sense perception to be considered trustworthy, physical and cognitive health, as well as location and time, are important factors; but this is not the case for MP.[105] There is also, (as Kretzmann pointed out in the quote above), universal participation in SP, but not, apparently, for the sensus divinitatis, and this represents an important disanalogy.[106]

A second type of major objection to Reformed epistemology is that on its general scheme of epistemic justification, all kinds of crazy and contradictory beliefs can end up being justly held by different people. This

103. Grigg, "Crucial Disanalogies," 392.
104. Kretzmann, "Mystical Perception," 90.
105. Gale, "Cognitivity of Mystical Experiences," 429.
106. Ibid., 439.

has sometimes been called "The Great Pumpkin Objection" following Charles Schulz's Peanuts comic strip, where every Halloween Linus waits in a pumpkin patch with the belief that the Great Pumpkin appears once a year on Halloween to those who are absolutely sincere in their hearts and believe in him. Even if Linus has friends who wait with him, they may not experience the Great Pumpkin, because they are not sincerely anticipating his arrival in their hearts. His appearance is not a publicly evident manifestation, but individual and "basic." Those who use this objection find that it passes the criteria laid down by Reformed epistemologists

Plantinga actually provides the most helpful working understanding of the Great Pumpkin Objection, as well as identifying a sub-argument that he calls the "Son of the Great Pumpkin Objection." The original objection was that virtually anything could be considered basic and therefore immune from objection, which would have obviously negative entailments for knowledge.[107] As a development of this position, the "Son of the Great Pumpkin Objection" did not maintain that almost anything could be considered basic, but that one community could have their own sets of basic beliefs, while other communities could have basic beliefs that were entirely contradictory to each other. Thus the objection was that one community could have one set of basic beliefs, while another community could have a set of basic beliefs that could not possibly be reconciled with that of the first community. For example, voodoo practitioners could have one set of basic beliefs, and Christians another, and even if it were recognized that their beliefs were contradicted by the other community, they could still hold to their beliefs as properly basic and reject the beliefs of the others.[108]

It is in adjudicating such contrary religious beliefs that the importance of the disanalogies between religious beliefs and other recognized foundational beliefs becomes important. In such a case, theists would have to demonstrate that their beliefs are analogous to other basic beliefs, while also showing how the competing religious belief is not thus analogous. Grigg states: "In other words, a meaningful defence against the Great Pumpkin dilemma entails showing that belief in God is analogous to certain commonly agreed upon examples of proper basicality in a way that belief in the Great Pumpkin is not."[109] Here there is the twin

107. Plantinga, *Warranted Christian Belief*, 345.
108. Ibid., 345–47.
109. Grigg, "Crucial Disanalogies," 401.

difficulty of having one's own religious beliefs pass the standards of common basicality for foundational beliefs, and also demonstrating that the competing religious belief fails the same test.

The dilemma is part of a wider concern that has been expressed about the Reformed epistemologists. This concern is that they are working out an epistemology that is of interest to Christian believers, but has no importance to those who are outside of the Christian community. Michael Martin argues that for Reformed epistemology, basic beliefs are only evaluated on the basis of the Reformed position. So this means that voodoo beliefs, for example, are rejected as properly basic. But, Martin asks, what would stop the voodoo community from using their basic beliefs to simply reject the Reformed claims? Both would merely claim that their beliefs were basic, and then from the vantage point of their own community, reject the claims of the other.[110]

Consequently, communities could make their own sets of criteria for basic beliefs, and then use these sets to reject the beliefs of other communities, while the same thing was going on in the opposite direction. It is also not clear why this standard for belief acceptance or rejection could only be applied to theistic or religious communities. Martin attempts to turn Plantinga's logic back on his own head. First, he quotes Plantinga's words that:

> The Christian will of course suppose that belief in God is entirely proper and rational; if he does not accept the belief on the basis of other propositions, he will conclude that it is basic for him and quite properly so. Followers of Russell and Madelyn Murray O'Hare [sic in Martin] may disagree; but how is that relevant? Must my criteria, or those of the Christian community, conform to their examples? Surely not. The Christian community is responsible to its set of examples, not to theirs.[111]

Next, Martin argues that, if he accepted the logic of Plantinga's remarks just cited, he and other atheists could justifiably hold that atheism is properly basic, regardless of what Christians think:

> So long as belief that there is no God was basic for them, atheists could also justify the claim that belief in God is irrational relative to their basic beliefs and the conditions that trigger them with-

---

110. Martin, *Atheism: A Philosophical Justification*, 272.
111. Ibid., 270.

> out critically evaluating any of the usual reasons for believing in God. Just as theistic belief might be triggered by viewing the starry heavens above and reading the Bible, so atheistic beliefs might be triggered by viewing the massacre of innocent children below and reading the writings of Robert Ingersoll. Theists may disagree, but is that relevant? To paraphrase Plantinga: Must atheists' criteria conform to the Christian communities' criteria? Surely not. The atheistic community is responsible to its set of examples, not to theirs.[112]

Martin's words just cited are in response to a quotation he cited from Plantinga, which reads: "Clearly in Martin's view if the Christian community can take this stance towards atheism, the atheistic community can take this stance towards theism. The same follows for every community that has beliefs incommensurable with other communities."

For the Reformed epistemologists, a further problem that the Great Pumpkin Dilemma generates is that their consistency with rational justification is situational. As Wolterstorff asserts:

> It has long been the habit of philosophers to ask in abstract, nonspecific fashion whether it is rational to believe that God exists, whether it is rational to believe that there is an external world, whether it is rational to believe that there are other persons, and so on. Mountains of confusion have resulted. The proper question is always and only whether it is rational for this or that particular person in this or that situation, or for a person of this or that particular type in this or that type of situation, to believe so-and-so. Rationality is always situated rationality.[113]

One result of this line of thinking is that two people, X and Y, may with justification both hold to belief A at time t_1, but as person X grows in knowledge they come to a new position at time t_2 where they are no longer able to rationally hold to belief A, while person Y, whose knowledge has not changed in regards to A continues at time t_2 to still be rationally justified in holding to the original form of belief A. In terms of the Great Pumpkin, this means, according to Bredo Johnsen, that the Reformed epistemologists should show that nobody in any circumstances could be justified in holding such beliefs.[114] Yet it seems that, given situated ratio-

---

112. Ibid., 273.
113. Wolterstorff, "Can Belief in God Be Rational," 155; emphasis in original.
114. Johnsen, "Basic Theistic Belief," 461.

nality and the standards of epistemic blamelessness that the Reformed epistemologists use, it is quite possible that at some specified time a particular individual could be justified in believing in the Great Pumpkin.[115]

Yet, as far as anyone knows, there are no communities of people who believe in the Great Pumpkin, and there no individuals with that belief either. If there were then perhaps an inquiry would have to be made about the status of their beliefs, and whether or not they really could qualify as basic.[116] The investigation might turn up that they were, but this is pure speculation. As Appleby remarks: "If the world were radically different, this conclusion might not obtain. But, crucially, it isn't."[117] Epistemology and basic beliefs can be investigated on the basis of what actually obtains and what people actually believe, rather than through hypothetical thought experiments.

Voodoo communities, where voodoo beliefs are accepted, actually do obtain, however, and thus they are a concrete instantiation of the Pumpkin dilemma. The solution for Plantinga is to adopt the position that the respective beliefs in the voodoo community and in the Christian community can be arrived at in the same way (through testimony, for example), but that if the original beliefs were generated falsely, then they are not warranted. If the first person to hold a belief did not have genuine warrant for that belief, then their holding that belief cannot be warranted if it is based on their testimony.[118] Furthermore, if Christian beliefs are actually true, then voodoo beliefs cannot be warranted.

There is an extremely important distinction to bear in mind. A belief can be formed in a basic manner, but this only confers prima facie justification. The accumulation of evidence and counter-argument can lead to the belief, even though basic, being defeated.[119] One problem with the Great Pumpkin Dilemma is that such a belief may be "properly basic with respect to justification," or "properly basic with respect to rationality," but it is not "properly basic with respect to warrant."[120] Plantinga's model for warrant is dependent on truth, whereas not failing in any epis-

---

115. Ibid., 462.
116. Appleby, "Reformed Epistemology," 137.
117. Ibid.
118. Plantinga, *Warranted Christian Belief*, 347.
119. Ibid., 343–44.
120. Koehl, "Reformed Epistemology and Diversity," 173.

temic duties (i.e., being justified), or holding a belief in a basic way that is rational, is not the same as having a warranted belief. It is very easy to confuse de jure and de facto issues, but ultimately factuality is necessary for warranted belief.

The most difficult objection for Reformed epistemology, however, comes in the form of religious pluralism or religious diversity (although this is in many ways an extension of the previous objection, so many of the same points could apply). Pluralistic religious beliefs are not merely hypothetical (like communities where belief in the Great Pumpkin is a serious option) but are an actual phenomenon in the real world. The difficulty of religious pluralism strikes at the Reformed epistemologists' case in general, and it is also important for the more narrow considerations of socially accepted doxastic practices, and beliefs being warranted and properly basic. Alston clearly understands the important challenge religious diversity poses for his work: "I have saved the most difficult problem for my position—religious diversity—for a separate chapter."[121] Plantinga frames the problem in the following way:

> But what about the facts of religious pluralism, the fact that the world displays a bewildering and kaleidoscopic variety of religious and antireligious ways of thinking, all pursued by people of great intelligence and seriousness? There are theistic religions, but also at least some nontheistic religions (or perhaps nontheistic strands of religion) among the enormous variety of religions going under the names "Hinduism" and "Buddhism." Among the theistic religions, there are Christianity, Islam, Judaism, some African religions, and still others. All of these differ significantly from each other. Furthermore, there are those who reject all religions. Given that I know of this enormous diversity, isn't it somehow arbitrary, or irrational, or unjustified, or unwarranted (or maybe even oppressive and imperialistic) to endorse one of them as opposed to all the others?[122]

But what is it that is so challenging about pluralism and religious diversity? Reformed epistemologists hold that basic beliefs are subject to potential defeaters, and can be overwhelmed. One such defeater is another religious belief that, all things being equal, enjoys as much theoretical potential for justification as your own religious belief. If you meet some-

---

121. Alston, *Perceiving God*, 255.
122. Plantinga, *Warranted Christian Belief*, 437–38.

one who has a different religious belief, you must have a good reason for believing that your belief is superior in order to be justified in continuing to hold it.[123] J. L. Schellenberg argues:

> Religious believers sensitive to the issue of religious diversity must find some plausible way of arguing that the "facts" of pluralism assumed by the critic and (for the sake of argument) by Alston are not facts after all—that there are no incompatibilities of the sort in question (at least not on fundamental matters) and/or that there are strong independent reasons for viewing one of the relevant alternatives—their own—as epistemically preferable to others.[124]

For example, a medical researcher may conduct a test that yields a certain result, and then they are justified in believing that the result they discovered is true. Yet if they meet three other researchers who ran equal tests and achieved three different results, none of them is justified in believing that their result is true.[125] If the internal markers in different believers are equally good,[126] then most believers will appeal to external evidences to adjudicate their differences.[127] But some see that this is a move away from externalism and proper basicality. Many also doubt that such compelling external evidence will be found.

Alston, for his part, argues that since different religious communities have different socially established doxastic practices, the issue is not one of internal inconsistency for generated beliefs, but of inter-inconsistency between the social communities.[128] He argues that, on one level, it is possible to conceive of these differences as owing to the object of the experience. Mystics of different religions may be in touch with the Ultimate, but since the concept of the Ultimate differs in cultures and religions, they may interpret their experience in unique ways.[129] That which is being experienced may be the same, but the content and concepts used to understand and express the experience might be very different. The im-

---

123. Willard, "Plantinga's Epistemology," 287.
124. Schellenberg, "Reply to Alston," 159.
125. Feldman, "Plantinga on Exclusivism," 87–88.
126. Ibid., 96.
127. Willard, "Plantinga's Epistemology," 283.
128. Alston, *Perceiving God*, 256.
129. Ibid., 258–59.

mediate experience may be of God, but the wider, doctrinal beliefs may be in conflict.[130]

Yet why should the Christian stick with their own beliefs, just because of the pragmatic value of continuing in the socially established doxastic practices of their community? There is another option available: the option of rationally investigating the claims of other religions, or exploring their practices.[131] In fact, an argument has been made that both Hindu and Muslim MP could enjoy the same pragmatic argument that Alston uses, and this for completely contradictory beliefs.[132] Here again the difficulty that Reformed epistemology has with dealing with the claims of other religions emerges. But it is at this point that it also needs to be remembered that Reformed epistemology can investigate evidence and arguments, and look at potential defeaters to prima facie justified beliefs.[133] This can be applied to other religions, in an attempt to demonstrate that their beliefs can be defeated. If this is the case for Christian belief, theoretically it could be used to defeat the beliefs of other religions.

One further response to Alston is that the Christian community itself has widely varying "procedures, mechanisms, or authorities"[134] to settle disputes about the beliefs generated by CMP. Roman Catholics can appeal to tradition and papal authority, whereas Fundamentalists try to look exclusively to the Bible.[135] Thus in the Christian community, there is not one simple authority that is commonly appealed to in order to settle disputes. Pluralistic beliefs are not just a problem between religions, but fall within the bounds of Christianity itself. Part of Alston's response is to affirm that there are different degrees in which a community can share a practice like CMP, but there is simply no agreed-upon standard by which one can determine when a shared practice is used so differently as to no longer be truly shared.[136] There are rough edges that cannot be smoothed away.

---

130. Ibid., 260.
131. Quinn, "Towards Thinner Theologies," 162.
132. Gale, "Overall Argument," 148.
133. Alston is identified as being particularly concerned with experience being supported by evidence by Pritchard, "Reforming Reformed Epistemology," 56.
134. Tilley, "Religious Pluralism," 165.
135. Ibid.
136. Alston, "Response to Critics," 176.

Plantinga notes that for the Christian believer, different religious practices are not equal, since the Christian has the sensus divinitatis, and the internal instigation of the Holy Spirit.[137] This means that the diversity in religions does not prove that there is equality amongst the religions. It is quite logically possible to argue that there are no different religious contexts that are equal to Christianity. While it is true that there are more people in the world who are not Christians than those who are, it is also true that truth is not determined by popular vote—and if it were, there are more Christians than philosophers who espouse pluralism, which would then defeat the pluralist's position.[138] What is most important is that there are no sound arguments from the fact that people do not agree on a certain proposition to the conclusion that the proposition is false, or that others can only accept it if they are morally or epistemologically deficient.[139] This move by Plantinga does not deal so much with the particulars of differing religious beliefs, but with an attack on the validity of the postmodern basis for the question in the first place.

There are two more points that Plantinga makes about religious pluralism that are worth mentioning. The first is that, given the Christian worldview, religious pluralism can be accounted for, not on the basis of equally veridical and warranted religious experiences in different religions, but as a sad indictment of the fallen human condition.[140] Now, the believer may be shaken by religious pluralism, and come to lose some existential benefits of comfort and peace, and they may even have their degree of warrant lessened, but this is not the only eventuality.[141] This is because, in the second place, there can be an analogy drawn between religious pluralism and moral or ethical pluralism. If you hold a certain act to be immoral, but then discover that others do not believe it is immoral, this does not by itself have to force you to abandon your original view. It may cause you to do deeper thinking on the issue, but this deeper thinking may lead you to become even more convinced that your position is correct; you may even gain assurance that you are correct. The same is at least logically possible for the Christian who considers the claims of other

---

137. Plantinga, *Warranted Christian Belief*, 453.
138. Ibid., 438 n. 18.
139. Ibid., 456.
140. Ibid.
141. Ibid., 456–57.

religious adherents.[142] As the Christian reflects on their beliefs and experiences, and compares them to the claims of other religions, the Christian may find their confidence in their faith growing rather than declining.

The response of Reformed epistemology to the problem of religious pluralism is what one would expect, given their response to the Great Pumpkin Dilemma and their focus on an internally consistent Christian religious epistemology. An accounting for other religious beliefs happens from within the Christian worldview. Especially in the Reformed view, total depravity can account for cognitive malfunction.[143] Through sin, our cognitive perception of God is distorted, and the deliverances of the sensus divinitatis can be resisted.[144] It may even be partially damaged by sin, and beyond this the knowledge that is produced can be suppressed by the sinner.[145] Yes, Plantinga recognizes that a theist and an atheist can have the same sense perceptual experience of seeing the starry sky, but only one will find the sensus divinitatis forming theistic belief.[146] Here is an example of how different religious beliefs can arise (they are distorted versions of genuinely Christian belief), that is internally consistent with the Reformed Christian worldview. This model will not likely be compelling to anyone outside the Christian community, but as has been seen, the Reformed epistemologists are working to show that, on Christian principles, belief in God and the great things of the gospel can be properly basic.

REFORMED EPISTEMOLOGY AND THE EVIDENTIAL CASE FOR THE RESURRECTION

This section will examine the position Reformed epistemology takes in relationship to the evidentialist case for the resurrection. It will proceed by looking at two related but differentiable aspects of the issue. The first subsection will be concerned with the wider topic of natural theology. Narrowing down from there, the second will look at the historical case in particular. For both sections, the details of the specific arguments of natural theology, or the specifics of a historical case for the resurrection, will not need to be mentioned. Reformed epistemologists have overarch-

---

142. Ibid., 457.
143. Ibid., 180.
144. Ibid., 205.
145. Ibid., 210.
146. Grimm, "Cardinal Newman," 500 n. 9.

ing theoretical reasons for their stance in regards to these areas, a stance that bypasses the smaller nuts and bolts details of particular arguments, and applies in general to the whole enterprise.

It is important to remember that the basic contention of the Reformed epistemologists is that belief in God is produced immediately or non-inferentially. Theistic belief is not grounded in other beliefs. Even the great, catholic Christian beliefs are not built on other foundational beliefs. They too are produced immediately and accepted without rational deduction. Rather than being secondary, tertiary, or even higher, theistic belief is primary and foundational. It is produced and held without argument, evidence, or inference.

Such a view of the nature of theistic belief will have an obvious impact on the importance one ascribes to natural theology. Whatever the arguments that are worked out in philosophy of religion, or whatever evidence is presented in Christian apologetics, such arguments and evidences are, strictly speaking, unnecessary for the believer to be warranted in holding their theistic beliefs. Any other understanding would relegate theistic belief to the realm of the nonfoundational, which is precisely what Reformed epistemology seeks to avoid. This is of course a controversial stance, and it is not the whole story concerning the relationship between argument, evidence, and Reformed epistemology. In fact, this relationship is complex, and there have been charges made that the Reformed epistemologists have an inconsistent and vacillating understanding of the role of theistic proofs and evidences. But to take things in proper order, now is the time to turn to Reformed epistemology and natural theology.

Natural Theology

Natural theology was not originally used to prove the existence of God, but rather to work out an understanding of God and his creation. As has been correctly noted: "In its formative stages, then, natural theology was not simply a detached analysis of an impersonal natural backdrop to human historicity but was reflection upon all existence, including human history, in the light of its *assumed* relation to God."[147] For Christian medieval philosopher/theologians like Anselm and Aquinas, natural theology was not an attempt to prove their faith; it was an attempt to work

---

147. Brown, "Plantinga and Natural Theology," 8; emphasis in original.

through their faith so they could understand it better.[148] Such thinkers "were engaged in the transmutation project of altering belief (faith) into knowledge."[149] Natural theology was not, then, a philosophical enterprise that was detached from God. It was (or at least it could be), a theological enterprise where logic, reason, and evidence were used to exposit God's creation, attributes, and existence. It could, therefore, be a deeply religious pursuit, not at all detached, skeptical, or neutral. Long before the Enlightenment, issues of faith and reason were being wrestled with in a wide variety of different ways.[150]

There is another way in which natural theology can be understood, however. In its strongest form, a natural theology must first prove that God exists, and then it can set creation in its relationship to him. The proof might be certain or probabilistic, but its initial goal is to provide a demonstration of the existence of God. In a weaker sense, natural theology's goal may not consist of seeking to prove that God exists; rather, it may try to prove that belief in God is rationally acceptable, where rationality is understood in terms of Enlightenment standards.[151] It is not thinking rationally about theism; it is reasoning to theism, or demonstrating that belief in theism is rational. This is a very different project indeed from that of the early Christian philosophers, and a variety of questions can be asked about it. One vital question is whether or not any natural theology actually succeeds in establishing its intended goal. Do any attempts at constructing such a natural theology actually prove the existence of God? A second very important question is whether or not such a project can be successful, even in theory. It is possible that no existent natural theology, no matter how rigorous, has succeeded to date, but that one will succeed in the future. It is also possible, however, that such success will never be forthcoming; it may be an impossible task. Third (but this does not exhaust possible important questions) is the matter of whether or not such a project is wise or appropriate. Even if a particularly elegant and coercive natural theology could be worked out, it still remains an open question as to whether or not it should be worked out. Is God in favor of such a pursuit, or is it dishonoring to him for human beings to try to prove to

---

148. Wolterstorff, "Can Belief in God be Rational," 140–41.
149. Ibid., 141.
150. Mulhall, *Faith and Reason*, 7.
151. Plantinga, *God, Freedom, and Evil*, 2.

their satisfaction that he is actually there? This latter question will only be asked by those who believe that God does in fact exist, of course; but in Christian communities, it is a valid question.

In general, Reformed epistemology does not just reject particular arguments in natural theology, it rejects the entire theory behind natural theology.[152] The rejection takes place for at least two reasons: one, because it is unnecessary, and two, because it is inappropriate.[153] Because of the nature of Reformed theology, natural theology cannot be necessary. Hoitenga explains: "Natural theology, that is, an inferential approach to the existence and nature of God apart from revelation, is unnecessary, say Reformed thinkers, because God can be known, and originally is known, by the direct acquaintance of the mind."[154] It is inappropriate because of this (i.e., God is already known and does not need to have his existence discovered or demonstrated by rational argument), and it is also inappropriate because God is a transcendent being, unlike all other things.[155]

Plantinga examines the thought of Bavinck, Calvin, and Barth and finds agreement in the Reformed camp that natural theology is rejected.[156] He writes:

> In rejecting natural theology, therefore, these Reformed thinkers mean to say first of all that the propriety or rightness of belief in God in no way depends upon the success or availability of the sort of theistic arguments that form the natural theologian's stock in trade. I think this is their central claim here, and their central insight. As these Reformed thinkers see things, one who takes belief in God as basic is not thereby violating any epistemic duties or revealing a defect in his noetic structure; quite the reverse. The correct or proper way to believe in God, they thought, was not on the basis of arguments from natural theology or anywhere else; the correct way is to take belief in God as basic.[157]

This paragraph represents not merely the thought of certain Reformed thinkers, but also is representative of Plantinga's own position.

---

152. Beilby, *Epistemology as Theology*, 26.
153. Hoitenga, *Faith and Reason from Plato to Plantinga*, 219.
154. Ibid.
155. Ibid., 220.
156. Plantinga, and Wolterstorff, eds., *Faith and Rationality*, 63–73.
157. Ibid., 72.

Furthermore, there may also be emotive or existential reasons for rejecting natural theology. If one does not believe that the arguments in natural theology are successful, or if one believes that they yield at the most a probabilistic value that is much less than 1, then one is basing their beliefs on what will seem to be an unsure base. The casualty in this case may not be the believer's belief, but the believer's assurance of the veracity of their belief. Laura Garcia writes: "I see Plantinga's project as in large measure an attempt to preserve this assurance of faith and to show how it can be rationally justified even in the absence of compelling evidence for what believers hold."[158] Evidence for this is found in Plantinga's statements that to be justified in terms of natural theology, the believer has to keep checking arguments from contemporary philosophers against belief in God. This, says Plantinga, can lead to "a faith that is unstable and wavering, subject to all the wayward whim and fancy of the latest academic fashion."[159] Given the lack of success many people evaluate natural theology to have in demonstrating the existence of God, doubt or lack of assurance is a very real possibility. Rationality and emotions are linked in a wide array of complex relationships.

Even in cognitive terms, natural theology is only going to be of limited use to a relatively small number of people. Plantinga has a footnote where he mentions, "Natural theology, as Aquinas says, is pretty difficult for most of us; most of us have neither the leisure, ability, inclination, nor education to follow those theistic proofs."[160] This remark seems manifestly true. On a personal note, Kelly James Clark describes his grandmother as a simple, devout Christian believer.[161] He maintains that she could not follow any of the theistic proofs even if she wanted to, but she does not have to because God created her and placed her in a cognitive environment where she could know him without following complicated chains of reasoning. Her belief is fully rational, but it is not derived from reasoning, the point that Reformed epistemologists are striving to communicate.[162] In this understanding, even if natural theology were successful, it would be only helpful to a very select group of individuals.

---

158. Garcia, "Natural Theology and the Reformed Objection," 113.
159. Plantinga, *Faith and Rationality*, 72.
160. Plantinga, *Warranted Christian Belief*, 171 n. 5.
161. Clark, *Return to Reason*, 157–58.
162. Ibid., 156.

The prospects of natural theology's success grow even dimmer, according to Alston, when it is required to underwrite the claims of a full religion. In reality:

> At the most optimistic estimate, natural theology is radically insufficient as a basis for the system of belief of a functioning religion. At best, it does not tell us nearly enough about what God is like, what he has in mind for his creation, what he has done and is doing to carry out his purposes, what he requires of us, what he has in store for us, and other matters that are of central concern to the religious life. Therefore we are forced to have recourse to communications from God and to our experience of God to get some purchase on these matters. The bulk of the putative knowledge of God that one finds in a religious tradition comes from these latter sources... We have to rely on our knowledge of God to determine what sources of belief about God are reliable ones. This involves epistemic circularity, but, as I have been pointing out, this doesn't distinguish religious knowledge from other areas of human knowledge, including the most prestigious ones.[163]

For a religion, then, like Christianity for example, natural theologians would have to combine their philosophical case for theism with other evidence for revelation and Christian doctrine. This is the paradigm used by the classical apologists. Natural theology alone, however, narrowly defined as philosophical as opposed to historical argument, cannot establish the truth of the Christian religion.

Despite the rejection of natural theology by Reformed epistemology, there is some change in how it has been evaluated. The trend has been noted that Plantinga was more critical of natural theology early in his career, but has become more positive about it in his later work.[164] Plantinga himself now remarks that arguments from natural theology may tip towards theism, all things considered, even though the strength of the arguments is not coercive.[165] It has also been observed that, from the beginning, Alston was less opposed to natural theology than some others.[166] For example, Alston states concerning natural theology: "As for myself, though I have no tendency to suppose that the existence of God

---

163. Alston, "On Knowing That We Know," 38.
164. Sudduth, "Reformed Epistemology and Christian Apologetics," 315–16.
165. Plantinga, *Warranted Christian Belief*, 131.
166. Meeker, "Alston's Epistemology," 93.

can be demonstratively proved from extrareligious premises, I find certain of the arguments to be not wholly lacking in cogency. In particular, I think that there is much to be said for the ontological, cosmological, and moral arguments, in certain of their forms. However I will have no time to argue that here."[167] He also writes in regards to neutral starting points: "But I believe that the attempt to argue from neutral starting points for the truth of Christian beliefs deserves much more serious consideration than is commonly accorded it today in philosophical and (liberal) theological circles. I believe that much can be done to support a theistic metaphysics, and that something can be done by way of recommending the 'evidences of Christianity.'"[168]

Alston does not elaborate on his view, or sketch how these arguments might be formed. As will be seen in the section in this chapter on an internal analysis of Reformed epistemology, there are only certain areas that this school of thought delves into. Silence, or lack of time spent in other areas, does not mean that these other areas are considered completely unimportant or without merit.

So while there is a rejection of natural theology as a total package or project, the relationship between it and Reformed epistemology is not mutually exclusive. More will be said about this later in a subsequent chapter, but for now it is sufficient to observe that natural theology—if its purpose is to prove the existence of God—can be viewed as a failure in practice, and can even be held to be a failure in theory, without this perspective making it completely useless or devoid of other purposes. It may not accomplish what some wish it to, but this does not mean that it cannot be used in a different but still meaningful way. Some of the analysis will revolve around issues of intention: what is the philosopher trying to make these arguments prove? What is the stated purpose or goal of the natural theologian's project? What may be a failure when employed in one direction may be a success when employed in another.

The Historical Argument

Since Reformed epistemology objects to the natural theology that arises from evidentialism in both theory and practice, it is not surprising that it does not embrace historical-evidential arguments as convincing dem-

167. Alston, *Perceiving God*, 289.
168. Ibid., 270.

onstrations of the proof of Christianity or the existence of God. To do so would, again, violate the criteria of basicality that is the hallmark of the entire position. Historical arguments are by their nature evidential. They require reconstruction, evidence, and induction (or abduction). Beliefs that are based on historical considerations are not foundational by definition. They are invariably inferential and mediate. No matter how they are analyzed in Reformed epistemology, they cannot consistently be held to be necessary for grounding religious belief. Basic religious beliefs would be warranted apart from historical evidences, since the former are noninferential by nature.

Plantinga claims to have a great deal of respect for apologists who use the historical argument, and believes that it can have several functions, but it is not sufficient in terms of the evidential challenge.[169] For Plantinga, there is a crucial difference between the historical argument for Christian truth and historical arguments for other events. The claims concerning Jesus Christ, including the resurrection, are not like claims for events that are similar to what we are familiar with in our ordinary experience.[170] Even if a few ancient authors believed that these things were true, this fact would still not be strong enough to allow us to believe in them too.[171] Even if the noetic effects of sin were removed, and we could apprehend the historical case, argues Plantinga, "that case isn't strong enough to produce warranted belief that the main lines of Christian teaching are true—at most, it could produce the warranted belief that the main lines of Christian teaching aren't particularly improbable."[172]

Following Swinburne's case for theism, Plantinga notes that the historical, evidential case for Christianity can only be made on probabilistic lines. When total evidence is considered, God's existence may be more probable than not, but this still means that even if all the data for the historical case were in probability terms equivalent to the numeral 1, the total probability would still be tied to the probability for the existence of God in the first place.[173] Aside from special revelation, the historical case

---

169. Plantinga, "Internalism," 384–85.

170. This position demonstrates acceptance of a general principle of analogy for historical investigation.

171. Plantinga, *Warranted Christian Belief*, 270.

172. Ibid., 271.

173. Ibid., 272–74.

will not be successful in establishing the truths of Christianity with certainty; in fact, it cannot, because it trades in probability by its very nature.

Plantinga's main problem with the historical case, however, comes from the fact that the probabilities for a historical case where item is added to item must be multiplied together. Since the probability numerical values are decimals (or at the most 1.0, which functionally is never assigned), multiplication of these values will drive the total value lower, not higher. Plantinga expresses this problem in the following way: "The main problem for such a historical case, as I see it, is what we can call the principle of dwindling probabilities: the fact that in giving such a historical argument, we can't simply annex the intermediate propositions to K (as I'm afraid many who employ this sort of argument actually do) but must instead multiply the relevant probabilities."[174] Perhaps the clearest articulation of this problem comes from Timothy McGrew who writes to refute Plantinga's argument. He says: "Clearly the deflation takes place because we are multiplying numbers that lie between zero and one, and any very long multiplication of such numbers as Plantinga supplies will tend toward zero."[175] McGrew believes that Plantinga's case fails, but his expression of the main point of contention is quite exact and helpful.

By way of example, if the assigned probability value for A is 80 percent, this is expressed as 0.8 in decimal terms. If B also receives an assigned probability of 0.8, both are individually quite likely. (Perhaps A could stand for Jesus being a perfect moral teacher and B could stand for Jesus being buried for three days; A can represent anything, and so can B). But when the probability for both together is examined, it is no longer 0.8. The values are multiplied together, yielding a total probability of 0.64. If another historical item is added, C, and it too receives a value of 0.8 (which again is quite high), when C is put together with A and B, the resulting mathematical probability drops even lower. As Plantinga explains this phenomenon, the relevant probabilities dwindle rather than grow. The more elements required to make the case (and as was seen in the second chapter of this book, there are numerous elements in even the simplest historical case for the resurrection), the lower the overall probability will inevitably be.

---

174. Ibid., 280; emphasis in original.
175. McGrew, "Has Plantinga Refuted the Historical Argument," 10.

This analysis of the historical case has been vigorously challenged. Swinburne, in reply to Plantinga, argues that Plantinga's position is too strong. If it were consistently followed, rebuts Swinburne, then all the conclusions of history and science would grow weaker and weaker even as more and more evidence accumulated; but this seems to be an unacceptable entailment.[176] Furthermore, Swinburne argues that in his probabilistic case, he does not merely multiply independent conclusions, but rather he arrives at a particular conclusion, and then—and this is a critical step—he introduces new evidence at that stage to strengthen his case.[177] This additional evidence prevents the probability from dwindling, and thus renders Plantinga's objection to the historical argument unsustainable. It has been remarked to me that "This way of estimating likelihood depends on all the constituent likelihoods remaining orthogonal, so the 'negative' scores are multiplied; it doesn't take account of interior associations which in non-mathematical terms constitute likelihood!"[178] Perhaps the most strongly worded conclusion is that "Plantinga's critique of the historical argument is a failure—if not an abject failure, then at least a decisive one."[179] It seems extremely counterintuitive that more elements in a case lower the probability; this seems, in fact, to be the opposite of the criterion of comprehensiveness. If Plantinga's argument is fundamentally correct, one could be forgiven for thinking that it could almost be more an argument against the probability calculus itself, than against the method of historical argumentation.

Between the respective positions of McGrew, Swinburne, and Plantinga lies some middle ground. Jason Colwell notes that since Plantinga's argument posits each link in the chain of historical evidences as built off the preceding link, and the first historical link is grounded in background knowledge, it is the background knowledge that ultimately grounds the final link in the historical chain, resulting in low or weak probability.[180] Colwell's position is that if there is only one chain of evidence for a historical case, the resulting probabilities will dwindle, but he argues that "the lower bound may be significantly increased by simulta-

---

176. Swinburne, "Natural Theology," 540–41.
177. Ibid., 541.
178. Roger Grainger, personal correspondence.
179. McGrew, "Has Plantinga Refuted the Historical Argument," 24.
180. Colwell, "Historical Argument," 147.

neous consideration of several different sequences of propositions."[181] In this model, there is not simply one long chain of evidence to consider; there are several chains of evidence, which all lead to the same conclusion. This would strengthen rather than weaken the conclusion.[182] Multiple evidential chains would serve as independent arguments, and if they all pointed to the same conclusion, the probability of the conclusion would be reinforced and gain in numerical value, rather than descend. As Colwell remarks, "The essential principle involved is that whereas the law of dwindling probabilities decreases the probability of a conjunction, it increases the probability of a disjunction."[183]

RESURRECTION AND SCRIPTURE

In the extended Aquinas/Calvin model, the Christian is convinced that the great things of the gospel are true, and holds these beliefs non-inferentially. For those who accept the Christian gospel, no historical argument is necessary for their belief that the Bible is the Word of God.[184] Indeed, in order for a Christian's belief in Scripture to be warranted: "its epistemic status for them must be something different from a conclusion of ordinary historical investigation."[185] Here the contention is not merely that the Scripture as the Word of God can be held in a basic sense, it is the much stronger contention that this belief must be held in a basic sense, and not on the basis of a normal historical argument.

The basic belief, that the Scripture is the Word of God, is formed through the internal instigation of the Holy Spirit. There are several possibilities for how this belief can have warrant that are compatible with the extended A/C model.[186] One way is that the belief is not immediately that the Bible is true, or that a book from God is true. What the Holy Spirit may do is testify to the truth of a particular teaching or teachings in the Bible.[187] Eventually, this leads to the inference that the whole book has divine status, as the Holy Spirit continues to work and bring the Christian

---

181. Ibid., 147.
182. Ibid., 151.
183. Ibid., 154.
184. Plantinga, *Warranted Christian Belief*, 378.
185. Ibid., 379.
186. Ibid., 380.
187. Ibid., 379.

to believe that the Scriptures are from God.[188] Scripture is the testimony of God, and it is the Holy Spirit who gets us to see this.[189]

Reformed theology has often taken an acceptance of the Scriptures in their entirety as properly basic.[190] This is reflected in the Reformed creeds, which unanimously declare that Scripture is known as revelation by the testimony of the Holy Spirit.[191] Plantinga quotes the 1561 Belgic Confession's statement concerning the Protestant canon: "And we believe without a doubt all things contained in them—not so much because the church receives them and approves them as such, but above all because the Holy Spirit testifies in our hearts that they are from God, and also because they prove themselves to be from God."[192]

Reformed thought has often held that the Scriptures "prove" themselves, as the Belgic Confession says, not on the basis of external data, but on the basis of internal considerations. Reformed philosopher Paul Helm explains:

> The object of religious belief for Protestants such as Calvin is the Bible regarded as "self-authenticating" divine revelation. The reasons for believing the message of the Bible are not ecclesiastical—the testimony of the Church; or historical—that there is more evidence to support the truth of the Bible than its falsity; but they are reasons that are internal to the teaching of the Bible. The idea of self-authentication is a difficult one to get clear.[193]

The reason that "the idea of self-authentication is a difficult one to get clear" is because it does not mean that the Scriptures are incorrigible or self-evident as the term "self-authentication" means in philosophical studies. It is analogous, rather, to the way that someone who "has a sensation of sweetness is convinced of its sweetness."[194] The self-authentication of the Bible is subject to testing, and its historical reports are subject to falsification.[195] The main principle at stake, however, is that what au-

---

188. Ibid., 380.
189. Ibid., 252.
190. Wood, "Justification of Doctrinal Beliefs," 53.
191. Evans, "Evidentialist and non-Evidentialist Accounts," 166.
192. Plantinga, *Warranted Christian Belief*, 379.
193. Helm, *Varieties of Belief*, 104.
194. Ibid.
195. Ibid., 106.

thenticates the Bible is something internal to itself, and not an appeal to external evidences.

In Reformed thought, if there is going to be doctrinal knowledge of God, the Scriptures first need to be accepted as his Word.[196] Subsequent to this, it is through rational reflection on the teaching of Scripture that other theological and doctrinal beliefs are formed, and these formulations are grounded back on basic beliefs like the existence of God and the Bible as his Word. According to one scholar, the progression from accepting the Scriptures as God's Word to believing doctrinal propositions looks like this:

> Here at last may be the sort of grounds which automatically give rise to a corresponding belief in the truths attested to in Scripture. By the experience of the Holy Spirit's "bearing witness with our spirit" (Rom. 8:16) we spontaneously and immediately assent to portions of Scripture as the Word of God. So, in actuality, it is not a specific doctrine to which the testimony of the Holy Spirit gives rise. It is rather the wholesale acceptance of certain passages of Scripture as coming from God. So from our acceptance of the Scriptures, we proceed, through theological deliberation, to derive specific doctrinal beliefs. So then, we have the Reformer's affirmative answer to the question of whether or not our acceptance of the Scriptures is properly basic: yes, insofar as they arise or are activated by the Spirit's work within us, an experience presumably accessible to all believers.[197]

What is of the utmost importance, however, is that the initial acceptance of the Scriptures as God's Word only comes through the internal work and testimony of the Holy Spirit. It is only after this that the believer will be able to be warranted in holding further doctrinal beliefs.

Theoretically, there is no reason why a believer cannot accept, by way of a basic belief, the Bible in total as God's Word. As should now be familiar, this position does not lend itself to convincing skeptics that the Bible is the Word of God. It is not "dialectically useful"[198] because the skeptic will not receive any argument in this case that they are likely to find convincing. But on the issue of internal or personal justification, this model may

---

196. Alston, *Perceiving God*, 38; Wood, "Justification of Doctrinal Beliefs," 52.
197. Alston, *Perceiving God*, 59.
198. Ibid., 62.

succeed.[199] The Christian may be able to gain assurance that their beliefs are intellectually credible through this model, but, again, those who are outside of the Christian community will not see anything here that they find compelling in terms of accepting Christianity as true. Those outside may admit that, on the basis of the Christian's own worldview principles, Christians are justified in holding their belief, but that as outsiders they see absolutely no reason to adopt that set of beliefs personally.

INTERNAL ANALYSIS OF APOLOGETIC COGENCY

As has been seen, one of the criticisms that has often been made against Reformed epistemology is that it does nothing to establish the truth of Christianity.[200] It deals in negative apologetics exclusively, rather than positively attempting to demonstrate the existence of God.[201] Swinburne identifies the chief problem of early Reformed epistemology as its wholly negative character.[202] Swinburne also identifies this same problem as a major defect of Plantinga's *Warranted Christian Belief*. He agrees that Plantinga has shown that Christian belief can be warranted if it is true, but states that Plantinga provides no reason for why anyone who is not a Christian should think that it is true.[203]

Reformed epistemology is concerned, naturally enough, with epistemology. A careful scholar of Plantinga has actually coined the term the "Plantinga Thesis": "PT: There is no plausible epistemological theory that rules out theistic belief as a category of epistemologically appropriate belief."[204] Sennett continues by adding the explanation: "In other words, Plantinga maintains that any epistemological theory entailing that theistic belief qua theistic belief is irrational, unjustified, or in some other sense an epistemic ne'er-do-well is a theory which will show itself to be defective and unacceptable."[205] Thus the "Plantinga Thesis" is not that Plantinga is attempting to prove the existence of God or the truth of Christianity;

---

199. Ibid.

200. Fumerton, "Plantinga, Warrant, and Christian Belief"; Meeker "Alston's Epistemology," 90.

201. Sudduth, "Reformed Epistemology and Christian Apologetics," 299.

202. Swinburne, Review of *Faith and Rationality*, 51.

203. Swinburne, "Plantinga on Warrant," 206–7.

204. Sennett, "Introduction," xvi.

205. Ibid.

Reformed Epistemology

what he is doing is endeavoring to show that Christianity is epistemologically acceptable, and any epistemology that makes belief in Christianity impossible to justify is going to be unsustainable. Epistemological issues do not revolve around establishing the truth of beliefs, but only the rationality of holding beliefs.[206] In other words: "We can begin by noticing that although proper basicality is not truth-guaranteeing, it is, generally speaking, rationality-guaranteeing."[207] The aim of the Reformed epistemologists, consequently, is to establish the latter rather than demonstrate the former.

Plantinga's argument is based on a massive contingency: if God exists, then Christian belief is probably warranted.[208] What he does not do, however, is provide initial reasons to believe that the existence of God is actually true. Alston characterizes and evaluates Platinga's position:

> Plantinga's defense of his position is carefully crafted and very much to the point. Nevertheless, except for his negative critiques, the defense is an internal one. It consists of taking one's stance within the doxastic practice in question and defying all comers to dislodge him. This is valuable, but it would also be worthwhile to have some positive reasons in support of the practice that appeal to more widely shared assumptions. This is what I have tried to do with my defense of the rationality of socially established doxastic practices.[209]

Plantinga is self-consciously aware of this limitation to his work, but believes that his project is a reflection on the limitations of philosophical analysis. At the end of his Warrant trilogy, he writes concerning Christianity: "But is it true? This is the really important question. And here we pass beyond the competence of philosophy, whose main competence, in this area, is to clear away certain objections, impedances, and obstacles to Christian belief. Speaking for myself and of course not in the name of philosophy, I can say only that it does, indeed, seem to me to be true, and to be the maximally important truth."[210]

---

206. Sudduth, "Reformed Epistemology and Christian Apologetics," 308.
207. Appleby, "Reformed Epistemology," 133.
208. Plantinga, *Warranted Christian Belief*, xii.
209. Alston, *Perceiving God*, 197.
210. Plantinga, *Warranted Christian Belief*, 499.

There is a human condition that passes from establishing rationality to still desiring to know if something is true.[211] In fact, as Swinburne suggests, what worries most atheists and many theists is whether or not Christianity is actually, really true.[212] Yet, it is still important to know if something is conceptually rational, even if one does not know whether or not it is true.[213] Plantinga, in a reply to Swinburne, notes that he is dealing with whether or not Christian belief should be accepted as epistemologically permissible, and this must happen previous to Christianity being taken on evidence as being true.[214] One cannot believe that Christianity is true if one cannot believe that it is ever justified to hold that belief in the first place.

In defending this position, he argues that his project is valuable, even though it does not cover everything.[215] He also jokingly remarks that his third book in his trilogy was 500 pages long, and he should not be taken to task for failing to make it longer.[216] Furthermore—and this is crucial—he also reminds his disputants that, in his judgment, he does not know of any good argument from public evidence that proves the truth of Christianity.[217] Thus his argumentation has dealt with developing a Christian epistemology from within the Christian tradition. It has an apologetic purpose, but this purpose is embedded in the purposes of Christian philosophy and Christian epistemology.[218] In fact, he does not even argue that he proves that Christian belief is warranted, because its being warranted depends on its being true.[219] The objections he is concerned with are de jure, not de facto; but if Christianity is de facto wrong, belief in it cannot be warranted.

Negative apologetics are not, of course, useless. The Reformed epistemologists, and Plantinga in particular, are quite adept at using philosophy of religion to defeat the defeaters that are urged against their claims. In fact, two scholars who find several problems with Plantinga's

---

211. Appleby, "Reformed Epistemology," 139.
212. Swinburne, "Plantinga on Warrant," 207.
213. White, "Can Alston Withstand the Gale," 144.
214. Plantinga, "Rationality and Public Evidence," 216.
215. Plantinga, "Internalism," 399.
216. Ibid., 398.
217. Ibid., 399.
218. Plantinga, "*Warranted Christian Belief*: A Precis," 328.
219. Plantinga, "Internalism," 387.

model of warranted Christian belief find his answers to putative defeaters of Christianity's epistemic status "always interesting and frequently convincing."[220] For Reformed epistemology, it is in the arena of negative apologetics that arguments from natural theology can be most profitably employed, and the tools of analytic philosophy most helpfully used to defend Christianity. Gary Habermas cites the defense of Christianity against its detractors as an area in which Reformed epistemology excels, while still having serious reservations concerning Reformed epistemology's lack of a positive case for the truth of the Christian faith.[221]

Perhaps the clearest example of Reformed epistemology's engagement with putative defeaters for Christianity involves the atheist argument from evil. Responding to this argument was a large part of Plantinga's seminal work *God, Freedom, and Evil*. Chapter 14 of *Warranted Christian Belief* carries on his work in this regard, showing that he has kept up with developments in this argument, and has thought through responses. Even more recently, Plantinga has engaged in a written debate with Michael Tooley, where Tooley articulates and defends a deontological version of the argument from evil.[222] Clearly Plantinga has continued to think and write on the problem of evil, without (unsurprisingly) convincing everyone that he is correct in his position. As with many philosophical arguments, it does not seem likely that a universally accepted resolution for this one is on the horizon, but Plantinga continues to demonstrate that Christian belief can still be warranted in the face of alleged defeaters like the argument from evil and suffering.

It is also a logical possibility that even if a Christian thought that the evidence from evil seemed more favorable to atheism than theism, their basic belief in theism could still outweigh this counterevidence. This does not have to be the case in reality, but it is possible theoretically. Basic theistic belief could conceivably have intrinsic, built-in defeaters to opposing defeaters.[223] When it comes to the argument from evil, many people may consider it and find theism implausible, "But for those who widely (or even continuously) experience the presence of God, the experience of evil

---

220. Le Morvan and Radcliffe, "Plantinga on Warranted Christian Belief," 350.
221. Habermas, "An Evidentialist's Response," 297.
222. Plantinga and Tooley, *Knowledge of God*.
223. Quinn, "Foundations of Theism Again," 39.

does not alleviate that experience of God."[224] In the Bible, both Job and the prophet Habakkuk struggle with the injustice of evil, but neither one of them approaches accepting atheism as a result. Again, this does not have to be necessarily the case for the modern Christian, but it is a logical possibility that they will find themselves in a similar epistemic position, where they are intellectually thinking through evil, existentially suffering, and still finding their belief in God intact. This may even be our epistemic duty. As Wolterstorff says: "Perhaps it is our duty to believe more firmly that God exists than any proposition which conflicts with this, and/or more firmly than we believe that a certain proposition does conflict with it."[225]

In the final analysis, Sudduth argues that Reformed epistemology is simply not a full school of apologetics; it is a project that deals with epistemological issues that have definite entailments for Christian apologetics.[226] In response to Habermas, who cites the lack of positive evidences as a major problem for Reformed epistemology, Sudduth replies that establishing the truth of Christianity is just not the goal of Reformed epistemology (the repetition of this point is intentional: it must be understood). In this regard, Sudduth claims that the complaint of Habermas (and others) is illegitimate; it is like complaining that Toyota vehicles are substandard because NASA cannot use them for space exploration.[227] What is really problematic is not the lack of positive apologetics in Reformed epistemology, it is misunderstanding Reformed epistemology as a separate school of apologetics that is trying to accomplish everything necessary for a full apologetic. If the project of Reformed epistemology were understood and accepted on its own terms and for its own contributions, it would not be faulted for failing to support weight it was never engineered to bear.

CONCLUSION

Sudduth's analysis is surely right, and it lines up perfectly with statements we have already seen by Alston, Plantinga, and Sennett to the same effect. The major implication for this study, then, is that Reformed epistemology is not going to establish the truth of the resurrection, or the truth of

---

224. Pargetter, "Experience, Proper Basicality, and Belief in God," 157.
225. Wolterstorff, "Can Belief in God be Rational," 177.
226. Sudduth, "Reformed Epistemology and Christian Apologetics," 309.
227. Ibid., 308-9.

the inspiration and inerrancy of Scripture. What it does, if successful in reaching its own goals, is make believing in the resurrection and Scripture epistemologically justified on the basis of non-inferential, basic beliefs. It is an open question as to whether or not these beliefs are true; if they are, then holding them is warranted, and if they are not, then nobody is warranted in believing in the great things of the gospel. Reformed epistemology is not representative of a complete apologetic methodology, and yet since it articulates a way in which the doctrines of the resurrection and Scripture could be potentially held in a warranted manner, it contains enough elements that are relevant to our focus that it may emerge as the most cogent option for Reformed apologetics. Its partial focus does not disqualify it from consideration, since its scope still covers the great things of the gospel, or the major doctrines of the Christian faith. After all, it may be impossible to prove these things through natural theology or historical evidences, and if this is the case, then something like that which is offered in Reformed epistemology may be the best way of defending Christian beliefs. It may be possible that Christianity will only be able to make a case for internal rationality, and never be able to prove itself to those outside of the faith community.

4

Presuppositionalism

INTRODUCTION

Presuppositionalism is a school of thought that attempts to bring all human thinking into subjection to the authority of the Word of God. Methodologically, presuppositional apologists endeavor to achieve this goal by demonstrating that all human thought that does not submit to the Word of God is fallacious and untrustworthy. In the view of presuppositionalists, it is literally impossible for human knowledge to obtain apart from the existence of the triune God and his revelation to humankind. The apologetic encounter ultimately relies on the impossibility of the contrary—experience in this world is intelligible, but this is impossible on any modal scheme that is contrary to Christian theism. Since only Christian theism (which here must include biblical trinitarianism) can account for the intelligibility of human knowledge and experience, and all other alternatives can be shown to fail in this regard, Christian Theism is vindicated by default as the true position.

Since the goal in a presuppositional apologetic is to show the nonbeliever that their worldview (whatever the details) is necessarily incoherent, and that in contrast the Christian worldview is necessary for there to be coherence, the main emphasis is on negative apologetics. The apologist attempts to demonstrate that the non-Christian worldview is intellectually unsustainable and incapable of being rationally articulated. The non-Christian is invited to prove that the Christian worldview is internally incoherent, but this is something that they cannot succeed in doing. Ideally, the Christian presuppositionalist exposes the inconsistency, contradictoriness, and incoherence of the other worldview, and then the non-Christian tries but necessarily fails to expose the philosophical flaws in the Christian worldview. They fail in this attempt because it is impossible to be successful; after all, Christianity is held to be perfectly cogent and logically compelling. Thus the apologist defends the faith by destroying the coherence of the contrary position, and then supervising the failure that comes when the coherence of the Christian worldview is attacked (at least in idealized presuppositional practice).

POSITIVE AND NEGATIVE EPISTEMOLOGICAL CONSIDERATIONS

As will be demonstrated, presuppositional apologetics denies that a convincing case for Christianity can be built up in the manner used by evidentialists. This denial does not merely stem from a lack of confidence in the logic of the theistic arguments and the particular historical evidences for Christianity (although this is part of the rationale), but from a basic epistemological position that is different from the assumed epistemology of evidential thought. In order to use rational argumentation, and to understand putative facts in the domain of science or history, worldview level considerations must be taken into account. Epistemology and metaphysics must both be coherent in their totality, and they can only be coherent if they are properly aligned. Human thinking must be in contact with an externally objective order, and this order must be constituted in felicitous ways for human cognition if intelligibility is to exist, or even be logically possible. But if epistemology and metaphysics are not related in proper ways, then the very use of logic and rational thought itself is at the least called into doubt (resulting in skepticism), or at the most rendered impossible. For the presuppositionalists, rather than relying on arguments to build up a case for the existence of God or the truth of Christianity, the baseline is that the Christian worldview in its totality must be accepted in order for cognitive activity to be meaningful. Autonomous thinking does not prove the validity of the Christian worldview: the Christian worldview alone is necessary for the validity, or even the possibility, of human thinking.

Both proponents and opponents of presuppositional apologetics recognize that Cornelius Van Til, the unquestioned pioneer of this school of thought, was not very systematic in his treatment of themes.

His insights are scattered throughout his literary corpus, and were never brought together into a user-friendly resource. Presuppositional apologetics today, however, is rather homogenously related to Van Til's work. While there are intra-presuppositional debates (between Bahnsen and Frame, for example) on some of presuppositionalism's finer points, on balance the presuppositional camp is fairly consistent and uniform. Thus the following section will not exposit or trace the thought of Van Til, and then the thought of Frame, or the thought of Bahnsen. Wherever necessary, points of debate between presuppositionalists will be identified, but on balance it is safe to identify a common presuppositional position in general terms. (This is more the case, of course, when presuppositional thought is being contrasted with other apologetic methodologies, than if presuppositionalism were the only subject in view.) As a further corollary to this, not every thinker who agrees with a point will be cited in each instance. Unless there is a good reason, the citations will not refer to Van Til, Bahnsen, Frame, and others all at the same time. Rather, they will be identified when they make a point in a particularly forceful or clear way.

Rationality apart from God

Presuppositionalism denies that human experience is rational or intelligible apart from the existence of the triune God. The human predicament makes autonomous epistemological formulations and metaphysical comprehension impossible. As Greg Bahnsen explains:

> Apologetical disputes between believers and unbelievers depend upon, include by reference, and arise out of conflicting epistemologies. Conflicts over the theory of knowledge in turn incorporate, function within, and must address differing world-and-life views (with divergent concepts of man as a knower), if they would be resolved. The bold defense of the faith offered by Van Til's presuppositionalism is that the unbeliever's worldview fails to provide an adequate or workable theory of knowledge in terms of which the non-Christian can intellectually challenge the truth of Christianity. His presuppositions preclude the unbeliever from making claims to know anything intelligible or meaningful.[1]

---

1. Bahnsen, *Van Til's Apologetic*, 311. Various authors are quoted in this chapter and other parts of the book who, as was the convention when they wrote, use the term "man" as a generic term for humanity in general. I have retained their words (without trying to mark this usage with [sic]) while using gender-inclusive language in my own comments.

This is a basic line in presuppositional apologetics. The non-Christian worldview cannot account for human knowledge. Narrow epistemological issues cannot be resolved without reference to wider philosophical considerations.

To claim that non-Christian thought cannot account for human knowledge is obviously quite controversial, and in need of elaborate defense. Perhaps the first issue is that of reductionism. What can it mean to speak of a singular non-Christian worldview? Are there not multiple and mutually exclusive worldviews that, even though they are not Christian, still are irreducible to one another? Is it not the case that pantheism and materialism, for example, are too different to be considered the same? For the presuppositionalists, the provisional answer would be yes, but in the final analysis the answer is no. It can easily be admitted that there are numerous, contradictory manifestations of worldviews. Ultimately, however, presuppositionalism holds that all worldviews boil down to two: the Christian and the non-Christian. The simple, bottom line stance is that "Christianity interprets reality in terms of the eternally self-conscious divine personality; non-Christian thought interprets reality in terms of an existence independent of God."[2] No matter which non-Christian school of thought one is presented with, they are all suppressing the truth of God, and are rebelling against the knowledge that they have of him, as stated in Romans 1:18.[3] The contrast is as absolute as it is simple. One either accepts the truth of the Christian worldview, or one adopts a singular worldview of rebellion, suppression, and truth-distortion. Formulations of the one rebellious worldview will have contradictory accidental features and propositions, but these contingent properties do not change the underlying core issue, which is that all non-Christian worldviews stand in opposition to God.

Operating from the non-Christian worldview (regardless of its secondary details) means that, by definition, the individual is excluding the existence of the triune God. For the presuppositionalists, this spells disaster for genuine epistemology. There is an integral link in presuppositionalism between human epistemology and metaphysics. It is impossible to accept, as non-Christian philosophy does, the ability of human beings to decide on epistemological strategies for discerning reality apart from

---

2. Van Til, *Defense of the Faith*, 38.
3. Frame, *Cornelius Van Til*, 232.

knowing what metaphysically obtains.[4] Ontology and epistemology must be related together in full worldview systems in order for epistemological principles to be justified. Epistemological considerations cannot be thought through without reference to the wider universe in which such thinking occurs. Furthermore, the concerns of anthropology, such as the type of being that humans are, and the type of brains that they have, will contribute much to understanding human rationality, and the rules that govern it.

Van Til argues that all non-Christian thought must view the universe as chaos or chance, but decipherable to human rationality, and exhaustively comprehensible to human logic.[5] The dialectic is between the rational and irrational. The human mind is simultaneously posited as the final authority for knowledge, while recognizing that in its finite nature the mind is not capable of being trustworthy in this capacity.[6] Ontologically, people cannot be sure that they are in a position to comprehend and identify reality. What they identify is a universe that is governed by chance, where anything can obtain.[7] They also identify themselves as ultimate metaphysically for understanding the universe; this metaphysics places humanity in the highest epistemic position.[8] That which is logically possible is a larger set than that which is actual, and humans can comprehend it.[9] But, "If the universe is open, the facts new to God and man constantly issue from the womb of possibility. These new facts will constantly reinterpret the meaning of the old."[10] Constant reinterpretation of these facts and revision of knowledge means that nothing can be concretely held to as factual today; nobody knows what future facts may emerge that will annihilate all previous interpretation.

Basically, the thrust of the presuppositional method at this point is that all non-Christian thought must bring epistemology and metaphysics into a coherent relationship. In reality, however, on the basis of the non-Christian's own position, it is impossible for such coherence to ob-

---

4. DeMar, *Pushing the Antithesis*, 118–20.

5. Van Til, *Defense of the Faith*, 216.

6. Bahnsen, *Van Til's Apologetic*, 316.

7. Van Til, *Defense of the Faith*, 242. This assertion will be examined later in this chapter.

8. Ibid., 157.

9. Van Til, *Christianity and Idealism*, 8.

10. Ibid., 9.

tain. The non-Christian position begins with epistemology, but can only set forth arbitrary rules, or follow a consensus for rationality. But on the basis of what the non-Christian's metaphysics are, human epistemology is doomed to failure. The human mind is adrift in a sea of chance and chaos, where anything can happen, and where new facts may emerge that destroy all previous human interpretations of putative facts. There will always be a breakdown in non-Christian worldviews, because the epistemology of the worldview will inevitably conflict with the metaphysics of the worldview.

Human comprehension of the universe invariably runs aground on the shoals of the problem of the one and the many, otherwise known as the problem of unity and diversity. In the history of philosophy this has not been a minor problem. On the contrary: "To judge from our sources, early Greek metaphysics revolved around the problem of the one and many."[11] The one and the many is not an archaic philosophical problem relegated to the study of the history of Western thought. From the early Greeks until the present it has persisted as a basic and important philosophical problem.[12] The solution offered by presuppositionalism "is often considered to be the centerpiece of Van Til's apologetic."[13] In Van Til's estimation, any attempt to solve the problem of the one and the many immediately shows the difference between Christian and non-Christian philosophies.[14] It was also, in his estimation, the issue that could sum up the whole problem of philosophy.[15]

Anderson articulates the heart of the problem very clearly when he writes:

> The question naturally arises (as it did in ancient Greece) as to which aspect of reality is *ultimate*: unity or plurality? Suppose, on the one hand, that *plurality* is ultimate. It follows that reality consists at bottom of an aggregate of things that are utterly *dissimilar* and *unrelated* to each other (anything serving to connect them would amount to a more ultimate unifying principle, which *ex hypothesis* does not exist). Yet, as I noted above, nothing can be known *in principle* about utterly dissimilar and unrelated things.

11. Halper, "One-Many Problem," 630.
12. Rushdoony, "One and Many Problem," 339.
13. Anderson, "If Knowledge Then God," 61.
14. Van Til, *Defense of the Faith*, 25.
15. Ibid.

> Suppose, on the other hand, that *unity* is ultimate. It follows that reality is fundamentally *monistic*: It is one undifferentiated thing. Once again, however, nothing can be known *in principle* about such a thing because there can be nothing from which to distinguish it. In either case, because reality cannot be cognized at its most basic level, the prospects for understanding any *part* of it are bleak (not least because in both cases the very notion of a part would be unintelligible).[16]

While the quoted material from Anderson is an excellent description of the problem, no presuppositionalist has surpassed Frame for clarifying and explaining the problem. Human beings seek to understand the universe, and this requires both the ability to distinguish objects from each other, and the ability to relate them to each other in a meaningful way.[17]

Taking a common example, Frame begins to exemplify the problem of the one and the many by considering a dog named Fido. There are other beings that are classified as dogs, on the basis of differences with other beings and similarities amongst themselves. The category of dog, however, is not self-explanatory. As the category of dog is thought through, "we learn that dogs can be grouped into still larger classes: canines, mammals, living beings, beings, being. This process is called 'abstraction'. Each of these steps may be seen as going deeper into the reality, the essence of things. Philosophizing about 'being as such' seems to be the consummation of human knowledge."[18] Identifying and categorizing requires more conceptual powers and rigor than is normally assumed.

To really understand Fido, then, it seems that he must eventually be named into the category of pure being. Yet when this consummate level of abstraction is reached, it becomes apparent that nothing cognitively meaningful is actually being said about Fido. The dog's personal distinguishing characteristics (height, weight, color, etc.) are not included in the definition of the category "dog," and so this designation is incomplete.[19] What is worse, the higher up the levels of abstraction you go, the less you know about Fido. The consummate level in this process of abstraction is pure "being," which "covers everything. But it includes nothing

---

16. Anderson, "If Knowledge Then God," 62; emphasis in original.
17. Frame, *Cornelius Van Til*, 71.
18. Ibid., 72.
19. Ibid.

specific."[20] It is actually the same as nothing. There is simply no content to this category, and so climbing up the ladder of abstraction in this direction literally leads to no knowledge whatsoever.

Recognizing that moving from specifics to the most general category of being results in an epistemological dead end, other philosophers have attempted to salvage knowledge by moving in the opposite direction and seeking knowledge not in the category of unity (i.e., being) but in the category of ultimate diversity. Starting with Fido, we break him down into smaller constituent parts, rather than abstracting him into higher levels of beings and being. We do not really know Fido as such; all we know of him has been put together by our minds from visual and sense experiences. We have had certain visual impressions of his color, or felt certain sensations, like warmth and wetness from a lick.[21] In order to properly understand Fido, we keep breaking him down into smaller constituent parts, and the experiences we have had with him.

Our perception of Fido is really how we have perceived smaller units or elements of him, and related them into larger and more complex patterns. To really have knowledge of Fido, then, is going to require analyzing his elements down to their irreducible termination point. Frame explains:

> Let us imagine that we could trace the elements of the elements of the elements to the point where we could discover some ultimate element of human experience, as scientists have sought for ultimate particles in the physical universe. Let us call that element "ultimate matter," for it would be much the same as Aristotle's "prime matter." What would it be? If it were identifiable, describable, like Fido, then it would be subject to further analysis and would not be the ultimate constituent of experience. Evidently, then, if it were really ultimate, nothing could be said about it. To put the point differently: it could have no qualities, because it would be the bearer of all qualities. So it seems that the very notion of an ultimate component to experience is self-contradictory (as was, indeed, Aristotle's concept of prime matter). The ultimate component is both nothing and something.[22]

The termination point in reducing Fido (or anything else) into smaller and smaller elements is a blank nothingness. The termination

20. Ibid.
21. Ibid., 73.
22. Ibid., 73–74.

point in analyzing Fido into wider and wider spheres of being is likewise a blank nothingness. "In the end, there is no difference between 'being in general' and 'ultimate matter.' Both concepts are empty, uninformative, unintelligible."[23] In the final analysis, absolute unity destroys particularity, and absolute particularity destroys unity. Furthermore, "if both are somehow true, then all is chaos, and nothing is true."[24]

All worldviews must find a way to satisfy the theoretical, in-principle epistemological challenge of the one and the many. Van Til's apologetic forcefully argues that only the Christian worldview is capable of solving this dilemma. This is because the ontological Trinity stands at the center of Christian thinking.[25] Van Til argues thus: "Using the language of the One-and-Many question we contend that in God the one and the many are equally ultimate. Unity in God is no more fundamental than diversity, and diversity in God is no more fundamental than unity. The persons of the Trinity are mutually exhaustive of one another."[26] Rather than abstractions into ultimate unity or plurality, the Christian worldview sees the triune God as concretely existing, and as such his existence provides not an abstract universal, but a concrete one.[27] Furthermore, there are not abstract universals that must be related to each other, but only one self-contained concrete universal where the one and many are "a self-complete unity."[28] For the Christian worldview, diversity can be meaningfully related to unity because diversity and unity are co-ultimate in the ontological Trinity.

It is important to remember that the Trinity was not invented or put forward as a philosophical postulate in order to answer this dilemma. The doctrine of the triune Godhead is not a philosophical solution to a purely abstract philosophical problem. On the contrary, the triune God is part of the biblical revelation, yet his ontology provides the only satisfactory answer to the epistemological dilemma of unity and plurality, and this not on the basis of a philosophical model, but on the basis of genuine existence. This is an example of how metaphysics and epistemology are

23. Ibid., 74.
24. Ibid.
25. Van Til, *Defense of the Faith*, 25.
26. Ibid.
27. Ibid., 26.
28. Ibid., 25.

Presuppositionalism

inseparable. In unfolding the necessary existence of the Trinity to solve the problem of unity and plurality, Van Til believed that all he was doing was following the Bible, rather than primarily engaging in philosophy.[29] In his estimation the solution of the one and the many problem was an entailment of theology, rather than the result of a philosophical treatise engineered to solve the problem.

While presuppositionalists hold that all non-Christian philosophies will necessarily fail to account for genuine human knowledge by failing to find a coherent solution to the one and the many dilemma, they also hold that human beings, as they are in non-Christian thinking, will never be able to justify their knowledge because they are not omniscient. Human beings have set up comprehensive knowledge as the standard for real knowledge.[30] In this they are right, for "It is true that there must be comprehensive knowledge somewhere if there is to be any true knowledge anywhere but this comprehensive knowledge need not and cannot be in us; it must be in God."[31] Nobody argues that they know everything, and yet many argue that they do know some things. Why then is omniscience required for genuine knowledge to be possible?

All objects are understood by comprehending the interlocking sequence of relationships that they bear to one another.[32] Thus, in order to understand any component part or singular object, one needs to also understand all else that the object stands in relation to. This set would comprise the entirety of knowledge. If this whole set is not comprehended exhaustively, then the alleged knowledge that one has cannot be held with confidence. It is completely within the realm of both theoretical and factual possibility that additional comprehension would radically overturn previous interpretation and understanding of received "facts."

If reality is not pre-interpreted and exhaustively comprehended by anyone, then no knowledge is possible as long as the timeline of the universe continues to unfold. As already noted, Van Til wrote: "If the universe is open, the facts new to God and man constantly issue from the womb of possibility. These new facts will constantly reinterpret the meaning of the old."[33] Reality stands in need of interpretation, and it is humans who

---

29. Van Til, "Response by C. Van Til," 348.
30. Van Til, *Defense of the Faith*, 41.
31. Ibid.
32. Frame, *Cornelius Van Til*, 74.
33. Van Til, *Christianity and Idealism*, 9.

must rely on their own minds and experiences to be the ultimate arbiters of factuality in the universe. This is an impossible burden, an epistemic challenge that cannot be met. As long as facts emerge from the possible, it is always imaginable that a new fact will destroy the way all humans understood reality before the issuance of that new fact.

The resulting situation for the non-Christian amounts to this: omniscience of all facts, both present and future, is necessary for knowledge to obtain. All things must be comprehended in their current relationships to all other things, but they also must be comprehended in the relationship they will sustain to all future facts as well. The former is practically impossible, while the latter is theoretically impossible for human thinkers. Yet, since both present and future exhaustive knowledge is necessary for any current knowledge whatsoever, human beings are left in an impossible epistemological situation, where they simply are not in a position to have any real knowledge at all. In this understanding human belief cannot be justified, and therefore cannot be considered knowledge.

These are obviously immense claims that are made by the presuppositionalists. They may also seem to be fairly abstract, even when fleshed out in working examples (like with Fido and the ladder of abstraction). It may sound as if Van Til would be a supporter of postmodernism, although the comparison is more superficial than substantial.[34] Postmodernism rejects metanarratives, acknowledges that all supposed facts are really subjected to interpretation, and understands all perception to be situationally relative and perspectival. This results in a lack of confidence at the least, and at the most a frank rejection of human knowledge in favor of a relativism inclining towards epistemic skepticism. Presuppositionalism agrees that human beings are not so situated that they can have knowledge apart from God, but maintains fervently that humans do know things truly on the basis of the Christian worldview. Humans have knowledge because God has knowledge, and they can learn to interpret reality in light of God's previous interpretation of it. Rationality is impossible on any view other than the Christian one, but in the Christian worldview rationality and knowledge are possible; this view will be the subject of the next section.

---

34. Edgar, "Introduction," 8–11.

Rationality in the Christian Worldview

Presuppositionalism holds that although human beings are not, and never will be, omniscient, they can have genuine knowledge because God is omniscient and exhaustively comprehends all things. For God, all possible facts are already known, and they are interpreted prior to their instantiation.[35] God knows everything that will come to pass before it does, and so every fact is pre-interpreted. He does not wait to collect new data to work into his intellectual system; the meaning of every fact is pre-assigned its significance by the evaluation of God. For God, understanding precedes the instantiation of temporal facts, whereas for human thinkers, the fact must be instantiated, recognized, and then understood.

As long as human beings believe themselves to be in the position of interpreting facts for the first time, their lack of complete comprehension will destroy their claims to have knowledge. In pre-lapsarian Eden, however, human beings were created to recognize that they were creatures, to know that their knowledge was partial, but to understand that their partial knowledge was nevertheless true because it was anchored in the full knowledge of the omniscient God.[36] This guaranteed that data was meaningful, and that it was rationally comprehensible. God already exhaustively knew how each fact related to every other fact, and how they cohered in an intelligible, meaningful system. Ultimate reality was not a contingent surd, but profoundly coherent and knowable. Human epistemology was made rational by the metaphysics of God's created order, and the internal rationality of the Godhead.

In the original state of pre-lapsarian Eden, Van Til states that:

> [M]an would naturally, by virtue of his thought activity, know and come to know ever more fully the true state of affairs about the universe in general and about himself in particular. He would in the field of metaphysics, know and recognize the fact that he was a creature. Hence he would know, in the field of knowledge, that, in the nature of the case, he could be no more than a re-interpreter. That is, he would recognize at once that the possibility of predication presupposed the existence of God as absolute.[37]

---

35. Van Til, *Christianity and Idealism*, 9.
36. Van Til, *Introduction to Systematic Theology*, 70.
37. Ibid.

This is a fully-packed paragraph of Van Tillian themes. In it Van Til brings together the relationship between metaphysics and epistemology, identifying the connection between what humans are and how humans can know. He notes that they can truly know facts, and increase in their knowledge. But this is only possible because they are creatures, and are not the primary interpreters of the universe and all the facts therein. They are striving to re-interpret the facts that have already been pre-interpreted and given their meaning by God. Unless this is recognized, predication becomes impossible. (More will be said on the impossibility of predication apart from the presupposition of God below.) Their reinterpretation does not have the goal of finding a different way of understanding facts than the way that God does, but rather they are to be secondary reinterpreters who strive to understand every fact as closely as possible to the way that the primary first-interpreter, God, understands them.

All knowledge is original to God. Human knowledge is derivative, and can only be reconstructive of God's thoughts.[38] Human beings are to think the thoughts of God after him. Their thinking is to be self-consciously analogical. For presuppositionalism, analogical thinking is a finite reconstruction of God's thinking; it is knowledge only because our thoughts are based on God's thoughts.[39] Human thinking is patterned after, and reflective of, the thinking of God, and it is only because humans bear the image of God that they are in an epistemic position to truly know anything whatsoever.[40]

Even when humans succeed in thinking God's thoughts after him, however, they still only do so in an analogical rather than a univocal sense. Owing to the nature of God there is a categorical difference between the Creator's knowledge and the creature's knowledge. This distinction is necessary and unbridgeable. Nevertheless, humans are to think God's thoughts after him.[41] They will never understand any proposition or fact in precisely the same way that God does, but all their understanding and knowledge is to be patterned after the thoughts of God, and all their interpretations are to reconstruct God's interpretations as accurately as possible. Epistemological success can never erase the qualitative difference

---

38. Bahnsen, *Always Ready*, 50.
39. Frame, *Cornelius Van Til*, 92.
40. Ibid., 93.
41. Ibid., 115.

that exists between the thoughts of God and the derivate, reconstructive thoughts of human beings.

Yet it is only the Christian worldview that allows for even this measure of epistemological success. The richness of the mind of God and of his revelation allow for every manner of human epistemic activity to be grounded in a legitimate foundation. Bahnsen very clearly expresses how presuppositionalists see the extent of this relationship when he writes:

> God knows Himself, of course, perfectly and comprehensively. He knows His holy character. He knows all propositional truths and possibilities, as well as their conceptual or logical relations. He knows His plan for every detail of creation and history, as well as the relations between all events and objects. His understanding is infinite and without flaw. Moreover, it is in terms of His creative and providential activity that all things and events are what they are. God's thinking is what gives unity, meaning, coherence, and intelligibility to nature, history, reasoning, and morality. In terms of this picture of the knowing process, man can search for causal relationships and laws (thinking God's thoughts after Him about His providential plan). He can think in terms of shared properties, similarities, or classes (thinking God's thoughts after Him about the patterns, classifications, or kinds of things He creates and providentially controls). He can draw logical inferences (thinking God's thoughts after Him about conceptual and truth-functional relations). He can make meaningful normative judgments (thinking God's thoughts after Him about the demands of His righteousness). He can account for man's mind knowing extramental objects (thinking God's thoughts after Him about created man's control over the created environment in which God placed him). He can account for the public or objective character of the truth available to many finite minds (thinking God's thoughts after Him about the community of minds created and providentially planned to reflect His thinking), etc.[42]

What is very obvious from Bahnsen's writing here is that for presuppositionalism human thinking must be patterned after God's thoughts, and this has entailments for every single aspect of human cognition. On the basis of the Christian worldview, humans have the right and the ability to actually think and know, because of the relationship in which they stand to the omniscient, revelatory deity. There is not a sphere of human

---

42. Bahnsen, *Van Til's Apologetic*, 223.

investigation or mental activity that is not ultimately justified only when it is grounded in the reality of God's nature and revelation.

If it is the case, as presuppositionalism maintains, that the existence of God and the Christian worldview must be true in order to ground human knowledge and justify human thought, then any worldview other than the Christian one will by default fail to account for intelligibility in experience and thought. The truth of the Christian worldview is, in other words, a transcendental necessity for human experience and thought to be coherent. It is an epistemic precondition that Christianity be true in order for there to be, even in the theoretical realm, any justified true belief. As such, the hallmark of the presuppositional method is to argue transcendentally for the truth of the Christian worldview.

Transcendental arguments have been a philosophical topic of discussion since the time of Kant. Frame notes that Kant's inquiry was concerned with "What are the preconditions of meaning and rationality? Granting that knowledge is possible, in other words, what must we presuppose to be true? Kant concluded that we must make certain assumptions about space and time and about the 'categories' (unity, plurality, cause, effect, etc.) that the mind applies to experience."[43] There is still debate not only about whether or not Kant was successful in his argument, but even about how his argument was actually structured.[44] The interest is not merely historical either. Interest in constructing transcendental arguments grew throughout the mid-twentieth century,[45] and they are—as the reader is sure to realize—still discussed today.

Still, transcendental arguments are very hard to formulate, and their success is still harder to evaluate. Moltke Gram succinctly identifies the heart of the issue: "The problem about transcendental arguments is whether there are any."[46] It has indeed been argued that it is debatable whether any arguments that have been labeled as transcendental really are.[47] As a result, transcendental argumentation is suspect both in theory and in practice. Even granting that such a style of argument may be pos-

---

43. Frame, *Cornelius Van Til*, 133.
44. Brueckner, "Transcendental Argument," 925.
45. Wilkerson, "Transcendental Arguments," 201.
46. Gram, "Transcendental Arguments," 15.
47. Chisholm, *Foundations of Knowing*, 95.

Presuppositionalism

sible, it does not follow that any argument that has been constructed has actually ever been transcendental.

Brueckner provides a dictionary definition:

> *Transcendental argument*, an argument that elucidates the conditions for the possibility of some fundamental phenomenon whose existence is unchallenged or uncontroversial in the philosophical context in which the argument is propounded. Such an argument proceeds deductively, from a premise asserting the existence of some basic phenomenon (such as meaningful discourse, conceptualization of objective states of affairs, or the practice of making promises), to a conclusion asserting the existence of some interesting, substantive enabling conditions for that phenomenon.[48]

Kant's formulation tried to show that certain objects must exist in order for self-conscious experience to be valid.[49] The following explanation is especially clear: "Making statements about the external world presupposes not only a prior distinction between oneself and that world, but also a method for differentiating, within one's experience of it, external objects and attributes—properties and relations of which external objects are the bearers."[50]

Two elements of Korner's explanation are particularly worthy of emphasis. The first involves an actual state of affairs that is differentiable from the individual subject. There is a presupposition of a legitimate subject/object relationship. This is in no way indicative of an acceptance of some form of naïve realism, but it does necessitate a givenness to the universe, the reality of an external state of affairs. Such an external order is mind-independent and exists apart from the perception of the perceiving subject.[51] In this reality there is diversity; the external state of things is not blankly monadic. So not only does the mind-independent reality exist, it is divisible and internally differentiable. Thus there can be subject/subject and object/object relationships. A variety of items bear unique properties, and sustain relations to each other. This given order that is parsed by the

---

48. Brueckner, "Transcendental Argument," 925; emphasis in original.
49. Brueckner, "Transcendental Arguments I," 552.
50. Korner, "Impossibility of Transcendental Deductions," 317.
51. This is true even if a noumenological realm is sealed off from direct access, and we can only know by direct acquaintance our inner phenomenological world of experience and interpretation.

149

human mind is a transcendental necessity for the genuineness of human experience, including intelligible thought and knowledge.

The second element worthy of noting from Korner is that there is also a presupposition made concerning methodology. Granting that the external world of objects, properties, and the relations pertaining therein exists and can be parsed by human beings, there must also be a presupposition made concerning the method by which the parsing is to be accomplished. Human minds must have the ability to actually engage the mind-independent world with enough accuracy to make possible the identification of differentiable aspects of the world. They must be able to predicate, but this requires a sound theory and practice of predication. Analyzing the external world can only be done under the presupposition that humans are in possession of analyzing equipment that is sufficiently calibrated to do the job, and that they are able to use it properly to discover what the world is like. Otherwise, there could be no rational commitment to meaningful discourse or intelligible experience about the external world order. Why believe, after all, that one knows anything whatsoever about the world if one does not believe they have the right tools to investigate it properly, or the right mechanisms and procedures for carrying out the investigation? In order for human experience to be coherent, it is necessary both for the external world to exist with certain differentiable objects bearing certain properties, and also for the human subject to have the noetic and sensory equipment required to perceive the external world by the proper methodological procedures that allow for predications to be rationally acceptable.

Importantly, the very reason why there is a problem is because the solution exists.[52] Humans ask themselves questions about epistemology, metaphysics, and ontology (ontology here and for the remainder of this book, when it is used in conjunction with metaphysics, will designate personal being in distinction from impersonal being, or the nature of sentient beings like God and humans rather than impersonal natural laws and metaphysical states of affairs), and struggle to find answers and solutions. But their mental activity presupposes certain non-negotiable states of affairs. Transcendental arguments try to demonstrate that the very act of questioning demands an already given answer. The very act of questioning is itself predicated upon certain realities. Human thought

---

52. Strawson, *Individuals*, 40.

and predication simply depend on certain factors obtaining. They are not ultimate but dependent on other things. Philosophers asking philosophical questions are only justified in their activity because there are bedrock, inescapable realities that make their investigations rationally possible. A transcendental approach endeavors—even if it is not successful—to demonstrate what these necessary presuppositions are. It says that, although you may not be able to tell exactly what it is, the very fact you are able to think and predicate proves that x must obtain.

The momentous claim of the presuppositionalists (in Christian apologetics) is that the existence of the triune God and the truth of the Christian worldview is what must be presupposed in order to make human experience intelligible, and that this can be demonstrated by a transcendental argument. Van Til describes transcendental arguments in the following way: "A truly transcendental argument takes any fact of experience which it wishes to investigate, and tries to determine what the presuppositions of such a fact must be, in order to make it what it is."[53] Using this transcendental method, the reasoning process will bring human thinkers from their own experience to God.[54] Everything that exists can only ultimately be understood in the relationship that it bears to God. Only the ontological Trinity solves the problem of the one and the many; only the universe as God's creation guarantees its coherence; only the notion of humans as rational image bearers of God gives grounds for confidence in human knowledge. If any of those three points is denied, the denial entails the destruction of epistemology. Justifying predication transcendentally requires the truth of the Christian worldview.

The transcendental approach, then, is the essence of the Christian presuppositional apologetic. But one of the more controversial areas in presuppositionalism lies in grounding the rules of logic itself in the mind of God. Is it really possible that basic logical rules are dependent upon God? If they are not, then it would seem that any creature that can comprehend them can engage in rational reflection apart from the existence of God. In many ways this can be seen as the epistemological equivalent of the Euthyphro dilemma regarding morality. If the gods declare something is holy because it is holy, then others may be able to make that evaluative judgment independently from the gods. And if the object is

---

53. Van Til, *Survey of Christian Epistemology*, 10.
54. Ibid., 201.

holy simply because the gods declare it to be holy, then holiness seems entirely arbitrary; the gods could have said that rape or wanton destruction is holy, and their fiat decree would have made it so. What, then, is the right way of understanding the relationship between the triune God and the existence of logic? Are logical relationships merely recognized by God, and are thus potentially capable of being recognized by other beings, or has God simply declared that certain modes of thought will be considered structurally acceptable, and hence rationality is arbitrary? Or, as with the Euthyphro dilemma, is there another position, a third way towards resolution?

The dependence of logic on the mind of God was the subject of an internet debate between Michael Martin and John Frame. Sketching their arguments will be helpful in showing two different conceptions of logic. The exchange began not as a debate but with an article that Martin wrote in 1996 for *The New Zealand Rationalist and Humanist* that was subsequently put online in 1997.[55] Martin (1997a)[56] begins by writing: "Some Christian philosophers have made the incredible argument that logic, science, and morality presuppose the truth of the Christian world view because logic, science and morality depend on the truth of this world view." Not only does Martin find this position untenable, but he tries to argue that, since this view is false, if Christianity entails this view then it is false as well. Where logic is concerned, Martin asserts that the principles of logic are necessarily true, but if they were dependent on God then they would be contingent. As contingent, the principles of logic could be changed by God. If this was the case, then God could make the law of noncontradiction false, a position Martin labels absurd. To demonstrate its absurdity, Martin provides the example of God simultaneously making New Zealand south of China and not south of China, something that seems intuitively impossible. Concluding his section on logic, he writes (1997a): "So, one must conclude that logic is not dependent on God, and,

---

55. The online material that Martin wrote is copyrighted in 1997, while the online material that Frame wrote was copyrighted in 1996. Martin's online material is copyrighted in 1996 as well, but the online source where I found it was granted copyright permission by Martin the following year, in 1997. I accessed all these sites on January 15, 2010.

56. For ease of reference, references to their respective articles will be placed in parentheses in the text, and consecutively numbered in letter sequence a, b, c, etc. In the bibliography, the date includes the appropriately corresponding letter.

insofar as the Christian world view assumes that logic so [*sic*] dependent, it is false."

Frame was sent Martin's article, and provided a very brief response. Frame (1996a) wrote: "Logic is neither above God nor arbitrarily decreed by God. Its ultimate basis is in God's eternal nature. God is a rational God and necessarily so. Therefore logic is necessary. Human logical systems don't always reflect God's logic perfectly. But insofar as they do, they are necessarily true." These sentences constituted Frame's entire reply. Perhaps the most important point, which is an extremely close analogue to morality and the standard of goodness, is that "rational" is something that God is in his very nature. Logic is necessary because it is part of the necessary being and essence of God. God is the standard of logic and rationality, and human systems of logic are more or less true (or necessary) in their relationship to God's nature.

Martin (1997b) was not persuaded by Frame's point. He responded by arguing that logic is above God. God cannot break the law of noncontradiction, and the law of contradiction would hold even if God did not exist. If logical rules are dependent on God's nature, then a change in the nature of God would require a change in the rules of logic. The law of noncontradiction may become invalid if God were other than what he is, but Martin finds this absurd. Frame (1996b) responded by arguing that "God presupposes logic, and logic presupposes God" because "God's nature is the ultimate basis for logic." He holds that logic cannot exist without God. Furthermore, because God's nature is necessarily the way that it is, Frame can agree with Martin that it is absurd to imagine God being different, and in this way to imagine logical rules being different. Frame (1996b) ends his section on logic by stating: "The chain of justification, of course, must end somewhere. Else we justify A by reference to 'independent standard' B, B by 'independent standard' C, ad infinitum. My chain ends in the personal God of the Bible. Martin's ends in an abstract law of contradiction or abstract system of logic. Or does that too require an 'independent standard'?" For Frame, Martin's appeal to abstraction sets up an infinite regress of justification, looking for the final, authoritative standard for logic. By contrast, Frame's final standard for logic is found in the necessary being and nature of God.

Martin (1997c) in response maintained that Frame had given no reason for locating logic in the nature of God, and that Frame's position entailed that if God did not exist, logic would not exist. This seemed clearly wrong to Martin, and he noted that unless an ontological argument for the existence of God was successful (which Martin denies), there was no reason to agree with Frame. In his reply, Frame (1996c) reaffirmed that logic is an attribute of God's being, and that God exists necessarily. Frame argued that if a necessary being did not exist, it would be impossible to know what would obtain. Talking of the non-existence of a necessary being is incoherent; imagining such a world is impossible. Frame also noted that, on Christian presuppositions, the ontological argument is valid, but not on Martin's. According to Frame, Martin ends up relying on "rough-hewn intuitions," on what just seems clear and right to him.

At this point, the positions were clearly articulated, and the debaters were not moved. Martin (1997d) simply did not believe that Frame had given any reason for holding his position. Frame (1996d) noted that many theologians and philosophers have held that God's existence is necessary, and that to deny the existence of a necessary being renders all meaning vacuous. The Scriptures, according to Frame, give data that indicates that God is a necessary being. He also noted (Frame 1996d): "We should also keep in mind that TAG [transcendent argument for the existence of God] (as, e.g., in Bahnsen's formulation) asserts another relationship between God and logic: theism can account for the universality and necessity of logic, while nontheistic accounts cannot." The two agreed to let Martin have the final word, and Martin (1997e) restated his position that there is no reason to think logic is dependent on God's nature, and there is also no reason to think that God is a necessary being. In the end, Martin found presuppositionalism to make many assertions about the relationship between the character of God and the principles of logic, but to be lacking in argument or proof.

In my judgment, there is nothing incoherent in identifying logic as an attribute of a necessary being, but this position is going to be counter-intuitive to many, and almost impossible to argue persuasively. By "persuasively" is not meant "validly," but "convincingly." The same is true of the moral argument where God is posited as the standard of goodness. Can torturing babies be right? It would seem that this could never be the case: God could not arbitrarily decree that it be so, even if goodness itself is dependent on him. Likewise, it is impossible for the law of non-contradiction to fail to be true, and any scheme that seems to make the law of non-contradiction contingent, or possibly changeable, will be greeted with dismissal by any except the most Pyrrhonian skeptic (who is still dependent on the law). In my view, Frame is likely right when he says that, for the presuppositionalists, the best way forward is to identify God as a necessary being on the one hand, and on the other to argue that other accounts of logic will be caught in an infinite regress of justification, always appealing to another standard. (This same argument is used for God being the standard of goodness: if we identify something as "the good" and are asked for a justification for that identification, we are caught in an infinite justificatory regressive situation.) Presuppositionalists assert that their standard stops with God, and may certainly inquire as to what justification the other party has for stopping at their chosen standard.

Nevertheless, this position seems far easier to express than convincingly establish or defend. Rather than trying to demonstrate the essential grounding of logic in the nature of God, however, the presuppositionalist can turn from this more abstract discussion to the relationship between the principles of logic and the human mind. Van Til writes: "We have seen that the very question between theists and antitheists is to the foundation of the law of contradiction . . . We hold that they have falsely assumed that the self-contradictory is to be identified with that which is beyond the comprehension of man. But this takes for granted that human categories are ultimate categories—which is just the thing in question."[57]

This is a critical point for Van Til. Human beings accept the logic that they identify in their minds as ultimate, so that their thoughts are construed as the final arbiters for possibility. Recognizing logic is seen as an innate ability, rather than a gift from the Creator.[58] Yet human logic can only be as reliable and stable as the universe in which it is found. Questions of ontology and metaphysics again rise up and must be answered. Why do human beings think that the processes of their minds actually fathom the extent of the possible? Van Til states:

> According to the Christian story, logic and reality meet first of all in the mind and being of God. God's being is exhaustively rational. Then God creates and rules the universe according to his plan. Even the evil of this world happens according to his plan. The only substitute for this Christian scheme of things is to assert or assume that logic and reality meet originally in the mind of man. The final point of reference in all predication must ultimately rest in some mind, divine or human. It is either the self-contained God

---

57. Van Til, *Survey of Christian Epistemology*, 206.
58. Van Til, *Defense of the Faith*, 173.

of Christianity or the would-be autonomous man that must be and is presupposed as the final reference point in every sentence that any man utters.[59]

If the final reference point for logic and rationality takes place inside the mind of human beings, there is no reason to believe that the human mind is sufficient to bear the burden of epistemological rationality. The fact that the human brain goes through certain processes and has certain functions does not entail that it is capable of ultimately legislating theoretical reality, or even that it is in touch with the actual state of affairs that obtains. If logic first engages reality at the intersection of the interpreting human mind, logic itself must be called into question.

Bahnsen is very helpful in specifying the relationship between metaphysical reality and logic in the human mind:

> If the laws of science, the laws of logic, and the laws of morality are not seen as expressions of the unchanging mind of God, then the notion of universal and absolute "laws" or the concept of order in the contingent, changing world of matter makes no sense whatsoever. In what way could anything truly be universal and law-abiding when every event is isolated and random? If universality is supposed to be objective, then there is no justification for holding it on the basis of man's limited experience, whereas if universality is subjective (internal to man's thinking), then it is arbitrarily imposed by man's mind on his experience without warrant.[60]

For presuppositionalists it follows that: "Given the non-Christian assumption with respect to man's autonomy the idea of chance has equal rights with the idea of logic."[61] As humans exist apart from God, they are not in a position to exhaustively understand the universe, and the universe is pure contingency. It is impossible to justify human thought patterns concerning reality, let alone to make human thought patterns the highest standard for determining what is possible, given the non-Christian position. The finiteness of human beings, and the chaos that birthed them, destroys the foundation for rationally espousing rational thought. In the final analysis, all human logic will be subverted and collapse into the dialecticism of rationality/irrationality.

---

59. Ibid., 215.
60. Bahnsen, *Van Til's Apologetic*, 110 n. 65.
61. Van Til, *Defense of the Faith*, 125.

In presuppositionalism the action of debating any of these epistemological positions asserts the essential rightness of one of them. The very fact that there is a rational debate, then, is indirect proof of Christianity. Intelligible discourse, relying on sensory data, memory, and logical interpretation, demands that reality is what the Christian says that it is. If the non-Christian is right, then there is nothing to debate, and no epistemological reason to accept that they are right. Their position is far worse than self-stultifying; it is self-referentially incoherent. But the nature of the case is such that the non-Christian cannot be right; they are proving by their actions what they deny by their theory and anti-theistic formulations. Human experience is intelligible, as the discussion demonstrates. Yet that same discussion can only be coherent if the non-Christian is wrong. The fact of the matter is, then, that if the non-Christian wins the debate, they actually lose it, and if the Christian wins the debate, the non-Christian still loses. The debate depends on the foundation of the Christian worldview, because rational discourse is only coherent given the precondition of Christian truth. And this is the unique feature of a transcendental argument: by setting out the necessary preconditions for intelligibility, either a positive or negative conclusion from certain premises demonstrates the truth of the presupposition.[62]

If this is the case, as the presuppositionalists maintain, then it follows that the apologist has liberty to begin with any fact whatsoever in the defense of the Christian worldview. As Van Til explains: "When we approach the question this way we should be willing to start anywhere and with any fact that any person we meet is interested in. The very conviction that there is not a single fact that can really be known unless it is interpreted theistically gives us the liberty to start anywhere, as the proximate starting point is concerned."[63] Every single thing that exists in the universe and everything that is experienced by humans depends on the existence of God as a presupposition to account for its coherence and knowability. The presuppositionalists are adamant that there is nothing that can be known apart from the existence of the God of the Bible. And, as Van Til notes, this can only be demonstrated by means of an indirect, transcendental argument.[64]

---

62. Collett, "Van Til and Transcendental Argument," 270–71.
63. Van Til, *Survey of Christian Epistemology*, 204.
64. Van Til, *Defense of the Faith*, 109.

This belief provides the presuppositional apologist with the unique ability to defend the faith in conversations or from topics that seem extremely removed from spiritual matters. There is nothing that is off topic when it comes to God, since all things relate to him and can only be interpreted in the relationship that they sustain to him. Anything, no matter how remote it seems, can serve as a proximate starting point for a discussion about the truth of Christianity. Such a conversation does not need to be forced or connected by tenuous logic, since everything is integrally related to all else, and finds its definition rooted in God.

Presuppositionalists distinguish between beginning (i.e., proximate, or immediate) starting points and the ultimate starting point, which is God. Bahnsen writes: "In the process of knowing anything, man begins with his own experience and questions—the 'immediate' starting point. However, that which man knows metaphysically begins with God (who preinterprets, creates, and governs everything man could know), and God's mind is epistemologically the standard of truth—thus being the 'ultimate' starting point."[65] Human beings must begin where they are, but that cannot be where their discussion terminates. According to Van Til, "There is a sense to be sure, in which we must start 'from below.' Psychologically we must start our process of interpretation with ourselves. We cannot escape from ourselves and jump into the being of God. But this is not the point at issue. The real question is one of epistemology and not of psychology. And in epistemology we must begin 'from above.' That is, we must presuppose God."[66]

Psychologically and metaphysically the starting point is in the human being, but to justify epistemology, the starting point must be grounded in the presupposition of God. Existential human experience begins in the human's perception (as far as the human is concerned) but reflection should make it clear that such experience is only intelligible if God is behind all such thought and experience. If an individual is not willing to admit to perceiving God (cf. Romans 1:18-21), this does not mean that their perceptions and thinking are not actually dependent on God. Human consciousness, in the nature of the case, will be the proximate point of departure, but God must be the ultimate reference point.[67] The phrase "starting point" has engendered misunderstanding, however,

---

65. Bahnsen, *Van Til's Apologetic*, 100 n. 33.
66. Van Til, *Christianity and Idealism*, 85.
67. Van Til, *Defense of the Faith*, 77.

and Frame argues that it is too ambiguous to be helpful and should be dropped from the discussion.[68] Regardless of terminology, however, the most important point to understand is that self-consciousness is the plane on which we exist and cogitate, but this plane can only be secondary and never ultimate as a starting point into reality. If human consciousness were the ultimate starting point, the existence of God would not be necessary for epistemology, but this is impossible given the inevitable breakdown in all non-Christian worldviews.[69]

The same consideration holds for all metaphysical and ontological realities of which the human is aware. Since any object is created, sustained, and pre-interpreted by God, it is only by analogical knowledge that humans can understand what it is. At the very end of the analysis, in order to understand any object, it must be understood as created by God. Even seemingly ordinary and mundane objects, when analyzed as exhaustively as possible, require ultimate termination points of interpretation. In order to understand an object like a baseball, there has to be knowledge of the game of baseball, and the psychology of game playing. But this would also require knowledge of sociology and history. It would require knowledge of physics, nutrition, biology, and ecology (the care of the outfield grass, for example). There are also economic factors, and even philosophical ones (i.e., the philosophy of competition). Even breaking down the baseball itself requires movement up or down the ladder of abstraction, which brings up the issue of unity and plurality. Understanding a baseball requires solving the problem of the one and the many.

Understanding any object also requires relating it to everything else. For the Christian, all objects are created and sustained by God. In order to understand an object, then, it must be understood in relationship to God. If this is not done, the object is misunderstood, and the supposed knowledge is not only fallacious, it is rebellious. Applying this idea to a common object can reveal how everything either affirms or denies God:

> For example, as any scientist knows, apples come from trees and are normally good for eating. But where do apple trees come from? Ultimately the secular scientist will say that trees are a product of evolution, that is, chance. In other words, apple trees are not designed by God. Thus, for the nonbeliever, apples are Creator-denying apples: to really understand apples is to deny the biblical

68. Frame, *Cornelius Van Til*, 292.
69. William Edgar, in Van Til, *Christian Apologetics*, 97 n. 20.

concept of God; apples *prove* that the God of the Scripture does not exist, and each apple is an evidence *against* such a God. Ultimately, the nonexistence of God becomes part of the *definition* of apples.[70]

Notaro is quick to point out that hardly anyone ever thinks out their definition of an apple this rigorously, but it is still the case that an ultimate definition would have to either affirm or deny the existence of God.[71] Defining an apple requires relating it to one's entire worldview.

One of the greatest misconceptions stemming from this contention is that it amounts to claiming that non-Christians do not know anything about anything. On the face of it, this is surely false. There are many non-Christians who know many things that Christians do not know. Non-Christians are found leading various fields, and certainly many non-Christian teachers know more about their subject matter than their Christian students. Those who reject the Christian worldview are still capable of achieving degrees, publishing books, and making rich discoveries and inventions. On a simpler level, even rather unintelligent non-Christians know their names, can add 1 + 1 to get 2, and can carry on a host of daily activities that require knowledge. It seems that presuppositionalism may deny something that is just obviously true.

This is a misconception of the presuppositionalist's position, however. Van Til was aware that this criticism might be raised if his position were misunderstood, and so he deals with it squarely. It is very important to understand this nuance in presuppositionalism, or else the entire method will be misunderstood. Van Til writes: "The first objection that suggests itself may be expressed in the rhetorical question 'Do you mean to assert that non-Christians do not discover truth by the methods they employ?' The reply is that we mean nothing so absurd as that. The implication of the method here advocated is simply that non-Christians are never able and therefore never do employ their methods consistently."[72]

The non-Christian can use the empirical method and rationally study nature and learn many things about it. But this study presupposes the uniformity of nature, and other things that the scientific method itself cannot demonstrate. It relies on certain assumptions to back up its methodology, but these assumptions are not grounded in anything substantial.

---

70. Notaro, *Van Til and the Use of Evidence*, 38–39; emphasis in original.
71. Ibid., 39.
72. Van Til, *Defense of the Faith*, 103.

Presuppositionalism

The uniformity of scientific laws depends on the creator and sustainer of them. There is nothing in methodological naturalism that would require scientific laws, which are descriptive of statistical correlations, to actually be unbreakable laws. Scientific study, unless it has some foundation for the laws and phenomena under investigation, provides no reason for confidence in either the intelligibility of the pursuit, or the intelligibility of the conclusions. The universe may be chaos and chance, and all observations to this point may be statistically anomalous. Non-Christians actually presuppose Christianity to underwrite their investigations: "They need to presuppose the truth of Christian theism in order to account for their own accomplishments."[73] Christian truth provides a worldview foundation where scientific research is legitimate and trustworthy. An eternal, all-knowing, all-wise, and immutable being's will is what guarantees the regularity of the world's laws.

Non-Christians do have justified beliefs at one level, however, because they can think God's thoughts as revealed in the natural world.[74] The reality of God's universe is inescapable, and so is the human rationality to which it gives rise. Van Til held that non-Christians could count but could not account for counting, and this was owing to the combination of their metaphysical placement in God's creation, and their rebellious epistemological principles. Autonomous human thought is thus again seen to be submerged in the dialecticism of the rational and irrational. It cannot escape from the confines of a universe limited by God's stamp of rationality, but all attempts to justify thinking apart from the existence of God lead to conclusions that affirm an inescapable irrationalism. Non-Christian thought is therefore perpetually bouncing back and forth between rationalism and irrationalism.

In order to properly understand the distinctions that presuppositionalism is making at this point, there needs to be a clear separation between metaphysical and epistemological common ground. While non-Christians understand many things to a point, they cannot justify their knowledge of anything. In fact, what they do know is predicated on Christianity, which they deny. Epistemologically their formulations and rules for learning are vacuous. Yet they cannot escape the objective metaphysical reality that God has created. He has constituted them to

---

73. Ibid.
74. Frame, "Presuppositional Apologist's Closing Remarks," 351–52.

know things, and discover things. The common ground believers and non-believers share is metaphysical rather than epistemological. They are both placed in God's universe, and share that in common. Furthermore, they are able to reason together, not because their epistemologies are the same in theory, but rather because the non-believer covertly borrows the epistemology of the believer without recognizing that fact. As Frame says: "Therefore, in [Van Til's] more extreme antithetical formulations, he declares that there is no common ground at all between believers and unbelievers. Of course, as we have seen, there is common ground, because the unbeliever is never consistent in his unbelief. There is no common ground in principle, but there is common ground in actual debate."[75] The unbeliever can reason and has understanding because of his or her metaphysical location (i.e., the universe created and governed by God), ontological constitution (i.e., the rational image bearer of God), and epistemological inconsistency (i.e., unwitting dependence on the Christian worldview to ground the validity of their epistemology).

Van Til is actually quite clear about the point of contact that he envisions between the Christian apologist and all others. He contrasts his position with that of Stuart Hackett, who takes a traditional approach:

> Hackett assumes that unless one finds a point of contact with the natural man by way of agreeing with him on his false views of man and the world then one has no point of contact with him at all. Against this position, I maintain, with Calvin following Paul, that my point of contact lies in the *actual state of affairs between men* as the Bible tells us of it. It is Hackett who has no *real* point of contact, for his lies in what men *imagine* (and, to be sure, "agree") to be the case. The Calvinist's point of contact is rooted in the *actual* state of affairs. All things are what they are because of their relation to the work of the triune God as reported in Scripture.[76]

It is, in Van Til's estimation, impossible to have a genuine point of contact if one denies Calvinistic theology and biblical metaphysics. Here the force of his apologetic comes to the fore: the triune God of the Bible exists, and the Scriptures are his word, so any other conception of reality is false. The apologist must work from the true position to oppose the false one, or else there will be no chance of a successful defense.

---

75. Frame, *Cornelius Van Til*, 305.
76. Van Til, "My Credo," 16–17; emphasis in original.

PRESUPPOSITIONALISM AND THE EVIDENTIAL CASE FOR THE RESURRECTION

This section will develop through two main subsections. Since classical apologetics, as was seen in Chapter 2, places the proof of theism as a prior step to arguing for the historical resurrection, the interaction that presuppositionalism has with theistic proofs is important to understand. After that, the particularly historical case for the resurrection will be examined from a presuppositional perspective. Both subsections will reveal some very interesting aspects of presuppositional thought. As should be expected, the macrostructures of the argument receive a great deal of emphasis compared to the smaller formulations of individual arguments. For example, all that was said about presuppositionalism above applies to every theistic argument that has been formulated.

Theistic arguments are by their very nature set up to be rational and logical, and presuppositionalism has particular things to say about logic and rational discourse, as has been already noted. A quotation from Bahnsen about the methodology of traditional apologetics will set the stage for what follows:

> The argument usually proceeds in two major steps. (1) Autonomous, self-sufficient, unaided reason (it is imagined) can establish from nature that there is most probably a supernatural realm as well—and, with further refinements, that a God of some sort exists. Theistic proofs are then followed by (2) appeals to natural and historical evidences (empirical facts) which inductively support the likelihood that the Bible is historically accurate, especially about Jesus, including His miracles and resurrection—and, therefore, is right about whatever else it says (because He believed that it was). This traditional method of defending the faith, thought Van Til, was lacking in both philosophical cogency and good theological foundations.[77]

Theistic Arguments

Styles of argument can be more or less appropriate to a particular discipline depending on its nature and subject matter. Apologetics tries to defend the Christian faith, and this faith has a given content. Thus the defense cannot adequately proceed unless it is calibrated to its subject.

---

77. Bahnsen, *Van Til's Apologetic*, 531.

Issues of theology cannot, therefore, be isolated or detached from apologetics. There is an interrelationship between the two that cannot be broken. One implication of this is that mistakes in theological formulations will result in poor apologetical formulations. Furthermore, the arguments advanced in defense of the faith may simply be incapable of proving what the apologist seeks to prove. In the presuppositional model, apologetics is primarily a theological discipline.

Van Til made this stance very clear: "We have seen that the proper method for Protestant apologetics is that of presupposition instead of the direct approach. But the theology of Rome and the theology of Arminianism do not permit such an argument. Roman Catholics and Arminians must of necessity argue by way of direct approach. As deformations of Christian theism they contain no challenge to the position of the natural man till it is too late."[78] Although a word like "deformations" is rather strong, this quotation makes the general point obvious. In Van Til's opinion not only was the apologetic of Roman Catholicism and Arminian Protestantism insufficient and inappropriate, but it stemmed not from a lack of philosophical sophistication, but followed primarily from theological error. The right way for defending the Christian faith must not be detached from what the Christian faith actually is. Bahsen writes, "Since apologetics is a defense of the truths presented in Christian theology, and since the method used for defending any system of thought grows out of the nature of that system, it is only natural that defective theology will beget a defective apologetical strategy."[79] Philosophy is not hermetically sealed from theology. Thus, for Reformed apologetics, the major distinctive features of Reformed theology are not of secondary importance. And since Reformed thought is by self-conscious definition neither Roman Catholic thought nor Arminian thought, it is not altogether unexpected that consistency would require that these respective theologies be wedded to different apologetic methodologies.

Building up a case for the Christian faith one step at a time, as is done in evidential approaches, was labeled by Van Til as a "block house" model.[80] In this model, a foundation was laid, and then the case was built point by point, as a house is constructed brick by brick. For presupposi-

---

78. Van Til, *Christian Apologetics*, 148–49.
79. Bahnsen, *Van Til's Apologetic*, 531.
80. Van Til, *Christian Apologetics*, 148.

tionalists, however, the case for Christianity cannot be successfully built in this manner. On the contrary: "the whole system should be presented and defended as a unit. Its epistemology should be defended in terms of its metaphysics and ethics (including anthropology and soteriology), and its metaphysics (including anthropology and soteriology) should be defended in terms of its epistemology."[81] Instead of trying to construct the Christian worldview, the presuppositionalist takes the entire Christian worldview as given, and defends it as an established system where each part receives its meaning from its relationship to the whole. The worldview is too internally dependent to build up from non-Christian definitions and understandings of metaphysics, epistemology, etc.

Since each element of the Christian worldview is only defensible when interpreted in Christian terms (i.e., if the non-Christian can define elements of the Christian worldview on their non-Christian terms, those definitions may not be defensible; but on definitions inherent in Christianity, the system and all its elements are defensible), the believer defends the faith by demonstrating to the unbeliever that the non-Christian worldview is incoherent. Then, the unbeliever is invited to stand inside the Christian worldview and demonstrate its incoherence on its own terms. The result, according to presuppositional thought, is that the Christian worldview will pass this test, while all other worldviews will fail.

Presuppositionalism denies that an evidential approach is even theoretically capable of establishing the Christian faith. Inside the presuppositional camp, however, there is a wide variety of debate concerning the effectiveness and utility of the individual theistic arguments.[82] Bahnsen claims that the traditional arguments are "really bad arguments as traditionally formulated."[83] Not only are they bad in terms of logical cogency, but Bahnsen also believes they lead to conclusions that are sub-biblical in terms of who God is, and as such they actually result in idolatrous thoughts about God.[84]

Traditional cosmological arguments rely on the rationality of cause and effect relationships. They are dependent on causes being identifiable. A traditional cosmological argument runs on the following lines, accord-

---

81. Bahnsen, *Van Til's Apologetic*, 268.

82. See the differences between Frame, *Apologetics to the Glory of God*, and Bahnsen, *Answer to Frame's Critique*.

83. Bahnsen, *Answer to Frame's Critique*, 34.

84. Ibid.

ing to Bahnsen: "*Each of the many parts* within experience has a *natural* cause; therefore *the whole* set of things has a *single* and *supernatural* cause."[85] There are three fallacious moves in this argument: it moves from parts to whole, from multiple causes to a single cause, and from natural causes to a supernatural one.[86]

Frame argues that the fact of causality depends on God, and since causal relations exist, God must exist.[87] Bahnsen argues at a deeper level that the very notion of causality must be defined in terms of the Christian worldview.[88] If causality is understood in terms of Aquinas or Aristotle, then Aristotelian conclusions can follow. Or, multiple creators can be proved as easily as one creator.[89] Either way, the traditional cosmological argument will arrive at a conclusion much less than the God of the Bible. Every other argument will try to add another element to the conclusion, but since each argument allows for a conclusion much less than the triune God, it is impossible for the cumulative case of these arguments to amount to him. And, if an argument or chain of reasoning cannot lead to the biblical God, then the worldview will ultimately be bankrupt in accounting for intelligible experience and rationality; without God, the worldview implodes.

According to Bahnsen a presuppositional cosmological argument is an application of the transcendental presuppositional argument to causation.[90] Causality is taken for granted in all human experience, and is fundamental to intelligibility. But non-Christian philosophers like Hume and Russell have shown that, given their worldviews, philosophically causality cannot be rationally accepted.[91] If causal principles are not acceptable, then inductive logic and reasoning about the future are irrational as well. The collapse is back into irrationality. As Bahnsen writes: "The unbelieving worldview cannot provide a cogent reason for what we necessarily assume in all of our reasoning. Thus, it is entirely unreasonable not to believe in God."[92] Rather than human reasoning about causal rela-

85. Bahnsen, *Van Til's Apologetic*, 618.
86. Ibid.
87. Frame, *Apologetics to the Glory of God*, 76.
88. Bahnsen, *Answer to Frame's Critique*, 38.
89. Ibid.
90. Bahnsen, *Van Til's Apologetic*, 618.
91. Ibid., 619.
92. Ibid.

tionships leading to the conclusion that God exists, it is human reasoning itself that is dependent on the existence of God for its legitimacy, since it presupposes the metaphysical truth of cause and effect relationships, and the epistemological truth of the human ability to recognize them. These preconditions only obtain if humans and the universe are as the Bible states they are in relation to God. In this way, a presuppositional apologist can approach the traditional cosmological argument, reformulate it, and employ it transcendentally.

A quick note on the teleological argument will be sufficient. The teleological argument turns on recognizing and evaluating ordered relationships. What sense does it make to speak of order or design or function or ends in a chance universe? How does the human knower epistemologically justify their recognition and evaluation of the "facts" of order? How do teleological observations fit into a system that has not resolved the problem of unity and plurality? For presuppositionalism, teleology as a theistic proof or evidence requires the Christian worldview to be coherent. Again, the teleological argument by itself does not provide evidence for the existence of God; the existence of God is required to provide the necessary justificatory principles or preconditions on which all teleological arguments depend. Classical, evidential approaches to apologetics simply have the cart before the horse: they actually presuppose what they are ostensibly designed to demonstrate.

Historical Evidence

At this point it will not be surprising to note that presuppositionalists do not believe that the evidential historical case in favor of the resurrection of Jesus Christ from the dead is sufficient to establish the truth of Christianity. If all facts, rational thought, and causality are necessarily coherent only in the Christian worldview, then any historical investigation will be dependent on the Christian worldview to be meaningful. It is impossible to pursue genuine historical research without relying on rational procedures and making certain assumptions about causal relationships, the uniformity of nature, communication and testimony, the reliability of the senses, etc. Granting that this is the case, and recognizing that presuppositionalism denies that any of these things are intelligible apart from Christianity being true, it obviously follows that the presuppositional approach is to present a transcendental argument for the rationality of even pursuing historical investigation, rather than examining piecemeal certain putative historical facts and the conclusions that can be drawn from them.

Beside the larger transcendental approach of the presuppositionalist, the stricter relationship between events and their significance or interpretation must be borne in mind. An event cannot be interpreted apart from the metaphysical reality in which it is contained. Van Til presents and comments on a dialogue that a traditional Christian apologist (Mr. Gray) may have with a non-Christian (Mr. Black). He writes: "For Mr. Black, history is something that floats on an infinitely extended and bottomless ocean of Chance. Therefore he can say that *anything* may happen. Who knows but the death and resurrection of Jesus as the Son of God might issue from this womb of Chance?"[93] Van Til believed that for an evidential apologist like Mr. Gray to be consistent and neutral in his methodology, and because Mr. Gray is "anxious to be genuinely 'empirical' like the unbeliever, he will throw all the facts of Christianity into the bottomless pit of Chance. Or, rather, he will throw all these facts at the unbeliever, and the unbeliever throws them over his back into the bottomless pit of Chance."[94] The state of affairs that actually obtains is critical for the historical investigation. If the unbeliever holds that the universe is Chance, what rational argument forces them to admit that the resurrection could only be what Christians interpret it as being? On the basis of Mr. Gray's apologetic, the unbeliever is perfectly within his rights to accept that Jesus came back from the dead, and assign this event a random, utterly insignificant meaning.

The presuppositionalist apologist, Mr. White, however, approaches the topic in a different way. He will not separate fact from meaning, but will insist that the factuality of the resurrection of Jesus Christ must be theologically interpreted in terms of the Christian worldview right from the start. It will not do to try to establish the historical fact of the resurrection, and then try to find a proper theological definition or interpretation for it.[95] In point of fact, Van Til casts Mr. Black as already fully accepting the historical fact of the resurrection of Jesus. Van Til puts the following words in Mr. Black's mouth:

---

93. Van Til, *Defense of the Faith*, 242.
94. Ibid.
95. Ibid., 239.

> "Now as for accepting the resurrection of Jesus," continued Mr. Black, "as thus properly separated from the traditional system of theology, I do not in the least mind doing that. To tell you the truth, I have accepted the resurrection as a fact now for some time. The evidence for it is overwhelming. This is a strange universe. All kinds of 'miracles' happen in it. The universe is 'open.' So why should there not be some resurrections here and there? The resurrection of Jesus would be a fine item for Ripley's *Believe It or Not*. Why not send it in?"[96]

Van Til here gives the historical evidence its maximum possible force, and has Mr. Black accept it as "overwhelming." But even if the data causes the unbeliever to accept the event as having happened historically, nothing philosophically constrains the unbeliever to accept the Christian interpretation. Apart from the epistemological and metaphysical-transcendental challenge of the presuppositional methodology, any fact or event can be chalked up to strangeness, openness, chaos, or chance. Statistical anomalies do not prove Christian doctrine. It is also possible, as Van Til pointed out, that one day scientific laws may provide an explanation for all miracles, including the resurrection, if such laws are truly neutral in character.[97] Ultimately, it is the unbeliever's view of probability and possibility that needs to be challenged.[98] This point will be touched on again under the heading of Resurrection and Scripture.

The dialogue that Van Til writes concerning the resurrection, historical facts, and meaning is not merely theoretical. Bahnsen finds biblical support for Van Til's position by expositing Acts 17, where Paul speaks to the philosophers at the Areopagus. Bahnsen writes:

> Without the proper theological context, the resurrection would simply be a monstrosity or freak of nature, a surd resuscitation of a corpse. Such an *interpretation* would be the best the Athenian philosophers could make of the fact. However, given the monism, or determinism, or materialism, or the philosophy of history entertained by the philosophers in Athens, they could intellectually find sufficient grounds, if they wished, for disputing even the *fact* of the resurrection. It would have been futile for Paul to argue

---

96. Ibid., 240.
97. Notaro, *Van Til and the Use of Evidence*, 51.
98. Van Til, *Christian Apologetics*, 190.

about the facts, then, without challenging the unbelievers' *philosophy of fact*.⁹⁹

Given their varied philosophical presuppositions, the Athenian philosophers could dispute the fact of the resurrection. Worse yet, they could only interpret it in accordance with their unbiblical philosophies. Thus Paul needed to bring the full Christian worldview to bear against their insufficient worldviews. In other words, the Athenian philosophers would respond just like Mr. Black, unless their entire worldview was challenged and defeated by the Christian one.

While this framework must always be kept in mind, presuppositionalists are not opposed to historical evidence, as is sometimes charged. Frame even goes so far as to say that he finds Habermas's evidence for the resurrection entirely persuasive, but then adds that he is not the one who needs to be persuaded!¹⁰⁰ It has also been noted that: "The name 'evidentialist' as opposed to 'presuppositionalist' is recognized as misleading when you see that there is no necessary conflict between Christian evidences and Christian presuppositions."¹⁰¹ Christian evidentialism is entirely coherent in a framework where Christian presuppositions are recognized. It is the attempt to successfully prove the presuppositions from the evidence that is impossible according to presuppositionalism.

Bahnsen provides a very balanced analysis of Van Til's position concerning the relationship between historical facts and presuppositionalism. Although the citation is somewhat long, it is worth quoting in full. In Bahnsen's book the words of Van Til are written in a different font than Bahnsen's words. To preserve this difference, the following quotation will place Van Til's words in *italics*, even though they are not written in italics in the original. Bahnsen writes:

> Presuppositional apologetics certainly does not imply that historical debates are unimportant; indeed, Van Til was a leading and effective critic of the Barthian and neoorthodox view of "superhistory," since it had the effect of "evaporating" ordinary history. For Van Til, history was not to be reduced by the apologist to something meaningless. *We are to argue that only the Christian can intelligibly provide an all-embracing pattern in and underneath the changing facts of history.*

99. Bahnsen, *Always Ready*, 251–52; emphasis in original.
100. Frame, "Presuppositionalist's Response," 136.
101. Notaro, *Van Til and the Use of Evidence*, 20 n. 17.

Presuppositionalism

And yet, despite all that, there have been those who have claimed that presuppositional apologetics is inherently antagonistic or indifferent to the use of evidences. But why, then, would Van Til have declared, "*I see induction and analytical reasoning as part of one process of interpretation. I would therefore engage in historical apologetics*"? He said this not only in his key apologetics textbook in 1955, but published it again (verbatim) in 1969 in another text; he certainly was not shy about endorsing historical study in defense of the truth of Christianity. But if that is so, somebody might wonder, why do we not find extensive historical argumentation in his publications? Van Til's answer was: "*I do not personally do a great deal of this because my colleagues in the other departments of the Seminary in which I teach are doing it better than I could do it.*" When you are working shoulder to shoulder with scholars like Machen, or Ned Stonehouse, or Edward J. Young, it makes sense to recognize a division of God-given gifts. Hence, Van Til focused on philosophical examination and let his colleagues develop the historical details, all as part of a common task of defending the faith. Van Til declared that the evidential work of such colleagues was imperative: "*Historical apologetics is absolutely necessary and indispensable to point out that Christ rose from the grave, etc.*"[102]

It is in the dialogue that Van Til constructed, where Mr. Black accepts the fact of the resurrection but fails to assign to it the Christian meaning, that this attitude becomes clarified. Evidence supports the claim of factuality for the resurrection, but only Christian presuppositions can provide the framework for intelligible historical investigation, and correctly interpret the meaning of the resurrection.

On balance, however, there is still a lacuna in presuppositional apologetics when it comes to historical argument and the use of evidence. Frame, as one of the last statements he makes in his book on Van Til's thought, asserts, "Students of Van Tillian apologetics need to be far better informed about Christian evidences."[103] Bahnsen concurs, noting that too much presuppositional thought has been directed towards meta-apologetics, rather than actually doing apologetics.[104] Evidence and argument need to be located in a wider worldview context, but in such a context they are vital rather than dispensable for apologetics.

---

102. Bahnsen, *Van Til's Apologetic*, 635–36.
103. Frame, *Cornelius Van Til*, 400.
104. Bahnsen, *Answer to Frame's Critique*, 1.

Resurrection, Scripture, and Reformed Apologetics

RESURRECTION AND SCRIPTURE

Presuppositionalists unanimously hold to the inspiration and inerrancy of Scripture.[105] Van Til, considering the necessary inerrancy of the Bible's original *autographa* and the current manuscript errors that occurred in transmission, uses the imagery of a bridge partially flooded. It makes a great deal of difference whether or not there is a solid foundation just under the surface of the water, or if it is water all the way down. If some errors have crept in over top of the inerrant original foundation, that is one thing; it is entirely different if the foundation itself is watery too, since then one could never know what was mistaken.[106] Precisely because a high view of Scripture was under attack, Van Til asserted that "the doctrine of infallible inspiration must therefore be unequivocally taught."[107] Furthermore, for Van Til, "for better or worse the Protestant apologist is committed to the doctrine of Scripture as the infallibly inspired final revelation of God. This being the case, he is committed to the defense of Christian theism as a unit."[108] This is the position that all presuppositional apologists take in regards to the Bible.

In many ways, the presuppositional approach to the role of the Scriptures in apologetics is very straightforward. Since the Christian is defending Christianity, and since Christianity is a full system, the entire system needs to be presupposed for the defense. For the Reformed Christian, the ultimate presupposition is the self-attesting Christ as revealed in his self-attesting Word.[109] Any other presuppositional foundation means that the individual's commitment is to an authority higher than God. No other standards can be used to measure God's Word, since the Word of God cannot be subordinated in authority to human judgment. If humans use their autonomous reason to judge the revelation of God, then their reason as opposed to God's Word is *de facto* authoritative. As Bahnsen expresses the case:

> In the nature of the case, God is the final authority. But if God's authority must be authorized or validated by the authority of human reasoning and assessment, then human thinking is more

---

105. Frame, "Presuppositional Apologetics," 208 n. 1.
106. See discussion in Frame, *Cornelius Van Til*, 127–28.
107. Van Til, *Survey of Christian Epistemology*, 158.
108. Van Til, *Defense of the Faith*, 105.
109. White, *What is Truth*, 42.

authoritative than God Himself—in which case God would not have final authority, and indeed would no longer be God. The autonomous man who insists that God can only be accepted if His word first gains the approval or agreement of man has determined in advance that God will never be acknowledged as God (the final authority).[110]

Without question, the biblical record contains as a major theme the idea that God is the Lord over all else. Amongst other things, this requires recognizing him as the ultimate authority. And if he speaks, therefore, his words are the highest authority.

The Word of God (i.e., the Scriptures) must be the final authority because it is used to judge the worth of all other sources of authority by which some people attempt to judge the Bible.[111] A special entailment of this position is that evaluating the Scriptures on the basis of naked reason or probability is illegitimate because the Bible must be first used to judge reason and probability. In the final analysis, whatever is used to judge something else is the real authority. The Bible is God's special revelation, and although general revelation bears the attribute of authority as well, special revelation is required to interpret the general (and even more so because of sin's presence in the world).[112] Human beings were never left to figure out the world on the basis of their own rationality; even before the fall into sin, God came into the Garden of Eden and gave special verbal revelation to Adam and Eve, so that they would properly interpret themselves and their surroundings.[113] Being dependent on God's verbal revelation is part of the human epistemological condition.

Presuppositional apologetics groups three items together in this area. First, the Bible does teach that it is the Word of God (e.g., 2 Tim 3:16), and so it does make a self-attesting claim to authority on the basis of its being the Word of God. Second, this presupposition should be the believer's most basic commitment (because it is the believer's final authority), and this should be identified and verbally acknowledged in appropriate apologetic contexts. Third, this whole worldview is then compared to the unbeliever's worldview, and it is indirectly or transcendentally demonstrated that the unbeliever's worldview collapses into

---

110. Bahnsen, *Van Til's Apologetic*, 95 n. 20.
111. Frame, *Cornelius Van Til*, 25.
112. Ibid., 118–24.
113. Bahnsen, *Van Til's Apologetic*, 195.

incoherence, while the Christian one does not. For presuppositionalism, one does not attempt to build up a case where the conclusion is that the Bible is the Word of God, after which the Bible can then be appealed to for authoritative interpretations of reality. On the contrary, the Bible is immediately accepted by the apologist, and the argument is that it is impossible to account for the intelligibility of human experience apart from the worldview which relies on the authoritative Scriptures.

Perhaps the main charge brought to bear against the presuppositional use of the Scriptures in apologetics is that it is painfully circular.[114] There are several counter-responses to this objection. The first is simply that all ultimate authorities are circularly recognized. It has been pointed out that this is an inescapable reality:

> The point is obvious! All epistemological authorities start with linguistic assertions that are self-referential. From these starting points a circular world-life view is developed. Since Babel and its pluriform communication, multiple views vie for men's allegiance. Man in his rebellion against God does not agree on one system, but has multiple alternatives. All of his systems share one thing in common—that the claims of God in the Bible cannot be true. Agreement extends to the ultimacy of man and his capacities as the only tolerable starting point for knowledge. Ultimate authorites [sic] cannot be validated by appeals to other authorities, for then ultimacy is obviously lost. Sinful man, with his autonomous ultimacy, reasons in a vicious circle, the result of which is his own intellectual and moral suicide.[115]

One author expresses the principle of circularity inherent in appealing to ultimate authorities very clearly by using example sentences such as: "My reason is my ultimate authority because it seems reasonable to me to make it so," and "Logical consistency is my ultimate authority because it is logical to make it so."[116] He is not endorsing the sentiments expressed in those remarks, but exemplifying the circularity that is inherent in appeals to ultimate standards. The examples help provide a material element to the formal (and correct) principle that all appeals to an ultimate authority can only be grounded in that authority. For the Christian, this means the Bible, which is self-attesting and the ultimate authority, must

---

114. Sproul, Gerstner, and Lindsley, *Classical Apologetics*, 318.
115. Grier, "Apologetic Value," 75.
116. Grudem, *Systematic Theology*, 79.

be used to judge itself. Circular, yes, but this is part and parcel of having an authority that is ultimate.

Presuppositionalists point out, however, that in regards to the Bible it is not a circularity that is stultifying. Frame, following Van Til, argues that because our experience of God's special revelation is dynamic and growing, it can be thoughtfully compared to a spiral more than a circle. In the spiral pattern, different facets of the revelation are seen, and previous knowledge informs subsequent interpretation and understanding. In spiralling, coherence and consistency are observed.[117] As Bahnsen writes: "'Circularity' in one's philosophical system is just another name for 'consistency' in outlook throughout one's system. That is, one's starting point and final conclusion cohere with each other."[118] It is contradictory to use a penultimate criterion for authority to establish the ultimate authority: presuppositionalism begins and ends with the same ultimate authority, and demonstrates its transcendental cogency and coherence in the apologetic process. It seems evident that human thinking can never be more authoritative than God's, and the presuppositionalist appeals for the believer to practice an apologetic that recognizes from the outset that nobody is in a position to stand in judgment on God or the authority of his Word.[119]

Frame even attempts to refine presuppositionalism's view of circular reasoning by arguing that it is not a vicious circle at all. Instead of a tight circularity, he sees it as a circularity that is somewhat linear: God's rationality makes human faith rational, which makes human reasoning rational.[120] Beginning with God's rationality allows the human thinker to discover and use the presuppositions that are necessary for comprehending the way things really are.[121] While Frame thought this new view of linearity instead of complete circularity was an exciting development for presuppositional thought, others have not found it as impressive.[122] Perhaps this is because the circle is not as tightly drawn as before, but it is still recognizably the same general shape.

---

117. Frame, *Cornelius Van Til*, 305–6.
118. Bahnsen, *Van Til's Apologetic*, 170 n. 42.
119. Bahnsen, *Always Ready*, 25.
120. Frame, "Presuppositional Apologetics," 210.
121. Ibid., 216.
122. Frame, "Presuppositional Apologist's Closing Remarks," 354.

The Scriptures, then, are not received as the Word of God on the basis of Jesus believing they were, and his resurrection proving his deity (and thus the accuracy of his thought). If that were the case, then the degree of confidence possible in accepting the doctrine of inspiration and inerrancy would depend on the degree of probability of the historical case for the resurrection. For presuppositionalism, like Reformed epistemology, the Scriptures are not accepted on the basis of any argument whatsoever. There is no chain of reasoning that ends in the conclusion that the Bible is the special revelation of God. On the contrary, the believer comes to accept the Bible on the basis of the internal work and testimony of God's Holy Spirit.

According to Van Til it is futile, as well as unbiblical, to ask the unbeliever to decide for themselves whether they will accept the Bible as the Word of God. He writes:

> The traditional method had explicitly built into it the right and ability of the natural man, apart from the work of the Spirit of God, to be the judge of the claim of the authoritative Word of God. It is man who, by means of his self-established intellectual tools, puts his "stamp of approval" on the Word of God and then, only after that grand act, does he listen to it. God's Word must first pass man's tests of good and evil, truth and falsity. But once you tell a non-Christian this, why should he be worried by anything else that you say. You have already told him he is quite all right just the way he is! Then the Scripture is not correct when it talks of "darkened minds," "wilful ignorance," "dead men," and "blind people"! With this method the correctness of the natural man's problematics is endorsed. That is all he needs to reject the Christian faith.[123]

The antidote to this dead end is to rely on the authority of the self-attesting Christ. In fact, Van Til could go so far as to say: "The self-attesting Christ of Scripture has always been my starting-point for everything I have said."[124] It is not autonomous human reasoning that comes to identify and accept the Bible as God's Word: it is the Holy Spirit who reveals this to human hearts.[125]

More will be said about the following position in the next chapter, but Bahnsen believes that human beings are constituted to recognize

123. Van Til, "My Credo," 11.
124. Ibid., 3.
125. Ibid., 4–5.

the revelation of God in both its general and special manifestations. He writes:

> Experience can "condition" us to identify a signature on a letter as the signature of a good friend. Similarly, God has so created men that, as it were, they are "conditioned" to see and understand His signature throughout the created world. The evidence is directly apprehended, and it is persuasive—leaving men without any excuse. What we have said here about God's revelation in the natural order is just as true of God's revelation in Scripture. Men are so constituted as to recognize these words as the authoritative voice of their Maker speaking to them. Scripture's divine quality is perceived directly, just as the sweetness of candy or the wetness of water is immediately experienced without discursive argumentation.[126]

It is the fact that discursive argument is not needed for defending the Scriptures as the Word of God that separates the Reformed epistemologists and the presuppositionalists from the traditional method. Bahnsen is very clear that even the miracles and the resurrection do not prove that Jesus is deity; for that truth we must rely on his word and interpretation of himself alone.[127] Bahnsen admits to circularity here, but holds that it is unavoidable. As Frame notes, the Scripture has to be self-attesting, since every other source that might be used to test it is itself judged and evaluated on the basis of God's Word.[128] This position is another exemplification of the presuppositionalists' commitment to the entire biblical worldview being the precondition for intelligibility in every way.

In the final analysis, then, presuppositionalism clearly breaks from the evidential method by refusing to try to move from the resurrection to the doctrine of Scripture. On the contrary, the historical factuality of the resurrection is *proved by its being part of the authoritative special revelation of God in his word, the Bible*. This is of the utmost importance, and the difference between the apologetic methods at this point is massive. Historical reconstruction and investigation does not prove the resurrection: the Scriptures prove the resurrection. From a slightly different perspective, the doctrines of Scripture and the resurrection are mutually reinforcing and supporting. Both are integral components of

---

126. Bahnsen, *Van Til's Apologetic*, 200–201.
127. Ibid., 201.
128. Frame, *Cornelius Van Til*, 125.

the Christian worldview, which is itself the transcendental requirement for intelligibility.

Since the Scriptures are God's word, and whatever God says is true and authoritative, the fact that the resurrection is recorded in the Scriptures is enough to prove that it took place. For presuppositionalism, it is methodologically incorrect to rest more weight on the authority of the apologist's historical argument for the resurrection than on the fact that the Bible claims the resurrection happened. God's authoritative word is far more reliable and trustworthy than any human historical reconstruction, and accepting the former cannot be based on accepting the latter first. The progression is not from historical argument to the doctrine of Scripture, but from the doctrine of Scripture to the resurrection. For classical and *evidential apologists, the argument for Scripture hinges on the argument for the resurrection. For Reformed epistemologists, the two doctrines do not need to be methodologically related in a particular order. For presuppositionalists, the fact that the Scriptures record the resurrection renders the probability of its factuality at 100 percent, and both doctrines cohere together in a non-negotiable, transcendentally necessary world and life view.

INTERNAL ANALYSIS OF APOLOGETIC COGENCY

Perhaps the most vexing issue when it comes to presuppositionalism is the same type of concern that surrounds transcendental arguments in general. Are there any? Do they work? *Can* they work? Even if presuppositionalism is logically valid, is it logically sound? Is it true? If it is true, then Christian apologetics cannot be defeated by rational argumentation, no matter how the specific arguments are formulated and deployed, since the very act of debating Christianity assumes that Christianity is in fact true. The debate is not about clusters of facts, but about the very nature of facts. If it is true that the essence of factuality is only coherent in the Christian worldview, then the presuppositional apologetic is demanded. But such a claim is, of course, extremely momentous, and relies on the complete impossibility of any other competing worldview accounting for the intelligibility of human experience.

The question has also been raised as to whether or not presuppositionalism is really even a form of apologetics, or whether it would be more accurately understood as a theological position, or as a theological view of apologetics.[129] There is no doubt that presuppositionalism sees itself as a philosophical and apologetical system that is based on a preexisting theological structure. Van Til self-consciously tried to work his apologetical methodology out of the theological, biblical framework of the Reformed faith. The development of his fullest apologetic work, *The Defense of the Faith* makes unmistakably clear that he labored to understand and present Reformed theology, and then tried to defend it with an apologetic that grew organically out of its principles.

Van Til himself believed that his first call was to be a preacher of the Word of God, and in discharging that responsibility he engaged in apologetics. He wrote:

> Ever since I can remember it was of this letter of Christ which my father read to me and to the family. It was also this letter which I heard in church, spoken by the minister of Christ. Every minister in those days had a V.D.M. degree: *Verbum Dei Minister*. When, therefore, I became a teacher of apologetics it was natural for me to think, not only of my Th.M. and my Ph.D., but above all my V.D.M. The former degrees were but means whereby I might be true to the latter degree.[130]

His work in apologetics was, therefore, not just on the basis of abstract theology, but on the basis of pastoral and practical theology. While a closer look at this relationship lies beyond the scope of this study, the reader should consult the recent biography of Van Til by John Muether for an excellent examination of the impact the practical life of the church had on Van Til's thinking.[131]

To ask whether or not presuppositionalism is really a school of apologetics, or a theological perspective on apologetics, is to immediately fall into the very dichotomy that Van Til abhorred. He was not trying to separate the two disciplines; for him, they could not be strictly separated. Theology and apologetics could be divided for heuristic reasons in the theological encyclopedia (as indeed theology could be subdivided), but ultimately philosophy had to be rooted in theology. Attempting to defend the faith philosophically apart from theological underpinnings would be a betrayal of the Christian worldview, since the Bible is the final author-

---

129. Habermas, "An Evidentialist's Response," 247.
130. Van Til, "My Credo," 8.
131. Muether, *Cornelius Van Til*.

ity for all things, and even the deeply philosophical topics such as metaphysics and epistemology could only be understood in light of Christian truth. In my judgment, Van Til would have viewed a strict "theology or apologetics" disjunction as indicative of a rampant misunderstanding of his entire position.

It is also not the case that the presuppositionalists only engage in negative apologetics aimed at demonstrating the inadequacy of an opposing argument, and totally eschew positive ones. This objection has been partly answered in the course of the discussion of presuppositionalism and evidence above. Nevertheless, it is true that presuppositionalism has a deserved reputation for focusing more on negative than positive apologetics. Habermas criticizes presuppositionalists for (1) talking about the value of evidence; (2) but then using the evidential arguments developed by evidentialists; (3) while insisting that the evidentialists use their evidence wrongly.[132] In Habermas's estimation, presuppositionalism is very good at negative apologetics, but is not strong in positive apologetics, which is the more important of the two.[133] His larger concern is that, if the evidentialists do not understand how to use evidence properly, the presuppositionalists should not simply engage in wholesale borrowing of their arguments, but reformulate them along proper lines.

Much of the discussion turns on linguistics. The legitimacy of the charge that presuppositionalists shy away from positive apologetics depends on how positive the argument must be. When presuppositionalists step onto their opponents' ground for argument's sake, and demonstrate how intelligibility breaks down in the non-Christian worldview, this is an exercise in negative apologetics. Since this is the tactic favored in presuppositionalism, it is not surprising, then, that a great deal of presuppositional thought will be spent on looking for internal inconsistencies and identifying the insufficient supporting presuppositions in those worldviews. Methodologically, the first step is negative.

But it must be borne in mind that the purpose of negative apologetics in presuppositionalism is to establish, indirectly by the impossibility of the contrary, that the Christian worldview is true. Presuppositionalism has not constructed many positive arguments for Christianity, but rather seeks to demonstrate transcendentally the necessity of the Christian

---

132. Habermas, "An Evidentialist's Response," 239–41.
133. Ibid., 241.

worldview for intelligibility. If successful, no argument could be more positive for establishing the truth of Christianity. Perhaps it would not be too far off the mark to suggest that a more accurate distinction in presuppositionalism's case than positive and negative apologetics would be between direct and indirect arguments. This is because the negative argument is preparatory for the transcendental argument, and not preparatory for direct arguments to establish the truth of Christianity.

On an internal analysis, presuppositionalism does not betray any obvious contradictions or inconsistencies. Intra-systematically it seems to contain mutually supporting and reinforcing axioms and propositions. While there are many Reformed theologians who are not presuppositionalists, I am aware of no non-Reformed theologians who ascribe to presuppositionalism. This raises the question of the accuracy of confessional Reformed theology: the support for presuppositional apologetics cannot be divorced from the strength of biblical support for Reformed theology. Presuppositionalism is self-consciously an attempt to understand the relationship between Reformed theology and apologetics. Theology is primary, and apologetics is built on the theological foundation. For those who assume or accept the validity of Reformed theology, presuppositionalism will be a live option; but for those who do not, it will likely be a non-starter. How presuppositionalism fares in the inter-systematic exchange will be reserved for the next chapter, but internally it seems capable of passing all the demands of logical coherence.

The most vexing issue for presuppositionalism is, in my judgment, the nature of logical principles. Internally, presuppositionalism can maintain its stance, but as an apologetic this one point is extremely hard to articulate and convincingly defend. Challenging human logical categories as ultimate is more promising, and pushing the problem of induction[134] is more promising yet, since these two issues do lend themselves to debating the intelligibility of human experience and thought. Also, difficulties with inductive logic have troubled Western philosophers since the time of Hume particularly, and there is no widely accepted resolution (many philosophers have even found Hume's problems with induction decisive).[135] In other words, it would seem that the best tactic for the presuppositional apologist in this area is to major on the subjective element of the human

---

134. For a definition of the problem of induction, see Salmon, "Problem of Induction."
135. Ibid., 746.

experience of logic, rather than the nature and necessity of logic itself. Arguing that the Christian worldview is transcendentally necessary to justify the use of human logic is more likely to be effective than arguing that logic is dependent on the character of God. In other words, arguing about the subjective human use of logic is more cogent than arguing about the objective status of logic's nature.

CONCLUSION

Presuppositionalism is distinct from classical apologetics and Reformed epistemology, and is most properly interpreted as a theological-apologetic methodology. It seeks to present the whole Christian worldview against the competing worldview of non-belief (in all its various manifestations), and demonstrate that all worldviews other than the Christian one are insufficient to account for reality. The triune God of the Bible is the transcendental precondition that makes human experience intelligible. As the Word of God, the Scriptures are self-attesting in their authority. Since all human thought must be submitted to God's authority, it is the Bible that stands in judgment on human deductions and usage of inductive logic. Only the Bible can provide human beings with the vantage point from which they can properly re-interpret facts after the mind of God. The apologist insists that, apart from this ground, there is nowhere to stand; that is the great proof that this ground is sound.

Having examined the three main competing schools of Reformed apologetics on their own, it is now time to focus on their relationships with each other, especially in terms of justifying a high view of Scripture that maintains the historic Reformed confessional position of inspiration and plenary inerrancy. The next chapter is directed to this end. It is time to compare and contrast the different methodologies at the most critical points, to see which methodology is most capable of cohering with Reformed theology.

5

Reformed Apologetics, Theology, and the Bible

INTRODUCTION

HAVING EXAMINED EVIDENTIAL APOLOGETICS, Reformed epistemology, and presuppositionalism in the last three chapters, it is now time for us to place them side by side to continue our search for the apologetic methodology most consistent with a high view of Scripture. The best choice for a defense of the Reformed Christian faith, which doctrinally includes a view of Scripture as inerrant, will be found in the apologetic methodology that exhibits a cogent relationship between apologetics and theology. If inerrancy is part of the Christian view that is being defended, the apologist must be able to defend that particular doctrine. It may be the case that this doctrine is defended late in the system, after other doctrines are established, but the only point to make now is that the doctrine must be capably defended at some point in the apologetic process. A Reformed apologetic eventually needs to defend Reformed doctrine; the Christianity being defended is not void of content, and it includes an inerrant view of Scripture.

The main body of this chapter will consist of three sections. In the first section, the major question to be answered is whether or not the principles of each apologetic methodology can logically make possible a compelling defense of the inerrancy of Scripture. The second section will examine two issues that each methodology must be concerned with: the nature and function of the pivotally important *sensus divinitatis*, and the issue of methodological and personal neutrality. In the third section, each system will be tested to determine which methodologies can justify their operating assumptions. These three sections contain relatively straightforward concerns, yet they are crucial tests for Reformed apologetic cogency.

METHOD AND THE DOCTRINE OF SCRIPTURE

Each Reformed apologetic methodology has its particular manner of arriving at or defending the doctrine of the inerrancy of Scripture. Organizationally, this section will reverse the order followed in the previous chapters, and look at presuppositionalism, then Reformed epistemology, and then the classical/evidential approach. Rather than arguing about the actual strength or soundness of each position, for the sake of argument each position will be allowed its maximum force and ideal explanatory power. In other words, the apologetic will be granted the status of being logically sound, up to the moment of defending or establishing the doctrine of the inerrancy of Scripture.

Presuppositionalism

Since presuppositionalism depends on the inerrancy of the Scriptures, it will be a rather obvious observation that, if presuppositionalism is granted its maximum force, then the doctrine of inerrancy is vindicated. The plenary inspiration of the original autographs guarantees their perfect truthfulness and accuracy. They are self-attesting and the highest court of appeal. Every test (e.g., logical consistency, induction) by which the Scriptures can be measured is actually tested and validated by the Scriptures. Thus human investigation does not demonstrate the inerrancy of Scripture; on the contrary, the inerrancy of Scripture is taken to be necessary to ground the legitimacy of human thought and investigation. While this position is, to put it mildly, controversial, if it is sound then the Reformed doctrine of inerrancy is secured.

Reformed Epistemology

Although there are more perspectives on inerrancy possible in Reformed epistemology than in presuppositionalism, the different views can be categorized in a fairly straightforward way. Unlike presuppositionalism, however, there is also the potential for an inerrancy-defeater to overwhelm the defense. This defeater is only potentially successful, but it is nevertheless real, and does present a challenge to Reformed epistemology's defense of the doctrine of inerrancy. Before identifying the potential defeater, however, three possible positions on inerrancy that are logically compatible with Reformed epistemology will be noted.

First, it is possible that the Reformed epistemologist will reject the plenary inerrancy of the Scriptures. The internal instigation of the Holy Spirit, testifying without mediation to the great things of the gospel, may produce Christian belief in the doctrines of the deity of Christ, the atonement, the resurrection, and other systematic elements of soteriology, without witnessing to the inerrancy of Scripture. The Spirit may testify that these things are true, and yet not testify that the historical record of these events is inerrant. A believer could, in this model, accept the Bible as the fallible record of human beings who recorded these doctrines in written form. Details may have become confused, but the great, central core of the Christian faith (i.e., the great things of the gospel) is clear enough to be accepted as true. Thus the Holy Spirit testifies to the reality of the events, but not to the perfection of the original record of the events.

Second, Reformed epistemologists may accept a view of partial or limited inerrancy. They may hold that the great things of the gospel were recorded without error, but that other matters concerning history, science, or trivial details are not necessarily 100 percent accurate. While some would contend that limited inerrancy is extremely problematic and logically fallacious, that is not the point here. The point is that limited inerrancy is compatible with the apologetic model of Reformed epistemology. In other words, Reformed epistemology's position underdetermines the issue of the inerrancy of Scripture.

Third, there does not seem to be any reason why a Reformed epistemologist could not accept the traditional Reformed doctrine of full plenary inerrancy. It is not entirely clear that the doctrine of inerrancy could not constitute one of the great things of the gospel, or perhaps why it could not at least occupy a secondary tier (i.e., not as important as the resurrection, but still important enough to be witnessed to by the Spirit). Furthermore, there does not seem to be any reason why the Spirit could not witness to a text like 2 Tim 3:16, and then through deduction, lead the Christian to believe that whatever is covered by that text (which may be taken as the entire canon), is in fact inerrant. So the inerrancy of the entire Bible is also a logically defensible possibility for the Reformed epistemologist.

As was previously mentioned, there is a potential inerrancy-defeater that the Reformed epistemologist must contend with. This is because there is only prima facie warrant given to Christian beliefs in Reformed epistemology, and this prima facie level of warrant can be undercut or overturned by defeaters. Since there are many who urge that the Bible contains discrepancies, errors, and other mistakes, the Reformed epistemologist will need to defeat this defeater (in any of its possible formulations) if they are to continue to be warranted in their belief in the doctrine of inerrancy.

Under further analysis, it is clear that any potential inerrancy-defeater will be irrelevant for the first position noted above, since there the doctrine of inerrancy has already been defeated, or was never accepted to begin with. Depending on the pitch of the defeater, it may also be rather irrelevant to the second position, since a limited inerrancy is already accepted. For the third position, however, the Reformed epistemologist will have to demonstrate that the objection is itself inaccurate, or in some other manner defeat the defeater. Now, it is logically possible that the testimony of the Holy Spirit will be of sufficient strength to outweigh the defeater, but it is more fitting to the model of Reformed epistemology to attempt to meet and defeat the defeater. Nevertheless, the stereotypical dear old saint, or a young believer who could never answer such objections, may still be warranted in holding to an inerrant Bible, on the basis of their experience and the testimony of the Spirit. The rationality of their belief will be, as Reformed epistemology maintains, relative to their situation.

Holding or failing to hold to the Reformed doctrine of inerrancy both seem to be compatible in a broad sense with Reformed epistemology. On the basis of the larger model, it is possible to defend the doctrine in its strongest form, although there is the potential for inerrancy-defeaters to arise that must be dispatched. Epistemologically the camp is wide enough to encompass a variety of theological and doctrinal perspectives on the inerrancy of Scripture. Reformed epistemology can logically be ascribed to by a great diversity of individuals who share similar views on epistemology and philosophy, but who differ substantially on the doctrine of Scripture. There is no *necessary* position on inerrancy in Reformed epistemology, but a great amount of room for contingent or accidental ones.

Evidentialism

To save time, it can be immediately noted that evidentialism, just like Reformed epistemology, underdetermines the doctrine of inerrancy. In other words, the methodological sequence of evidential apologetics does not need to lead to the doctrine of full inerrancy. As a matter of historical fact, evidentialists hold to each of the three positions identified in the previous subsection. Of course many people who hold to an evidential approach reject Christianity entirely; it is not surprising that some come to accept some of the truths of the Christian faith, while believing that the evidence cannot establish (and may even be totally against) the doctrine of inerrancy. The issue for evidentialism for our purposes is not whether or not it demands inerrancy (it does not) but whether or not the principles of its methodology can successfully lead to a defense of inerrancy.

Before proceeding, a careful distinction needs to be made. Evidentialism may be able to establish many things in theory that it cannot establish in practice. Take as an example a murder scene. Let it be supposed that two men decide to murder a third man. One of the conspirators videotapes the event, while the other kills the innocent victim. Startled when the police arrive, they run out with the video camera still filming. The entire episode is recorded with crystal clarity. There is no doubt (unless one wanted to postulate alien impersonators or some other desperate maneuver) that they are guilty. Evidentially, the case is as certain as can be.

There are other murder scenes, however, where there is simply not enough evidence to ever bring about a conviction. Think of a homeless person robbed and killed in the middle of the night in an alley with no witnesses, no known motive besides robbery, and no usable DNA traces. The killer may be local or visiting from another country. There is simply no possible way to investigate the murder in a successful manner; there is not enough evidence to lead to a suspect, let alone enough evidence to bring about a conviction. Theoretically there could be enough evidence, as in the first murder scenario, for the evidential/inductive method of investigation to arrive at a successful conclusion, but in real life experience such a method may not be able to lead to the desired result. All this goes to say there can be a rather wide divide between what a particular investigative method may achieve in the theoretical realm, and what it is actually able to achieve in practical, concrete situations.

Theoretically, a piece of literature could be justifiably held to be without error on the basis of an evidential approach. For example, if the piece of literature in question was a note that I passed to someone with only my name and phone number on it, one could imagine that this note could be validated as inerrant. Practically speaking, however, it is obvious that the Bible is extremely more complicated than a simple note. The Scriptures contain:

1. Names of people and places mentioned nowhere else in historical documents, or discovered in archaeological finds.

2. Speeches and conversations, many of which were written down centuries after the speakers had died.

3. Private motives and thoughts. The narrator is not depicted as guessing what someone was thinking, or surmising their motives, but rather saying exactly what someone thought or what motivated their behavior.

4. What God thinks and says in heaven. This would seem to require an even more specialized access than the previous point. Not only do some of the biblical writers claim to know some of the internal thoughts and motives of people, but they also claim to know some of the thoughts, motives, and words of God in the heavens. This stance assumes authorial knowledge beyond human potentiality.

5. Ethical and moral pronouncements. The Bible is not a collection of historical annals, where every statement is purely descriptive. It is also prescriptive and evaluative. It provides a standard of ideals, and a code of laws and ethics. Scripture does not merely present an arbitrary opinion on what seems good; on the contrary, it demands that good and evil be understood in terms of its own worldview.

6. Scripture deals with the future, and the consummation of the age. Since this has not yet happened, it cannot be investigated historically.

7. Theological interpretation. The Bible will describe an event, and then explain it in theological terms. An external observer, however, would not be able to see the one event and know exactly what it was for, and what God was accomplishing. The interpretation of the event is different from observing the event itself. Of all possible

interpretations the Scriptures will insist that there is one which is true to God's view and intention. Other interpretations that may be logically valid are nevertheless untrue.

What this means in the concrete case of the canon of Scripture is that there are a great many elements that are beyond the evidentialist's reach for verification. In fact, there is no necessary relationship between an inerrant description of an event and an inerrant interpretation of the same. A witness may be without error in saying that one person punched another, but they may be in error when they add that it was malicious, or in self-defense, or part of a game. Obviously, they might also be in error when they say what both persons were thinking, and what God said to an angel in heaven concerning the altercation, even though they accurately note that x punched y. It is a category confusion to flatten out this distinction.

A common move in evidentialism, as was noted in chapter 2, is to argue that Jesus Christ is divine, and he endorsed the inerrancy of the Scriptures. For the sake of argument, it will simply be granted that the New Testament contains remarks attributed to Jesus that entail that the Hebrew canon is inerrant. At this juncture it is possible to raise the objection that the New Testament Gospel manuscripts were written, at the least, decades after the life of Jesus. Is it utterly impossible that not every phrase or sentence attributed to Jesus was actually spoken by him? Even if the general reliability of the New Testament manuscripts is granted, it seems to require more than that in order to accept every word of the documents at face value. Nevertheless, let this point be granted for the sake of argument, and let it be taken as proven that Jesus absolutely did endorse the Hebrew canon as inerrant.

Another issue altogether, however, arises for the inerrancy of the New Testament. Perhaps it goes without saying that the opinion of Jesus on books that were not yet written is somewhat harder to prove using the evidential method than his spoken opinion on books that actually existed before his time. By way of example, one may be able to argue plausibly that Jesus accepted the full authority and inerrancy of the Pentateuch, while still doubting that a solid case can be made that Jesus endorsed the book of Revelation, or Second Peter, or Acts, as inerrant.

Furthermore, making an appeal to a verse like John 16:13—which states that when the Spirit comes he will guide the disciples into all truth—

is of extremely limited value for the evidential case for inerrancy. There are at least three difficulties. First, the immediate context is Jesus speaking to his disciples; this group does not include Paul, or Mark, or Luke, or the author of Hebrews, or anyone else besides the eleven. Second, there is an inferential step between being guided into all truth and writing an inerrant book or series of books. Jesus' words do not denote writing inerrant manuscripts; one may argue that this is the right connotation, but that is, again, inferential. His words may encompass writing inerrant books, but that is not on the basis of referential logical necessity. Third, the Gospel of John is, by all accounts, the latest Gospel written. What if John (assuming Johannine authorship) made a mistake in memory: what if John's own writing was not inerrant? It seems that there needs to be a hidden premise smuggled into the argument at this point; that the Gospel is without error needs to be assumed to ground inerrancy. This is circular.

The same consideration holds true for 2 Tim 3:16–17, the *locus classicus* for the doctrine of inerrancy. It can be immediately noted that many scholars reject Pauline authorship; if Paul did not write it, is this a challenge to its inerrancy? Again, though, the main thrust of the issue is that the document needs to be taken as without error in order for that verse to justify the inerrancy of other texts. Granting that an inductive case can be made that the New Testament sees itself as divinely inspired Scripture, the reader still needs to accept its self-attesting claim in order to use the data on inerrancy to establish the doctrine across the board.

At this point a summary of the difficulty can be offered. It can be fully granted that an evidential, historical case for the resurrection of Jesus Christ from the dead can be formulated successfully. But when the resurrection is accepted as a historical, factual event, this still does not demand that the *documents that record the event are completely without error*. Thinking again of a court case, it may be established as an absolute, incontrovertible fact that a murder occurred, but this does not mean that every (or even any) witness provided inerrant testimony. Historical events can be proved or defended successfully, even if there are errors in the witness accounts, or errors in the written records. Clearly an author could truthfully record that Jesus Christ was resurrected, and yet still make errors in writing an entire Gospel, most of which is engaged with words, prayers, sermons, events, people, and places having nothing directly to do with the resurrection event.

Summary

The evidential, inductive apologetic methodology is beset by too many difficulties to make a sure case for biblical inerrancy. Now, this does not necessarily mean that such a method cannot be the best apologetic strategy, since there might not be a better defense available. At the most, though, the defense will be probabilistic and provisional. There will also be a number of elements in the Scriptures that are simply outside the reach of the inductive method for verification. Reformed epistemology is theologically broader than the doctrine of an inerrant Scripture, but there is no reason why the two are incompatible. A defense of inerrancy can be made from the camp. Presuppositionalism takes the doctrine of inerrancy as a necessary support for human knowledge to obtain. If it is not true, then the Christian worldview is false, and all hopes for intelligibility are lost.

Out of the three camps, presuppositionalism and Reformed epistemology offer the models that are most congenial to the doctrine of inerrancy, with the evidential methodology simply insufficient for bearing the weight. Nevertheless, if the presuppositional system or Reformed epistemology are unsound, the evidential method may be left as the only option the apologist has. Yet it would seem that if this were the case, the evidentialist would be well advised to try to refute alleged errors and discrepancies, rather than trying to prove the inerrancy of Scripture. The most promising apologetic strategy for the evidentialist would seem to consist in denying that particular challenges to the doctrine of inerrancy were sound; defeating defeaters, and arguing that the Bible had not been shown to be in error would be the best way to defend inerrancy for the evidentialist. It is, of course, also true that failing to demonstrate inerrancy is not logically even close to the same thing as proving that the Scriptures are actually errant.

INTER-METHODOLOGICAL CRITIQUE AND DEBATE

This section could easily balloon in size, and it could also grow wearyingly repetitive, given that many points of critique and debate have already been mentioned in the previous chapters. In order to facilitate a manageable discussion, the scope of material will be restricted to two critical issues. The first issue is identifying the nature and function of the *sensus divinitatis*. This concept is crucial for apologetic methodologies. The second issue will be whether or not evidential approaches are more methodologically neutral than Reformed epistemology or presuppositionalism. While both of these issues are important in their own right, they are also linked in an important way. A relationship exists between the nature and function of the *sensus divinitatis* and the possibility of human epistemic neutrality.

The *sensus divinitatis*

It was noted in the third chapter of this book that in Plantinga's understanding, "the *sensus divinitatis* is a disposition or set of dispositions to form theistic beliefs in various circumstances, in response to the sorts of conditions or stimuli that trigger the working of this [natural] sense of divinity."[1] Thus the *sensus divinitatis* was designed by God to produce theistic beliefs in human beings when they are in certain situations and circumstances. If this design plan is successful (which it is, given God's design) it satisfies the requirements of Plantinga's model of warrant, and can generate justified beliefs.

Although this understanding of the *sensus divinitatis* is internally cogent in Plantinga's model, it has been the subject of intense criticism. There are two major Reformed points of critique: the first is that Plantinga's *sensus divinitatis* is not biblical, and the second is that it differs greatly from Calvin's teaching. Since the Aquinas/Calvin model is ostensibly linked with Calvin, a common understanding of the nature and function of the *sensus divinitatis* is very important. For those in the Reformed camp, it is vital that the Scriptures are given priority, and if Plantinga's model falters at the fence of sound biblical interpretation, his claims will be severely reduced in force.

What did Calvin have in mind when he discussed the *sensus divinitatis*? Without pretending to be exhaustive, a few careful citations can lay out the difference between Plantinga and Calvin very clearly. John Calvin wrote: "There is within the human mind, and indeed by natural instinct, an awareness of divinity. This we take to be beyond controversy. To prevent anyone from taking refuge in the pretense of ignorance, God himself has implanted in all men a certain understanding of his divine majesty . . . men one and all perceive that there is a God and that he is their Maker."[2] Calvin further remarks: "Men of sound judgment will always be sure that

---

1. Plantinga, *Warranted Christian Belief*, 172.
2. Calvin, *Institutes*, 1:43–44.

a sense of divinity which can never be effaced is engraved upon men's minds."³

Attention must be drawn to two significant differences between Calvin and Plantinga. The first is that, for Calvin, the knowledge of God that human beings have is universal. In Plantinga's model, the *sensus divinitatis* may function to produce theistic belief, but it does not have to. Calvin did not see the sense of deity as being *potentially produced*: it was something that was universally distributed across the human race. God himself, according to Calvin, planted this knowledge of himself in all people. Furthermore, no matter what happens, it cannot be erased or effaced from the mind. Plantinga looks at the *sensus divinitatis* as a disposition that may trigger the formation of theistic beliefs, but for Calvin the belief formation is not potential, or even just inevitably produced at some time; it is immediately present in all people. For Paul and Calvin, the issue is not that we have the potential to know God, it is that everyone actually does know God.⁴

In the second place, Calvin asserts that God himself places this knowledge inside the human mind, not that there is a faculty that has the function of producing this sense of deity. It is not a knowledge that is produced in certain circumstances by a cognitive faculty, or a set of dispositions. Plantinga sees the *sensus divinitatis* functioning in response to certain circumstances or stimuli, but for Calvin the sense of deity is immediately and ineradicably implanted by God. For Plantinga, the *sensus divinitatis* may not work in an atheist,⁵ but for Calvin, it may be properly said that there is no such thing as an actual atheist who is devoid of the knowledge of God. Taking these points together, then, for Calvin the *sensus divinitatis* is not a cognitive faculty, but the direct knowledge of God, and this knowledge is universally rather than partially distributed through the human race.

It is also worth observing that, in context, Calvin is not worried about the rationality of believing in God, since he simply holds that all people actually do know God through the *sensus divinitatis*.⁶ If Plantinga's view was really in line with Calvin's, one might expect that the *sensus di-*

---

3. Ibid., 45.
4. Oliphint, "Irrationality of Unbelief," 68 n. 22.
5. Grimm, "Cardinal Newman," 500 n. 9.
6. Helm, "John Calvin, the *Sensus Divinitatis*, and the Noetic Effects of Sin," 87–88.

vinitatis would play a key role at important, or at least relevant, junctures of the *Institutes*, but the concept is largely ignored. Instead:

> When he [Calvin] discusses the faculties of the created soul and the *imago dei* which it mirrored, he affirms that Adam knew God's benevolence naturally. However, he never discusses the *sensus divinitatis*. He does not list it as one of the faculties of the soul, or as part of the understanding or will. He never states that Adam knew God by reasoning about God's benevolence from the *sensus divinitatis*, or through the *sensus divinitatis* directly. In his crucial account of how we receive faith, Calvin emphasizes faith as the knowledge of God's benevolence toward us, its firmness and certainty, its ground in the promise of Christ, and the role of the Holy Spirit in sealing faith in the sinful human heart. He omits any mention of the *sensus divinitatis*, and accords it no role in bringing faith to faithless human beings.[7]

This is an argument from silence, but it is nevertheless an important point. Where Calvin does discuss the knowledge of God his understanding is significantly different from Plantinga's, and where it would be fully expected that he would discuss the *sensus divinitatis* (if Plantinga's definition were close to what Calvin had in mind), Calvin does not so much as mention it or allude to it. The fairest conclusion to draw from the data is that the *sensus divinitatis* in Reformed epistemology is far removed from what is found in Calvin.

Even if this is the case, however, it is possible that it is Calvin, not Plantinga, who is wrong (of course both may be incorrect). The second prong in the attack on Plantinga's understanding of the *sensus divinitatis* is that it fails to be biblical. This is also the more significant prong, since it has been rightly observed: "A Reformed apologetic is only Reformed to the extent that its tenets, principles, methodology, and so forth are formed and re-formed by Scripture."[8] Calvin will serve as a helpful bridge between the two attacks. In his commentary on Romans, Calvin writes that all people have "the true knowledge of God" but they suppress it.[9] This knowledge is engraved on the heart.[10] Calvin's comments come in his

---

7. Jeffreys, "How Reformed Is Reformed Epistemology," 427.
8. Oliphint and Tipton, "Introduction," 1.
9. Calvin, "Romans 1–16," 69.
10. Ibid., 70.

Reformed Apologetics, Theology, and the Bible

discussion of Rom 1:18–22 (verses 19–21 are of the most direct significance for the present purpose).

While it is true that "the interpretation of verses 19–20 has been the cause of endless controversy"[11] it is also true that there can be agreement on some of the major points Paul is making. One of the major points identified by the expositor D. Martyn Lloyd-Jones is that verse 19 teaches: "It is a universal fact that there is a sense of God in mankind."[12] Others have noted that: "To understand that Paul does not refer to a long process of reasoning by which people come to a knowledge of God's existence and power is critical. God has stitched into the fabric of the human mind his existence and power, so that they are instinctively recognized when one views the created world . . . the rejection of God is concurrent with the knowledge of him."[13]

Again, it appears that both the Bible and Calvin teach that every person naturally has the knowledge of God, rather than that such knowledge could be potentially produced by a cognitive faculty or disposition in propitious circumstances.

William Lane Craig simply finds the existence of the *sensus divinitatis* something very doubtful, and he fails to find any convincing biblical support for it.[14] One of the weak spots in Plantinga's model is that if someone does not accept the existence of the *sensus divinitatis*, there is nothing Plantinga can offer them to demonstrate its reality.[15] The two criticisms examined, namely that Plantinga's position on the *sensus divinitatis* is in accord with neither Calvin nor the Scriptures, are sound. This does not mean that it is not a workable *philosophical* model, or a usable *religious epistemic* model, but it does mean that it cannot find support by appealing to Calvin or the Bible. Given that such appeals are vital to Reformed epistemology, the lack of support in these sources is deeply problematic.

How should the sense of deity, which according to Calvin and Scripture all people innately have, be understood and used in apologetics? Van Til contends that: "It is to this sense of deity, even this knowledge of God—which, Paul tells us (Rom. 1:19–20), every man has, but which,

11. Morris, *Romans*, 78.
12. Lloyd-Jones, *Romans 1*, 368.
13. Schreiner, *Romans*, 86, who cites Wilckens in support.
14. Craig, "Classical Apologist's Response," 285.
15. Willard, "Plantinga's Epistemology," 286.

as Paul also tells us, every sinner seeks to suppress—that the Christian apologist must appeal."[16] The appeal to the knowledge of God that every person has is on the basis of the state of affairs that actually obtains. It is owing to the reality that everyone knows God that the apologist has a genuine point of contact for the apologetic encounter.[17] In the final analysis, according to Van Til, "only by finding the point of contact in man's sense of deity that lies underneath his own conception of self-consciousness as ultimate can we be both true to Scripture and effective in reasoning with the natural man."[18] The doctrinal link is the *imago dei*:

> The common ground between believers and unbelievers lies not in a supposed common epistemology but in a common bearing of God's image. This metaphysical common ground, involving as it does the *sensus deitatis*, becomes the proper point of contact in apologetics and evangelism. Men are accessible to the gospel because they are God's image-bearers and live in God's universe which constantly testifies to them of God. Here is the true genius of the apologetic method of Cornelius Van Til.[19]

A great difficulty, however, is that this knowledge of God is being actively suppressed by the unregenerate.[20] The task of the apologist is to bring to the fore not something that the unbeliever does not know, but something that they already know, but want to suppress and reject.

Although it is difficult to articulate, unbelievers paradoxically know God, yet culpably deceive themselves into consciously denying the knowledge that they possess. Bahnsen writes:

> All men know and hence believe that God exists. The revelational evidence is so plain that nobody can avoid holding the conviction that God exists, even though they may never explicitly assented to this belief. We are justified in ascribing such a belief to men on the basis of their observed behavior in reasoning (e.g., relying on the uniformity of nature), in morals (e.g., holding to ethical absolutes in some fashion), and in emotion (e.g., fearing death). Nevertheless, all men are motivated in unrighteousness and by fear of judgment to ignore, hide, and disavow any belief in

---

16. Van Til, *Christian Apologetics*, 109.
17. Ibid., 120.
18. Ibid., 121.
19. Turner, "Cornelius Van Til and Romans 1:18–21," 57.
20. Van Til, *Christian Apologetics*, 127.

the living and true God (either through atheism or false religiosity). By misconstruing and rationalizing the relevant, inescapable evidence around them ("suppressing it"), men bring themselves to believe about themselves that they do not believe in God, even though that second-order belief is false. Sinners can purposely engage in this kind of activity, for they also deceive themselves about their motivation in handling the evidence as they do and about their real intentions, which are not noble or rational at all. Thereby they "go to sleep" (as it were), forgetting their God. Because the evidence is clear, and because the suppression of the truth is intentional, we can properly conclude that all men are "without excuse" and bear full responsibility for their sins of mind, speech, and conduct.[21]

Given the elaboration of self-deception offered here, we can better appreciate what Paul says in Romans 1, namely that "knowing God," all people "suppress the truth in unrighteousness." And it can be asserted in a non-contradictory fashion that unbelievers culpably deceive themselves about their Maker.

Although atheists deny they actually believe God exists, Romans 1 states otherwise.[22] The suppression of the knowledge of God is the result of self-deception. Apologists know that the unbeliever knows God, and must try to clear away the rationalizations of deceit.

Methodological Neutrality

This section will examine the issue of methodological neutrality. It is on this topic that presuppositionalism is frequently criticized. A stark distinction emerges at this point between evidential approaches and presuppositionalism, since the former demand a common, neutral set of logical ground rules for discussing the existence of God and the rationality of the Christian worldview, whereas the latter refuses to acknowledge that neutrality is even theoretically, let alone practically, possible. The commonality that evidential schools claim is necessary for apologetics the presuppositionalists claim does not, and cannot, exist. At the heart of the issue this debate is not about differences of degree, but differences of kind.

---

21. Bahnsen, "Crucial Concept," 32.
22. Baker, "Romans 1:18–21 and Presuppositional Apologetics," 281–82.

An excellent example of searching for neutral, common ground rules is provided in the perspective of Sproul, Gerstner, and Lindsley when they write:

> Certain assumptions regarding the knowing process, for example, are virtually universal. These assumptions are shared by theists and nontheists alike, particularly when they are applied outside of the emotion-laden debate about the existence of God. We are not seeking at this point to construct or reconstruct an entire epistemology, but are seeking shared or common assumptions between theist and nontheist. We are not seeking those views which separate Kant and Paul, Descartes and Locke, Hume and Aquinas, Kierkegaard and Russel [sic], but for those assumptions which, despite their differences, they commonly hold . . . We are searching for assumptions which are neither arbitrary nor subjective, but which function by practical necessity, are objective, and are or should be nonnegotiables in any discussion of truth. In our effort to challenge assumptions, we are seeking to discover those assumptions which must remain intact if truth is to be possible. In a sense, we are proceeding in a kind of transcendental fashion by asking the question, "What are the assumptions necessary for life and knowledge to be possible?" At this point we are not inquiring about ontological prerequisites to life and truth, but epistemological prerequisites.[23]

Several points are worth noting. The first is that, underneath the cloud of contradictory and obscuring details, they believe that all philosophers share universal assumptions. These assumptions can be discovered and then utilized as a neutral, assumed starting point. The second point is that these principles are taken not as subjective, but objective. Third, the approach is stylistically transcendental, looking for non-negotiable preconditions for thought. Fourth, the principles are epistemic, not ontological or metaphysical.

As was noted in the second chapter, the three minimum, basic assumptions they find are: "1. the validity of the law of noncontradiction; 2. the validity of the law of causality; 3. the basic reliability of sense perception."[24] They note that these laws have been theoretically challenged from time to time, but all such challenges are *"forced* and *temporary."*[25]

---

23. Sproul, Gerstner, and Lindsley, *Classical Apologetics*, 71. See also 70–72.
24. Ibid., 72.
25. Ibid.; emphasis in original.

Admittedly, they also view the basic reliability of sense perception in a different light than the other two laws. Human senses are fallible, and so can only be generally, not perfectly, reliable.[26] This poses a very interesting question, to which they provide an even more interesting answer: "But with all these qualifiers, how can we be sure that our senses are even basically reliable and not totally distortive? We cannot. That is why we are left with the common sense necessity of assuming it."[27]

Leaving aside possible points of criticism for the present, there is a difference between basic, underlying epistemological principles and the use of these principles. Habermas remarks that "Contemporary apologists usually agree that no one can pursue evidence in a neutral manner, due to many sorts of biases and prejudices that color our thinking."[28] Clark states very strongly that reason is not neutral, and that nobody is unbiased or without prejudices for weighing evidence and argument.[29] There is no neutral perspective that one can occupy where everything is seen as it actually is. Thus, even if there are principles that are universally shared, consistently implementing them will not simply lead everyone to the same conclusions. Evidence is liked or disliked, and this strongly influences how much existential "weight" a claim is given. The history of philosophy should make exceedingly clear that interpretation of reality is not a matter of intelligent, trained specialists learning and then applying a few baseline rules that inevitably lead to shared conclusions.

For presuppositionalism, the search for epistemic non-negotiable principles underlying every person's thinking is as futile as expecting everyone to use these principles and end up thinking exactly the same way. As was noted in chapter 4, epistemology cannot be detached from metaphysics and ontology. It is now time to examine a little more carefully why this is the case.

What the human thinker is, and what the universe is, cannot be set aside while timeless, non-situated principles of thought are decided upon, or even merely identified. The strength of this position comes out most forcefully when the basic reliability of the senses is assumed, but it is also problematic for the law of causality. Just deciding that common sense

26. Ibid., 87.
27. Ibid.
28. Habermas, "Evidentialist's Response," 243.
29. Clark, "Reformed Epistemologist's Closing Remarks," 365.

makes accepting the basic reliability of the senses necessary does not in any way make the deliverances of the senses *accurate*. We might not be able to escape a circular reliance on the senses, but this has nothing to do with their contact with reality. Such an assumption attempts to merge the phenomenal realm and the noumenal realm, but this is too facile a maneuver. Things cannot just be uncritically taken to be what they seem to be to us, on the strength of the argument that since our reasons for justifying sense perception fail, we will just accept common sense, and call it rational.

If the universe is chaos, time, motion, and chance, there is no reason to think that causality obtains, nor reason to think that, if it did, our senses would reliably connect the proper causal relationships. Why think that, as a rule, human senses and rationality can, in a chaotic universe, identify the difference (if there is a difference) between causal relationships and correlational relationships? Metaphysics is inescapable for epistemology, and vice versa. What obtains, and the activity of justifying human thought, are inseparably related. Even if rejecting the Ligoniers's rules is forced and temporary for humans, this does not mean that these rules are either accurate or truth-producing.

In the actual apologetic encounter, however, the issue is not so much rules of thought as it is human, subjective bias. Van Til wrote a pamphlet entitled *Why I Believe in God*, which Bahnsen reprinted in his book *Van Til's Apologetic*. Van Til argues that everyone is conditioned to either believe in God or not to believe in God.[30] It is not a matter of either being taught to believe in God or being taught to be open-minded; it is a matter of being taught belief or unbelief. Education is connected and controlled by the Christian worldview or it is not. There is no such thing as being "without bias"; this is just another way of identifying a different kind of bias.[31]

If the Christian worldview is true, then the non-believer has a very real reason to want to reject it. The non-Christian has insulted their Creator, Sustainer, and Judge; as a result, they are not on "speaking terms" with God.[32] In weighing evidence, the non-Christian has assumed that they do not need God in order to decide whether or not he exists. They

---

30. Van Til, "Why I Believe in God," 126.
31. Ibid., 127.
32. Ibid., 132.

have assumed that they are sufficient for the investigation, and thus any fact that challenges their self-sufficiency will be disallowed.[33] Van Til states:

> For what you have really done in your handling of the evidence for belief in God, is to set yourself up as God. You have made the reach of your intellect, the standard of what is possible or not possible. You have thereby virtually determined that you intend never to meet a fact that points to God. Facts, to be facts at all—facts, that is, with decent scientific and philosophic standing—must have your stamp instead of that of God upon them as their virtual creator.[34]

With a tendentious use of logic and evidence, Van Til believed the non-believer would find a way to reject the Christian worldview.[35] At a deeper level, however, this destroys all chance for human intelligibility.[36] Regardless of the argument, the unbeliever finds a way to weigh the evidence and arguments in a manner that rationalizes holding that it is impossible or unnecessary to believe in God.

Taking the Reformed doctrine of total depravity seriously, Van Til's analysis seems correct on the level of the non-believer strongly desiring the falsity of the Christian worldview. This perspective is not unique to presuppostionalism. That sinners do not want God and judgment to be true can be accepted by apologists of any stripe. At this point, however, the link with the *sensus divinitatis* becomes important. All people *know* God, and yet do not want to know him. Evidence will be skewed in the direction of desire. Explanations will be afforded weight on the basis of the heart. In this post-lapsarian world, the Reformed position is that there is no person who uses their mental capacity in a neutral manner. Truth is distorted and suppressed, not because it is not known and plain, but because it is unpalatable to the unbeliever. Thus the bias of the unbeliever away from God is crucial in Reformed apologetics: the unbeliever is not neutral, and will not reason fairly and neutrally. The reason why unbelievers reject certain arguments and accept others is bound up with their suppression of the truth of the existence of God. Because they are emotionally

33. Ibid., 133.
34. Ibid., 138.
35. Ibid., 143.
36. Ibid., 142.

and spiritually hostile to God, they use their intellects to dismiss him. The root issue is spiritual and emotive, and only secondarily intellectual. Ironically, it is the existence of God that is necessary to understand this set of dispositions. To make the existence of God a neutral possibility, and then to expect the non-believer to autonomously reason to accepting the God of the Bible, is to deny total depravity. There should be no disjunction here between Reformed doctrine and Reformed apologetics.

THE JUSTIFICATION OF METHODOLOGICAL ASSUMPTIONS

The main thesis of this section is that none of the positions examined in this book can stand without coming to terms with the interface between presuppositions and evidence. Evidentialism does not exist in a presupposition-less sphere. Reformed epistemology strives to establish the rationality of Christian belief, but the original warrant is only prima facie and can be overridden by defeaters. Evidence and argument are required to defend the validity of continuing to hold to Christian belief in light of counter-evidence and counter-argument. Presuppositionalism, although standing one step behind putative evidence, still requires evidence and argument to maintain its position. It does not eschew argument, as the appeal to transcendental reasoning demonstrates, and it requires the deconstruction of the non-believer's worldview.

When pressed into dialectic camps, there are extreme differences between the various Reformed apologetic methodologies, as Chapters 2–4 made inescapably clear. They are by no means identical. Nevertheless, they are also capable of being related to each other in mutually beneficial and enriching ways. They provide unique frames of reference in which singular pieces of data and individual facts can be interpreted. From a Reformed perspective, it is arguable that the most promising apologetic methodology will operate from a biblical-theological framework (i.e., with biblical presuppositions), and will ramify this framework with as much evidence and rational argument as possible. Neither the scaffolding nor the bricks may be neglected in building a compelling and cogent defense of the faith.

Behind the search for, and presentation of, evidence and argument, there are assumptions that need to be made. As was mentioned above, the Ligonier apologists assume the law of non-contradiction, the law of causality, and the basic reliability of the senses. This may be justifiable on a pragmatic basis, or in terms of conventionalism, but it is doubtful that all three assumptions (noting the extreme weakness of the third even in comparison with the other two) can be justified in terms of pure rational thought, or pure empirical investigation. The law of causality has been extensively criticized, and in many ways our formulation of it is dependent on the basic reliability of our senses. Observation and then inference to causal explanation is too weighted to be an operating assumption at the outset. Even the law of non-contradiction can be doubted, when it is set in analogous relation to the supposedly self-evident axioms of Euclidean geometry.[37] As Pepper cogently observes, there are many "self-evident" facts that turn out to conflict with other "self-evident" facts, or suffer from internal inconsistencies. The final result is that the category of "self-evident" becomes suspicious. As has already been pointed out, self-evident epistemological standards like those found in classical foundationalism fail their own test.

It is also important to recognize that human rules of thought must be calibrated to metaphysical and ontological reality. The Reformed epistemologists, as outlined in chapter 3, have done an excellent job arguing that the trustworthiness of human cognition is dependent on what the brain is designed for, and how successful that design plan has been in both the subject's mini-environment and maxi-environment. A key insight here is that epistemology cannot float free from metaphysics. Human thought is not isolated in pure and detached Platonic forms. What the world actually is, and what humans actually are, cannot be laid aside when epistemological procedure is being considered.

As was seen in chapter 4, presuppositionalism makes the strong claim that a fundamental difference between Christian thought and non-Christian thought is over the nature of the law of non-contradiction. For the former, the law of non-contradiction is what God understands it to be, but for the latter, it is a rule used to legislate the bounds of the possible. Finite minds use their own understanding to disallow the infinite. Presuppositionalists also spend a great deal of energy arguing that metaphysics and ontology are prerequisites to epistemology. They are part of an inseparable whole, or a worldview. If the universe is brought into existence as a chance event, and if it operates with chance, causation is an incoherent concept. Humans may observe and make inferences, but

---

37. Pepper, *World Hypotheses*, 22–24.

there is no foundation for it; in fact, the inferences will be invariably mistaken, owing to the fact that an inference would be providing an ordered scheme, or positing causal relations that do not exist. Furthermore, if the universe is a chaotic string of random, unrelated events, then the events of the human brain are likewise not to be trusted. The very idea of an *inference* is illegitimate in such a universe, since brain states are unrelated to each other in any logical or coherent manner. Events may happen in the brain, but they would constitute nothing more than random, disconnected, successive events.

Basic metaphysics, ontology, and epistemology must be interrelated, and support each other in an unavoidably circular way. Plato and Hume had very different epistemologies, and if they had been able to debate, they would have been forced to engage their unique positions on metaphysics, since their respective epistemologies and metaphysics were inseparably linked.[38] Total worldviews as systems cannot be ignored. Every refinement in knowledge will be ultimately justified on the basis of assumptions, givens, or presuppositions; this may not be the case for proximate justificatory appeals, but it will inevitably be the case for appeals that stop before a looming infinite regress. It may be more psychologically restful to envision the refinements as asymptotic, or spiraling rather than tightly circular, but the end result is the same: advancements do not bring us beyond, but only rather back to, the inescapable bedrock cluster of what is, what we are, and how we think. Even when we find out we were wrong about something massively important, we discover that our previous error was discoverable only because of what actually is (metaphysics). In other words, we may believe many false things, but when their falsity is revealed it is because what actually obtains is conducive to discovering truth. Metaphysical reality was propping us up even when we were involved in formulaic error. We do not make discoveries of truth in spite of what is; we make them because of what is.

Presenting a set, system, or worldview involves the interrelationship of these three key components—what is, what we are, and how we think. The strength of the presuppositional apologetical model is that it refuses to even attempt to seal these areas off hermetically from each other. Such sealing is impossible, because the areas are organically interdependent. For the sake of heuristic philosophical convenience they can be separated

---

38. Bahnsen, *Van Til's Apologetic*, 263–64.

(the way the attributes of God can be separated in systematic theology), but they must go together as a cohesive whole in order to stand. This entire worldview is not built up from earth to heaven, either through rationalism or empiricism, since neither of these approaches (or eclectic combinations) can succeed in finding an Archimedean point for establishing the Christian worldview. On the contrary, the Christian worldview is delivered from heaven to earth by God, which is the only way that such a perspective could come to human beings. Revelation (as in the doctrine of Reformed theology, not the New Testament book) is necessary for the biblical worldview to be comprehended.

This biblical revelation discloses a metaphysical state of affairs that is not random; a human creature made in God's image; a human mind capable of true knowledge, through logic, empirical data, and inference; and an omniscient, omnipotent, omnibenevolent God who is himself Truth, and wants truth to be known and valued. In this worldview, metaphysics, ontology, and epistemology are related in such a way as to make human cognition intelligible. Upon further reflection, it seems that an individual is within their rights to conclude that the interrelationship between these three components as revealed in the biblical worldview is actually a necessary precondition for intelligibility. In other words, the Christian worldview is transcendentally required for human knowledge and experience to be coherent. The arguments about facts cannot be removed from the argument about fact, and factuality requires a cogently related metaphysic, ontology, and epistemology. The Reformed theologian can find the necessary worldview revealed; from this vantage point Christianity can be defended, and the inadequacies of other worldviews exposed.

These reflections are what ultimately provide an answer to the complaint that presuppositionalism insists on accepting the Bible's claim to be a special revelation from God, while rejecting other sources that also claim to be supernaturally revealed. What grounds does one have for accepting the Bible's claims, while rejecting the same claims when they are made for another book? John Warwick Montgomery phrases the objection in the following way: "Abu Qurra, having had contact with Muslim proselytizing, saw clearly what the presuppositional apologist so often forgets: that the religious situation is *pluralistic*. Fallen man is not confronted with but one alleged message from the Father; he hears a cacophony of conflicting religious claims. What is he to do?"[39] Or, as Kelly James Clark states the case: "Each person must decide (tacitly or explicitly) that a purported revelation *is* revelation. Each person must decide that what is being said in some particular holy writ *is* the voice of God."[40]

Earlier chapters detailed the position that receiving the Scriptures as the Word of God can be compared analogously to discerning the wetness of water or the sweetness of something sweet. And there is also the issue that was raised (in a linguistically awkward fashion) between proximate and ultimate starting points. If the Scriptures are comprehended for what they are, they will prove to reveal the worldview that is necessary to make sense of knowledge. The individual should realize that their rationality, which they have been using all their lives, has ever only been grounded and justified on the view of reality found in the Bible. In other words, to reject the Scriptures will logically entail a rejection of their own knowledge. While there is a plurality of books claiming inspiration and religious truth, only the Christian Scriptures present the way that everything *must be* in order for the rational judgments of human beings to be intelligible. The previous skepticism towards the Bible as special revelation should yield to the understanding that, all along, all coherence has been depending on the Bible's revelation being objectively true. Plurality of putative revelation can be met by the apologist on grounds other than the theistic arguments and historical evidences.

CONCLUSION

Evidential apologetics are not able to prove the inerrancy of the Scriptures. Even if the biblical writers who recorded the event of the resurrection of Jesus report the core of that historical event accurately, there are too many other details that are not proven to be true on that basis. Attempting to argue from the historicity of the resurrection to knowing all of Jesus' words, and knowing that Jesus endorsed the entire Old Testament canon as inerrant, and then knowing that this applied into the future for the books that would be accepted as the New Testament canon, goes beyond the boundaries of what an evidential methodology can adequately demonstrate. Evidentialism is not neutral, nor does it operate without foundational presuppositions. In the final analysis, there are too many

---

39. Montgomery, "Once upon an A Priori," 389.
40. Clark, "Reformed Epistemologist's Response," 262.

items in the Scriptures that simply fall beyond the scope of evidentialism's credentials for investigation and proof.

Reformed epistemology allows (if formulated in a particular way) for the inerrancy of Scripture as a doctrine to be accepted either as properly basic, or else on the basis of a deduction from a basic belief. On the basis of the way that it has been articulated, however, one can accept the resurrection and reject inerrancy. There are also critical problems concerning the *sensus divinitatis*: if such a disposition or faculty does not exist, the entire model fails to convince. Furthermore, the entire model allows for Christian belief to be *rational*, but it does not require that Christian belief be *true*. Thus inerrancy may be rejected as outside of the great things of the gospel, and even if it is accepted, it is seen as a rationally justified belief that may be false. There is a sound awareness, however, that epistemological warrant is not separable from human neurology and the metaphysical environment.

Presuppositionalism accepts the entire Christian worldview (as found in classical, creedal Reformed theology), including the doctrine of the inerrant Word. This worldview is dependent on revelation. Revelation is received, and then the world is interpreted on its basis. The claim is that since the actual state of affairs is what the Bible depicts it to be, it is foolish to try to work through reality as if it is not. Presuppositions are inescapable; if the apologist uses the non-Christian's presuppositions (which are false) the Christian worldview will never be successfully created. In fact, the non-Christian, having an ultimately false metaphysic, ontology, and therefore epistemology, will fail to be consistent, and cannot actually justify their claims of knowledge. The level of argument is transcendental, getting behind putative facts to assumptions, givens, and presuppositions.

Rather than atomization, the clash is between full worldviews. But full worldviews can only be articulated piece by piece. Individual elements need to be identified, and set in coherent relief. In my judgment, Reformed apologetic methodologies are set up in opposition to each other more than is necessary. If a presuppositional structure was adopted, and then individual pieces of evidence and rational argument were fitted into that structure, I believe Reformed apologetics could be very successful indeed. The evidence requires the ultimate backing of biblical presuppositions, but the evidence is not dispensable. If Reformed apologetics were likened to defensive battlements, the presuppositions would be the foundation, while the evidences would be the walls. The latter are supported by the former and dependent on it, but the former without the latter, even though it may be strong and immovable, is unable to provide for defense. In the short conclusion of this study, the possibilities for this position will be lightly sketched.

6

Conclusion

In the Gospel of Luke, Jesus tells a parable about a rich man and a poor beggar named Lazarus (Luke 16:19–31). The rich man lives in luxury, but in death he finds himself tormented in Hades. He wants his relatives who are still living to be warned about the torment that awaits them after death unless they change their ways and live righteously. The rich man beseeches Abraham to warn his brothers by sending Lazarus (who has also died but is receiving good things) to tell them about the afterlife, but Abraham replies: "They have Moses and the prophets; let them listen to them" (16:29). The rich man does not think this is sufficient, and responds: "No, father Abraham, but if someone from the dead goes to them, they will repent." Admittedly, this sounds quite plausible. Surely people would accept the message of the Scriptures if someone came back to warn them from the dead! Nevertheless, Abraham's reply is counterintuitive: "If they do not listen to Moses and the prophets, they will not be convinced even if someone rises from the dead."

What kind of evidence is required to convince people that the claims of the Bible are true? It would seem that, even if a person could return from beyond the grave, this would fail to convince those who are not willing to accept what the Scriptures teach. There is a human predisposition to interpret evidence in ways that attempt to somehow justify failing to accept the Christian worldview. A return from the dead could hardly be of better evidential value: but, according to Jesus, even this is insufficient to convince those who do not want to be convinced by Scripture.

Evidential apologetics has been subdivided into two approaches. One method begins with arguing for theism, and then moves to Christian evidences (with the main evidence being the resurrection), and the other approach begins with Christian evidence and argues back to theism (again, with the main evidence being the resurrection). Regardless of the particular evidential sequence that is favored, the apologetic importance of the historical case for the resurrection of Jesus Christ cannot be underestimated. There is a sense in which the resurrection is as central to apologetics as it is to theology. Yet, as has been seen, all apologetic methods that try to move from the resurrection to the doctrine of Scripture are insufficient. Rather than attempting the move from resurrection to Scripture, the proper Reformed apologetic method justifies belief in the resurrection on the basis of the testimony of the Holy Spirit through Scripture, or simultaneously holds them both together in a coherent whole. The theological-biblical set, or Christian worldview, is found to be transcendentally necessary for all human experience to be meaningful.

As chapter 4 indicated, presuppositionalists are not against evidence. In fact, evidence is an integral part of the presuppositional apologetic strategy. Since the presuppositionalist is willing to start with any fact, and since all facts are interrelated, individual facts are extremely relevant and important. It must be acknowledged that the best historical arguments that deal *directly* with the resurrection have been formulated by evidentialists. They have taken the resurrection as a fact open to historical investigation, and have investigated it with logic, data, and plausible reconstruction. All Christians should be thankful for how far these lines of evidence will take them.

Ultimately, however, in order to span the tremendous canyon between material events and the inference that God is the causal agent, more than evidentialism is required. There are distinct limitations to evidential, inductive, and rational investigations. This is not really a very profound criticism; it is simply the nature of things. As Kant brilliantly realized, there must be transcendental preconditions in order for human categorization and belief to be rational. A successful transcendental argument for the existence of God, as maintained by the presuppositionalists, is what provides the philosophical framework for the evidential, direct historical investigation of the resurrection. This relationship can, in my judgment, be mutually beneficial.

Presuppositionalism has been working on the transcendental approach, arguing for the whole of the Christian worldview, attempting to express the preconditions for factuality to be a coherent category.

Evidential apologetics has been rigorously formulating and tightening up arguments for the resurrection as a historical fact. The former provides the basis for human investigation to be intelligible; the latter provides evidence that the resurrection was a historical event. When these two approaches are combined, there is an indirect, transcendental approach that establishes a framework on which the direct, evidential considerations can be supported. While the latter may not be necessary in the strictest sense, it does serve the purpose of providing corroborating data. Perhaps the best apologetic method would be a presuppositionalism that truly takes individual pieces of evidence seriously, and understands its debt to evidential thinkers and apologists.

In this regard, it should be mentioned that Reformed epistemology, although not a complete apologetic system, has provided a very important reminder to the Christian community that many beliefs do not need to rest on argumentation to be justified. Many people are quite within their epistemic rights to accept the claims of Christianity, even if they have never heard any of the philosophical arguments for or against it. While the model for this warranted Christian belief is problematic (not least, as was seen in the previous chapter, in terms of the *sensus divinitatis*), it is a salutary reminder that apologists should be prepared to defend the rationality of an individual believing apart from their having self-consciously constructed rational arguments to justify their faith. If Christianity is true, the gospel can be (and in fact most often is) accepted on the basis of the internal instigation of the Holy Spirit, apart from any critical, philosophical analysis. Some Christians believe without rigorous, critical thought; professional apologists should make defending the ones in that position an important part of their agenda. After all, many children believe, and many adults without formal education believe: holding Christian truth must be warranted for them, even apart from philosophical, rational study. Perhaps ecclesiology figures into this equation. In the church, as one body, faith is rationally defended, even if not all individuals have the training and study to conduct this defense themselves. There are many parts and many gifts, but one body: another example of unity and diversity.

In the previous chapter the ability to move from the resurrection to the Reformed doctrine of the inerrancy of Scripture was examined. It was demonstrated that the evidential method is insufficient to prove that the Bible is actually inerrant. There are too many aspects of the Scriptures that are simply outside of the evidential field of discovery. The conclusions that are necessary go beyond the reach of what evidentialism provides. Reformed epistemology does not demand inerrancy, and may reject it. It is also subject to potential defeaters, and so is precarious for the defense of the inerrant Word.

Taking these thoughts into consideration, the conclusion of this book is that presuppositionalism is the best Reformed apologetic methodology, and that this is in fact demonstrated through examining the relationship between the doctrines of the resurrection and Scripture. Presuppositionalism takes the entire Reformed Christian worldview (inclusive of inerrancy) and defends the faith transcendentally. Nevertheless, a presuppositionalism that is truly appreciative of historical evidences, and is ramified with them, is better yet. The apologist should seek the strongest position, and this will include, rather than exclude, as much evidence and data as possible. Particular evidences may not be valuable enough to defend Christianity adequately by themselves, but this does not mean that they are valueless. As was seen in chapter 4, presuppositionalists say that evidence is important in the defense of the faith; this must not be just lip service, but must become more evidenced in their writings.

In researching this subject, I have been deeply impressed with the rigor and deep reflection of evidentialists on the historical data for the resurrection of Jesus Christ. Their contributions must not be dismissed or left out of the apologist's arsenal. Yet I find the need for reflecting on transcendental arguments to be necessary and inescapable. There must be something one step behind the evidential arguments; there must be preconditions for rationality. Epistemology, metaphysics, and ontology are not ultimately divisible; something must relate them that makes rationality possible, or all thinking and experience will be incoherent and unintelligible. The best defense of the faith is that, unless a theistic worldview is presupposed as a transcendental necessity, nothing at all can be known.

Going forward, then, presuppositionalists should spend even more time with evidences. As I quoted Frame in chapter 4, this was his recommendation at the end of his book on Van Til's thought.[1] Habermas also argues that presuppositionalists talk about evidence, and complain that evidentialists misuse evidence, but they never go on to show how to use evidence properly in a presuppositional model.[2] Kelly James Clark objects

---

1. Frame, *Cornelius Van Til*, 400.
2. Habermas, "Evidentialist's Response," 239–41.

that presuppositionalists have not proven that mathematics, logic, and all impersonal views of the universe are irrational apart from Christian theism.[3] Frame, for his part, acknowledges that much work remains to be done in presuppositional thought, and that more thinking and writing needs to take place.[4] Needless to say, the same is true for all apologetic methodologies. Much work yet remains to be done, and the Christian apologist (of whatever methodological conviction) must continue in the task of defending the faith. It is a task that is not complete, and as with theology, there is still light to be shed from God's Word to God's church.

---

3. Clark, "Reformed Epistemologist's Response," 260–61.
4. Frame, "Presuppositional Apologist's Closing Remarks," 353.

Bibliography

Alston, William. *Beyond "Justification": Dimensions of Epistemic Evaluation*. Ithaca, NY: Cornell University Press, 2005.
———. "On Knowing That We Know: The Application to Religious Knowledge." In *Christian Perspectives on Religious Knowledge*, edited by C. Stephen Evans and Merold Westphal, 15–39. Grand Rapids: Eerdmans, 1993.
———. *Perceiving God: The Epistemology of Religious Experience*. Ithaca, NY: Cornell University Press, 1991.
———. "Response to Critics." *Religious Studies* 30 (1994) 171–80.
Anderson, James. "If Knowledge, Then God: The Epistemological Theistic Arguments of Alvin Plantinga and Cornelius Van Til." *Calvin Theological Journal* 40 (2005) 49–75.
Appleby, Peter. "Reformed Epistemology, Rationality, and Belief in God." *International Journal for Philosophy of Religion* 24 (1998) 129–41.
Bahnsen, Greg. *Always Ready: Directions for Defending the Faith*. Phillipsburg, NJ: Presbyterian & Reformed, 1996.
———. *An Answer to Frame's Critique of Van Til: Profound Differences between the Traditional and Presuppositional Method*. Glenside, PA: Westminster Seminary Bookstore, n.d.
———. "The Crucial Concept of Self-Deception in Presuppositional Apologetics." *Westminster Theological Journal* 57 (1995) 1–32.
———. *Van Til's Apologetic: Readings and Analysis*. Phillipsburg, NJ: Presbyterian & Reformed, 1998.
Baker, Bruce. "Romans 1:18–21 and Presuppositional Apologetics." *Bibliotheca Sacra* 155 (1998) 280–98.
Basinger, David. "Christian Theism and the Concept of Miracle: Some Epistemological Perplexities." *Southern Journal of Philosophy* 18 (1980) 137–50.
Beck, W. David. "A Thomistic Cosmological Argument." In *To Everyone an Answer: A Case for the Christian Worldview*, edited by Francis Beckwith, William Lane Craig, and J. P. Moreland, 95–107. Downers Grove, IL: InterVarsity, 2004.
Beckwith, Francis. *David Hume's Argument against Miracles: A Critical Analysis*. Lanham, MD: University Press of America, 1989.
Beilby, James. *Epistemology as Theology: An Evaluation of Alvin Plantinga's Religious Epistemology*. Burlington, VT: Ashgate, 2005.
Bostock, Gerald. "Osiris and the Resurrection of Christ." *Expository Times* 112 (2001) 265–71.
Brown, Colin. *Miracles and the Critical Mind*. Pasadena, CA: Fuller Seminary Press, 2006.
Brown, H. "Alvin Plantinga and Natural Theology." *International Journal for Philosophy of Religion* 30 (1991) 1–19.

Bibliography

Brown, Raymond. *An Introduction to the New Testament*. New York: Doubleday, 1997.

Brueckner, Anthony. "Transcendental Argument." In *The Cambridge Dictionary of Philosophy*, edited by Robert Audi, 925–26. 2nd ed., Cambridge: Cambridge University Press, 1999.

———. "Transcendental Arguments I." *Nous* 17 (1983) 551–75.

Calvin, John. *Institutes of the Christian Religion*. Vol. 1. Edited by John T. McNeill. Translated by Ford Lewis Battles. Louisville, KY: Westminster John Knox, 1960.

———. "Romans 1–16." *Calvin's Commentaries*. Vol. 19. Grand Rapids: Baker, 1999.

Carnely, Peter. *The Structure of Resurrection Belief*. Oxford: Clarendon, 1987.

Carson, D. A. *Collected Writings on Scripture*. Wheaton, IL: Crossway, 2010.

Carson, D. A., and John Woodbridge, eds. *Scripture and Truth*. Grand Rapids: Baker, 1992.

Carson, D. A., and Douglas Moo, eds. *An Introduction to the New Testament*. 2nd ed. Grand Rapids: Zondervan, 2005.

Casey, Maurice. *Jesus of Nazareth: An Independent Historian's Account of His Life and Teaching*. New York: T. & T. Clark, 2010.

Chisholm, Roderick. *The Foundations of Knowing*. Minneapolis: University of Minnesota Press, 1982.

Clark, Kelly James. "A Reformed Epistemologist's Closing Remarks." In Cowan, ed., *Five Views*, 364–73.

———. "A Reformed Epistemologist's Response." In Cowan, ed., *Five Views*, 255–63.

———. *Return to Reason: A Critique of Enlightenment Evidentialism and a Defense of Reason and Belief in God*. Grand Rapids: Zondervan, 1990.

Coakley, Sarah. *Christ without Absolutes: A Study of the Christology of Ernst Troeltsch*. Oxford: Clarendon, 1998.

Collett, Don. "Van Til and Transcendental Argument." In *Revelation and Reason: New Essays in Reformed Apologetics*, edited by K. Scott Oliphint and Lane G. Tipton, 258–78. Phillipsburg, NJ: Presbyterian & Reformed, 2007.

Collins, C. John. *Science and Faith: Friends or Foes?* Wheaton, IL: Crossway, 2003.

Colwell, Jason. "The Historical Argument for the Christian Faith: A Response to Alvin Plantinga." *International Journal for Philosophy of Religion* 53 (2003) 147–61.

Cook, John. "Pagan Philosophers and 1 Thessalonians." *New Testament Studies* 52 (2006) 514–32.

Cover, J. A. "Miracles and Christian Theism." In *Reason for the Hope Within*, edited by Michael Murray, 345–74. Grand Rapids: Eerdmans, 1999.

Cowan, Steven, ed. *Five Views on Apologetics*. Grand Rapids: Zondervan, 2000.

Craig, William Lane. *Assessing the New Testament Evidence for the Historicity of the Resurrection of Jesus*. Lewiston, NY: Edwin Mellen, 1989.

———. "Classical Apologetics." In Cowan, ed., *Five Views*, 26–55.

———. "A Classical Apologist's Closing Remarks." In Cowan, ed., *Five Views*, 314–28.

———. "A Classical Apologist's Response." In Cowan, ed., *Five Views*, 285–90.

———. *Reasonable Faith: Christian Truth and Apologetics*. Rev. ed. Wheaton, IL: Crossway, 1994.

———. *The Son Rises: The Historical Evidence for the Resurrection of Jesus*. 1981. Reprint: Eugene, OR: Wipf & Stock, 2000.

Davis, Stephen T. *Risen Indeed: Making Sense of the Resurrection*. Grand Rapids: Eerdmans, 1993.

Dawid, Philip, and Donald Gillies. "A Bayesian Analysis of Hume's Argument concerning Miracles." *Philosophical Quarterly* 39 (1989) 57–65.

Bibliography

DeMar, Gary. *Pushing the Antithesis: The Apologetic Methodology of Greg L. Bahnsen*. Powder Springs, GA: American Vision, 2007.

Earman, John. *Hume's Abject Failure: The Argument against Miracles*. New York: Oxford University Press, 2000.

Edgar, William. "Introduction." In *Christian Apologetics*, by Cornelius Van Til, 1–15. 2nd ed. Phillipsburg, PA: Presbyterian & Reformed, 2003.

Evans, C. Stephen. "Evidentialist and Non-Evidentialist Accounts of Historical Religious Knowledge." *International Journal for Philosophy of Religion* 35 (1994) 153–82.

Feldman, Richard. "Plantinga on Exclusivism." *Faith and Philosophy* 20 (2003) 85–90.

Feldman, Richard, and Earl Conee. "Evidentialism." In *Epistemology: An Anthology*, edited by Ernest Sosa, Jaegwon Kim, Jeremy Fantl, and Matthew McGrath, 311–32. 2nd ed. Malden, MA: Blackwell, 2008.

Flew, Antony. *God and Philosophy*. New York: Hutchinson, 1966.

———. *Hume's Philosophy of Belief: A Study of His First Inquiry*. New York: The Humanities Press, 1961.

———. *There Is a God: How the World's Most Notorious Atheist Changed His Mind*. New York: HarperOne, 2007.

Fogelin, Robert. *A Defense of Hume on Miracles*. Princeton, NJ: Princeton University Press, 2003.

Forland, Tor Egil. "God, Science, and Historical Explanation." *History and Theory: Studies in the Philosophy of History* 47 (2008) 483–94.

———. "Historiography without God: A Reply to Gregory." *History and Theory: Studies in the Philosophy of History* 47 (2008) 520–32.

Frame, John. *Apologetics to the Glory of God: An Introduction*. Phillipsburg, NJ: Presbyterian & Reformed, 1994.

———. *Cornelius Van Til: An Analysis of His Thought*. Phillipsburg, NJ: Presbyterian & Reformed, 1995.

———. *The Doctrine of the Word of God*. Phillipsburg, NJ: Presbyterian & Reformed, 2010.

———. "Presuppositional Apologetics." In Cowan, ed., *Five Views*, 208–31.

———. "A Presuppositional Apologist's Closing Remarks." In Cowan, ed., *Five Views*, 350–63.

———. "A Presuppositionalist's Response." In Cowan, ed., *Five Views*, 132–37.

———. 1996a. http://www.reformed.org/master/index.html?mainframe=/apologetics/martin/framecontra_martin.html.

———. 1996b. http://www.reformed.org/master/index.html?mainframe=/apologetics/martin/frame_contra_martin2.html.

———. 1996c. http://www.reformed.org/master/index.html?mainframe=/apologetics/martin/frame_contra_martin3.html.

———. 1996d. http://www.reformed.org/master/index.html?mainframe=/apologetics/martin/frame_contra_martin4.html.

Fumerton, Richard. "Plantinga, Warrant, and Christian Belief." *Philosophia Christi* 3 (2001) 341–51.

Gale, Richard. "On the Cognitivity of Mystical Experiences." *Faith and Philosophy* 22 (2005) 426–41.

———. "The Overall Argument of Alston's *Perceiving God*." *Religious Studies* 30 (1994) 135–49.

Bibliography

Garcia, Laura. "Natural Theology and the Reformed Objection." In *Christian Perspectives on Religious Knowledge*, edited by C. Stephen Evans and Merold Westphal, 112–33. Grand Rapids: Eerdmans, 1993.

Geisler, Norman. *Christian Apologetics*. 1976. Reprint: Peabody, MA: Prince Press, 2003.

Geisler, Norman, and William Nix. *A General Introduction to the Bible*. Chicago: Moody, 1968.

Geivett, Douglas. "The *Kalam* Cosmological Argument." In *To Everyone an Answer: A Case for the Christian Worldview*, edited by Francis Beckwith, William Lane Craig, and J. P. Moreland, 61–76. Downers Grove, IL: InterVarsity, 2004.

———. "Two Versions of the Cosmological Argument." In *Passionate Conviction: Contemporary Discourses on Christian Apologetics*, edited by Paul Copan and William Lane Craig, 52–68. Nashville: Broadman & Holman, 2007.

Goetz, Stewart. "Belief in God Is Not Properly Basic." *Religious Studies* 19 (1983) 475–84.

Gowen, Julie. "Foundationalism and the Justification of Religious Belief." *Religious Studies* 19 (1983) 393–406.

Gram, Moltke. "Transcendental Arguments." *Nous* 5 (1971) 15–26.

Gregory, Brad. "No Room for God? History, Science, Metaphysics, and the Study of Religion." *History and Theory: Studies in the Philosophy of History* 47 (2008) 495–519.

Grier, James. "The Apologetic Value of the Self-Witness of Scripture." *Grace Theological Journal* 1, no. 1 (1980) 71–76.

Grigg, Richard. "The Crucial Disanalogies between Properly Basic Belief and Belief in God." *Religious Studies* 26 (1990) 389–401.

———. "Theism and Proper Basicality: A Response to Plantinga." *International Journal for Philosophy of Religion* 14 (1983) 123–27.

Grimm, Stephen. "Cardinal Newman, Reformed Epistemologist?" *American Catholic Philosophical Quarterly* 75 (2001) 497–522.

Grudem, Wayne. *Systematic Theology: An Introduction to Biblical Doctrine*. Grand Rapids: Zondervan, 1994.

Habermas, "Evidential Apologetics." In Cowan, ed., *Five Views*, 92–121.

———. "An Evidential Apologist's Closing Remarks." In Cowan, ed., *Five Views*, 329–44.

———. "An Evidentialist's Response." In Cowan, ed., *Five Views*, 291–301.

———. "Resurrection Claims in Non-Christian Religions." *Religious Studies* 25 (1989) 167–77.

———. *The Resurrection of Jesus: An Apologetic*. Grand Rapids: Baker, 1984.

Habermas, Gary, and Antony Flew. *Did Jesus Rise from the Dead? The Resurrection Debate*, edited by Terry Miethe. San Francisco: Harper & Row, 1987.

Habermas, Gary, and Michael Licona. *The Case for the Resurrection of Jesus*. Grand Rapids: Kregel, 2004.

Halper, Edward. "One-Many Problem." In *The Cambridge Dictionary of Philosophy*, edited by Robert Audi, 630. 2nd ed. Cambridge: Cambridge University Press, 1999.

Harrisville, Roy, and Walter Sundberg. *The Bible in Modern Culture: Theology and Historical Critical Method from Spinoza to Käsemann*. Grand Rapids: Eerdmans, 1995.

Haught, John. *Is Nature Enough? Meaning and Truth in the Age of Science*. Cambridge: Cambridge University Press, 2006.

Helm, Paul. "John Calvin, the *Sensus Divinitatis*, and the Noetic Effects of Sin." *International Journal for Philosophy of Religion* 43 (1998) 87–107.

———. *The Varieties of Belief*. New York: Humanities, 1973.

Hoitenga, Dewey Jr. *Faith and Reason from Plato to Plantinga: An Introduction to Reformed Epistemology*. New York: State University of New York Press, 1991.
Houlden, Leslie. "The Resurrection and Christianity." *Theology* 99 (1996) 198–205.
Houston, J. *Reported Miracles: A Critique of Hume*. New York: Cambridge University Press, 1994.
Howe, Leroy. "On the Resurrection and Lordship of Jesus Christ." *Asia Journal of Theology* 9 (1995) 318–30.
Hume, David. *An Enquiry concerning Human Understanding*. Oxford World's Classics. New York: Oxford University Press, 2007.
———. "Of Miracles." In *Philosophy of Religion: Selected Readings*, edited by William Rowe and William Wainwright, 492–99. 3rd ed. New York: Oxford University Press, 1998.
Jackson, William. *The Philosophy of Natural Theology: An Essay, in Confutation of the Skepticism of the Present Day*. London: Hodder & Stoughton, 1874.
Jeffreys, Derek. "How Reformed Is Reformed Epistemology? Alvin Plantinga and Calvin's 'Sensus Divinitatis.'" *Religious Studies* 33 (1997) 419–31.
Johnsen, Bredo. "Basic Theistic Belief." *Canadian Journal of Philosophy* 16 (1986) 455–64.
Koehl, Andrew. "Reformed Epistemology and Diversity." *Faith and Philosophy* 18 (2001) 168–91.
Korner, Stephan. "The Impossibility of Transcendental Deductions." *The Monist* 51 (1967) 317–31.
Kreeft, Peter. *Fundamentals of the Faith: Essays in Christian Apologetics*. San Francisco: Ignatius, 1988.
Kretzmann, Norman. "Mystical Perception: St Theresa, William Alston, and the Broadminded Atheist." In *Reason and the Christian Religion: Essays in Honour of Richard Swinburne*, edited by Alan Padgett, 65–90. Oxford: Clarendon, 1994.
Kuhn, Thomas. *The Structure of Scientific Revolutions*. 3rd ed. Chicago: University of Chicago Press, 1996.
Lake, Kirsopp. *The Historical Evidence for the Resurrection of Jesus Christ*. London: William & Norgate, 1907.
Le Morvan, Pierre, and Dana Radcliffe. "Plantinga on Warranted Christian Belief." *Heythrop Journal* 44 (2003) 345–51.
Langtry, Bruce. "Properly Unargued Belief in God." *International Journal for Philosophy of Religion* 26 (1989) 129–54.
Lewis, C. S. *Miracles: A Preliminary Study*. San Francisco: HarperCollins, 1947.
Lindars, Barnabas. "The Resurrection and the Empty Tomb." In *The Resurrection of Jesus Christ*, edited by Paul Avis, 116–35. London: Darton, Longman & Todd, 1993.
Lloyd-Jones, D. Martyn. *Romans, an Exposition of Chapter 1: The Gospel of God*. Grand Rapids: Zondervan, 1985.
Mackie, J. L. *The Miracle of Theism*. New York: Oxford University Press, 1982.
Martin, Michael. *Atheism: A Philosophical Justification*. Philadelphia, PA: Temple University Press, 1990.
———. *Atheism, Morality, and Meaning*. Amherst, NY: Prometheus, 2002.
———. 1997a. http://www.infidels.org/library/modern/michael_martin/tang.html.
———. 1997b. http://www.infidels.org/library/modern/michael_martin/matin frame/tang2.html.
———. 1997c. http://www.infidels.org/library/modern/michael_martin/matin frame/tang3.html.

Bibliography

———. 1997d. http://www.infidels.org/library/modern/michael_martin/matin frame/tang4.html

———. 1997e. http://www.infidels.org/library/modern/michael_martin/matin frame/tang5.html

Martin, Michael, and Rick Monnier, eds. *The Improbability of God*. Amherst, NY: Prometheus, 2006.

Martin, Michael, and Rick Monnier, eds. *The Impossibility of God*. Amherst, NY: Prometheus, 2003.

Mavrodes, George. "David Hume and the Probability of Miracles." *International Journal for Philosophy of Religion* 43 (1998) 167–82.

McDowell, Josh. *The New Evidence That Demands a Verdict*. Nashville, TN: Thomas Nelson, 1999.

McGrath, Alister. *Christian Theology: An Introduction*. Oxford: Blackwell, 1994.

McGrew, Timothy. "Has Plantinga Refuted the Historical Argument?" *Philosophia Christi* 6 (2004) 7–26.

McLeod, Mark. *Rationality and Theistic Belief: An Essay on Reformed Epistemology*. Ithaca, NY: Cornell University Press, 1993.

Meeker, Kevin. "William Alston's Epistemology of Religious Experience: A 'Reformed' Reformed Epistemology?" *International Journal for Philosophy of Religion* 35 (1994) 89–110.

Montgomery, John Warwick. "Contemporary Apologetics Lecture 3." Newburgh, IN: Trinity Theological Seminary, 2003. [audio cassette]

———. *Faith Founded on Fact: Essays in Evidential Apologetics*. Newburgh, IN: Trinity, 1978.

———, ed. *God's Inerrant Word: An International Symposium on the Trustworthiness of Scripture*. Newburgh, IN: Trinity, 1974.

———. "The Jury Returns: A Juridical Defense of Christianity." In *Evidence for Faith: Deciding the God Question*, edited by John Warwick Montgomery, 319–41. Dallas: Probe, 1991.

———. "Once upon an A Priori . . . :Van Til's Apologetic in Light of Three Fables." In *Jerusalem and Athens: Critical Discussions on the Philosophy and Apologetics of Cornelius Van Til*, edited by E. R. Geehan, 380–92. Phillipsburg, NJ: Presbyterian & Reformed, 1980.

———. *The Suicide of Christian Theology*. Newburgh, IN: Trinity, 1970.

———. *Where Is History Going? A Christian Response to Secular Philosophies of History*. 1969. Reprint, Newburgh, IN: Trinity, 2001.

Morison, Frank. *Who Moved the Stone?* London: Faber & Faber, 1930.

Morris, Leon. *The Epistle to the Romans*. Pillar New Testament Commentary. Grand Rapids: Eerdmans, 1988.

Morrison, Charles. *The Proofs of Christ's Resurrection: From a Lawyer's Standpoint*. Rev. ed. Andover: Warren F. Draper, 1885.

Moule, C. F. D., and Don Cupitt. "The Resurrection: A Disagreement." *Theology* 75 (1972) 507–19.

Muether, John. *Cornelius Van Til: Reformed Apologist and Churchman*. Phillipsburg, NJ: Presbyterian & Reformed, 2008.

Mulhall, Stephen. *Faith and Reason*. London: Duckworth, 1994.

Newman, Robert C. "Miracles and the Historicity of the Easter Week Narratives." In *Evidence for Faith: Deciding the God Question*, edited by John Warwick Montgomery, 275–302. Dallas: Probe, 1991.
Notaro, Thom. *Van Til and the Use of Evidence*. Phillipsburg: Presbyterian & Reformed, 1980.
O'Collins, Gerald. *Jesus Risen: An Historical, Fundamental and Systematic Examination of Christ's Resurrection*. New York: Paulist, 1987.
Oliphint, K. Scott. "The Irrationality of Unbelief: An Exegetical Study." In *Revelation and Reason: New Essays in Reformed Apologetics*, edited by K. Scott Oliphint and Lane G. Tipton, 59–73. Phillipsburg, NJ: Presbyterian & Reformed, 2007.
Oliphint, K. Scott, and Lane G. Tipton. "Introduction." In *Revelation and Reason: New Essays in Reformed Apologetics*, edited by K. Scott Oliphint and Lane G. Tipton, 1–10. Phillipsburg, NJ: Presbyterian & Reformed, 2007.
Overall, Christine. "Miracles as Evidence against the Existence of God." *Southern Journal of Philosophy* 23 (1985) 347–53.
Owen, David. "Hume *versus* Price on Miracles and Prior Probabilities: Testimony and the Bayesian Calculation." *Philosophical Quarterly* 37 (1987) 187–202.
Pannenberg, Wolfhart. *Basic Questions in Theology*. Vol. 1. Translated by George Kehm. Philadelphia: Fortress, 1970.
———. *Jesus—God and Man*. Translated by Lewis Wilkins and Duane Priebe. 2nd ed. Philadelphia: Westminster, 1977.
———. "Response to the Debate." In *Did Jesus Rise from the Dead? The Resurrection Debate*, edited by Terry Miethe, 125–35. San Francisco: Harper & Row, 1987.
———. *Toward a Theology of Nature: Essays on Science and Faith*. Louisville, KY: Westminster John Knox, 1993.
Pargetter, Robert. "Experience, Proper Basicality and Belief in God." *International Journal for Philosophy of Religion* 27 (1990) 141–63.
Pepper, Stephen. *World Hypotheses: Prolegomena to Systematic Philosophy and a Complete Survey of Metaphysics*. Berkeley: University of California Press, 1970.
Peterson, Michael, William Hasker, Bruce Reichenbach, and David Basinger. *Reason and Religious Belief: An Introduction to the Philosophy of Religion*. 2nd ed. New York: Oxford University Press, 1998.
Pinnock, Clark. *Set Forth Your Case: An Examination of Christianity's Credentials*. Chicago: Moody, 1971.
Pinnock, Clark, and Barry Callen. *The Scripture Principle: Reclaiming the Full Authority of the Bible*. Grand Rapids: Baker, 2006.
Plantinga, Alvin. *God and Other Minds: A Study of the Rational Justification of Belief in God*. Ithaca, NY: Cornell University Press, 1967.
———. *God, Freedom, and Evil*. Grand Rapids: Eerdmans, 1974.
———. "Internalism, Externalism, Defeaters and Arguments for Christian Belief." *Philosophia Christi* 3 (2001) 379–400.
———. "Rationality and Public Evidence: A Reply to Richard Swinburne." *Religious Studies* 37 (2001) 215–22.
———. *Warrant and Proper Function*. New York: Oxford University Press, 1993.
———. *Warrant: The Current Debate*. New York: Oxford University Press, 1993.
———. "*Warranted Christian Belief*. A Precis by the Author." *Philosophia Christi* 3 (2001) 327–28.
———. *Warranted Christian Belief*. New York: Oxford University Press, 2000.

Bibliography

Plantinga, Alvin, and Michael Tooley. *Knowledge of God*. Malden, MA: Blackwell, 2008.

Plantinga, Alvin, and Nicholas Wolterstorff, eds. *Faith and Rationality: Reason and Belief in God*. Notre Dame: Notre Dame University Press, 1983.

Polkinghorne, John. *Exploring Reality: The Intertwining of Science and Religion*. New Haven: Yale University Press, 2005.

Pritchard, Duncan. "Reforming Reformed Epistemology." *International Philosophical Quarterly* 43 (2003) 43–66.

Quarles, Charles. "The Use of the *Gospel of Thomas* in the Research of the Historical Jesus of John Dominic Crossan." *Catholic Biblical Quarterly* 69 (2007) 517–36.

Quinn, Philip. "The Foundations of Theism Again: A Rejoinder to Plantinga." In *Rational Faith: Catholic Responses to Reformed Epistemology*, edited by Linda Zagzebski, 14–47. Notre Dame: University of Notre Dame Press, 1994.

———. "Towards Thinner Theologies: Hick and Alston on Religious Diversity." *International Journal for Philosophy of Religion* (1995) 145–64.

Rowe, William. *Philosophy of Religion: An Introduction*. 4th ed. Belmont, CA: Thomson Wadsworth, 2007.

Rushdoony, Rousas. "The One and Many Problem—the Contribution of Van Til." In *Jerusalem and Athens: Critical Discussions on the Philosophy and Apologetics of Cornelius Van Til*, edited by E. R. Geehan, 339–48. Phillipsburg, NJ: Presbyterian & Reformed, 1980.

Salmon, Wesley. "Problem of Induction." In *The Cambridge Dictionary of Philosophy*, edited by Robert Audi, 745–46. 2nd ed. Cambridge: Cambridge University Press, 1999.

Schellenberg, J. L. "Religious Experience and Religious Diversity: A Reply to Alston." *Religious Studies* 30 (1994) 151–59.

Schlesinger, George. "Miracles and Probabilities." *Nous* 21 (1987) 219–32.

Schreiner, Thomas. *Romans*. Baker Exegetical Commentary on the New Testament. Grand Rapids: Baker, 1998.

Sennett, James F. "Introduction." In *The Analytic Theist: An Alvin Plantinga Reader*, xi–xviii. Grand Rapids: Eerdmans, 1998.

Sobel, J. Howard. "On the Evidence of Testimony for Miracles: A Bayesian Interpretation of David Hume's Analysis." *Philosophical Quarterly* 37 (1987) 166–86.

Sorensen, Roy. "Hume's Scepticism concerning Reports of Miracles." *Analysis* 43 (1983) 60.

Sproul, R. C. *Defending Your Faith: An Introduction to Apologetics*. Wheaton, IL: Crossway, 2003.

Sproul, R. C., John Gerstner, and Arthur Lindsley. *Classical Apologetics: A Rational Defense of the Christian Faith and a Critique of Presuppositional Apologetics*. Grand Rapids: Zondervan, 1984.

Stonehouse, Ned, and Paul Woolley, eds. *The Infallible Word*. Phillipsburg, NJ: Presbyterian & Reformed, 1967.

Strawson, P. F. *Individuals: An Essay in Descriptive Metaphysics*. London: Methuen, 1959.

Strobel, Lee. *The Case for Christ: A Journalist's Personal Investigation of the Evidence for Jesus*. Grand Rapids: Zondervan, 1998.

Sudduth, Michael. "Reformed Epistemology and Christian Apologetics." *Religious Studies* 39 (2003) 299–321.

Swinburne, Richard. *The Concept of Miracle*. London: MacMillan, 1970.

———. "Evidence for the Resurrection." In *The Resurrection*, edited by Stephen T. Davis, Daniel Kendall, and Gerald O'Collins, 191–212. New York: Oxford University Press, 1997.

———. *The Existence of God*. 2nd ed. New York: Oxford University Press, 2004.

———. "Natural Theology, Its 'Dwindling Probabilities' and 'Lack of Rapport.'" *Faith and Philosophy* 21 (2004) 533–46.

———. "Plantinga on Warrant." *Religious Studies* 37 (2001) 203–14.

———. *The Resurrection of God Incarnate*. New York: Oxford University Press, 2003.

———. Review of *Faith and Rationality*, ed. Alvin Plantinga and Nicholas Wolterstorff. *Journal of Philosophy* 82 no. 1 (1985) 46–53.

Tilley, Terrence W. "Religious Pluralism as a Problem for 'Practical' Religious Epistemology." *Religious Studies* 30 (1994) 161–69.

Troeltsch, Ernst. "Historical and Dogmatic Method in Theology." In *Religion in History*, translated by James Adams and Walter Bense, 13–32. Minneapolis: Fortress, 1991.

Tucker, Aviezer. "Miracles, Historical Testimonies, and Probabilities." *History and Theory: Studies in the Philosophy of History* 44 (2005) 373–90.

Turner, David L. "Cornelius Van Til and Romans 1:18–21: A Study in the Epistemology of Presuppositional Apologetics." *Grace Theological Journal* 2, no. 1 (1981) 45–58.

Van Til, Cornelius. *Christian Apologetics*. Edited by William Edgar. 2nd ed. Phillipsburg, NJ: Presbyterian & Reformed, 2003.

———. *Christianity and Idealism*. Philadelphia: Presbyterian & Reformed, 1955.

———. *The Defense of the Faith*. Phillipsburg, NJ: Presbyterian & Reformed, 1955.

———. *An Introduction to Systematic Theology*. Phillipsburg, NJ: Presbyterian & Reformed, 1974.

———. "My Credo." In *Jerusalem and Athens: Critical Discussions on the Philosophy and Apologetics of Cornelius Van Til*, edited by E. R. Geehan, 3–21. Phillipsburg, NJ: Presbyterian & Reformed, 1980.

———. "Response by C. Van Til." In *Jerusalem and Athens: Critical Discussions on the Philosophy and Apologetics of Cornelius Van Til*, edited by E. R. Geehan, 348. Phillipsburg, NJ: Presbyterian & Reformed, 1980.

———. *A Survey of Christian Epistemology*. Philadelphia: Den Dulk Christian Foundation, 1969.

———. "Why I Believe in God." In Bahnsen, *Van Til's Apologetic*, 121–43.

Waltke, Bruce. *An Old Testament Theology: An Exegetical, Canonical, and Thematic Approach*. Grand Rapids: Zondervan, 2007.

White, David. "Can Alston Withstand the Gale?" *International Journal for Philosophy of Religion* 39 (1996) 141–49.

White, James Emery. *What is Truth? A Comparative Study of the Positions of Cornelius Van Til, Francis Schaeffer, Carl F. H. Henry, Donald Bloesch, Millard Erickson*. Nashville: Broadman & Holman, 1994.

Wilkens, John. "A Summit Observed." In *The Resurrection*, edited by Stephen T. Davis, Daniel Kendall, and Gerald O'Collins, 1–4. New York: Oxford University Press, 1997.

Wilkerson, T. E. "Transcendental Arguments." *Philosophical Quarterly* 20 (1970) 200–212.

Willard, Julian. "Plantinga's Epistemology of Religious Belief and the Problem of Religious Diversity." *Heythrop Journal* 44 (2003) 275–93.

Wolterstorff, Nicholas. "Can Belief in God Be Rational If It Has No Foundations?" In *Faith and Rationality: Reason and Belief in God*, edited by Alvin Plantinga and Nicholas Wolterstorff, 135–86. Notre Dame: Notre Dame University Press, 1983.

Bibliography

———. "Epistemology of Religion." In *The Blackwell Guide to Epistemology*, edited by John Greco and Ernest Sosa, 303–24. Oxford: Blackwell, 1999.

———. "The Migration of the Theistic Arguments: From Natural Theology to Evidentialist Apologetics." In *Rationality, Religious Belief, and Moral Commitment: New Essays in the Philosophy of Religion*, edited by Robert Audi and William Wainwright, 38–81. Ithaca, NY: Cornell University Press, 1986.

Wood, W. Jay. *Epistemology: Becoming Intellectually Virtuous*. Downers Grove, IL: InterVarsity, 1998.

———. "The Justification of Doctrinal Beliefs." In *The Logic of Rational Theism: Exploratory Essays*, edited by William Lane Craig and Mark McLeod, 41–63. Lewiston, NY: Edwin Mellen, 1990.

Woods, G. F. "The Evidential Value of the Biblical Miracles." In *Miracles*, edited by C. F. D. Moule, 21–32. London: A. R. Mowbray, 1965.

Wright, N. T. *The Resurrection of the Son of God*. Minneapolis: Fortress, 2003.

Yasukata, Toshimasa. *Ernst Troeltsch: Systematic Theologian of Radical Historicality*. Atlanta: Scholars, 1986.

Zeis, John. "A Critique of Plantinga's Theological Foundationalism." *International Journal for Philosophy of Religion* 28 (1990) 173–89.

Index of Names

Alston, W. P., 87–89, 90–95, 103–4, 106, 111–13, 120–21, 127–28, 129–30, 132
Anderson, J., 139–40
Appleby, P. C., 110, 129, 130
Aquinas, T., 29, 99, 116, 119, 125, 166, 192, 198

Bahnsen, G. L., 136, 138, 146–47, 154, 156, 158, 163–66, 169–71, 172–73, 175–77, 196–97, 200, 204
Baker, B. A., 197
Barth, K., 118, 170
Basinger, D., 55, 57
Bavinck, H., 118
Beck, W. D., 29
Beckwith, F. J., 47, 58, 76
Beilby, J., 118
Bostock, G., 41
Brown, C., 9–10, 47
Brown, H., 116
Brown, R., 79, 80
Brueckner, A. L., 148–49

Callen, B., 5
Calvin, J., 99, 118, 125–26, 162, 192–95
Carnely, P., 17
Carson, D. A., 5, 42, 79–80
Casey, M., 42
Chisholm, R. M., 148

Clark, K. J., 86, 88, 119, 199, 206, 212–13
Coakley, S., 61–62
Collett, D., 157
Collins, C. J., 56
Conee, E., 78
Colwell, J., 124–25
Cook, J. G., 20
Cover, J. A., 54
Cowan, S. B., 4
Craig, W. L., 4, 18, 29, 43, 60, 66–67, 75, 195
Cupitt, D., 45

Davis, S. T., 4, 41
Dawid, P., 58
DeMar, G., 138

Earman, J., 48
Edgar, W., 144, 159
Evans, C. S., 126

Feldman, R., 78, 112
Flew, A., 24, 47, 56, 58
Fogelin, R. J., 48
Forland, T. E., 59
Frame, J. M., 5, 136, 137, 140–41, 143, 146, 148, 152–55, 159, 161–62, 165–66, 170–71, 172–73, 175, 177, 212–13
Fumerton, R., 105, 128

Gale, R., 106, 113, 130

225

Index of Names

Garcia, L. L., 119
Geisler, N. L., 4, 65–66, 67, 69–72, 75
Geivett, R. D., 29
Gerstner, J., 67, 69–71, 75, 78, 79, 174, 198–99
Goetz, S. G., 105
Gowen, J., 104
Gram, M. S., 148
Gregory, B., 59
Grier, J., 174
Grigg, R., 105–7
Grimm, S., 115, 193
Grudem, W., 174

Habermas, G. R., 4, 7, 17, 23–30, 32, 37, 58, 66, 68, 75, 131–32, 170, 179–80, 199, 212
Hackett, S., 162
Halper, E. C., 139
Harrisville, R., 61
Haught, J. F., 59
Helm, P., 126, 193
Hoitenga, D. J., 118
Houlden, L., 41
Houston, J., 50, 55, 58, 66
Howe, L., 46
Hume, D., 40, 47–58, 62, 76, 166, 181, 198, 204

Jackson, W., 53
Jeffreys, D., 194
Johnsen, B., 109–10

Kant, I., 47, 67, 148–49, 198, 210
Koehl, A., 110
Korner, S., 149–50
Kreeft, P., 44
Kretzmann, N., 106
Kuhn, T. S., 12

Lake, K., 60–61
Langtry, B., 84
Le Morvan, P., 131

Lewis, C. S., 53–54, 76
Licona, M. R., 4, 7, 17, 23–30, 37, 68
Lindars, B., 41
Lindsley, A., 67, 69–71, 75, 78, 79, 174, 198–99
Lloyd-Jones, D. M., 195

Mackie, J. L., 51–52, 54–55
Martin, M., 7, 37–52, 108–9, 152–54
Mavrodes, G. I., 47, 53
McDowell, J. D., 75
McGrath, A., 63–64
McGrew, T., 123–24
McLeod, M. S., 104
Meeker, K., 120, 128
Monnier, R., 37
Montgomery, J. W., 4, 5, 37, 67, 69, 71–73, 75–76, 205–6
Moo, D. J., 42, 79–80
Morison, F., 75
Morris, L., 195
Morrison, C., 37
Moule, C. F. D., 45
Muether, J. R., 179
Mulhall, S., 117

Newman, R. C., 53
Nix, W. E., 71
Notaro, T., 160, 169, 170

O'Collins, G., 44
Oliphint, K. S., 193, 194
Overall, C., 39
Owen, D. 48, 55

Pannenberg, W., 11, 18, 27, 41, 46, 61–64
Pargetter, R., 104, 132
Pepper, S. C., 203
Peterson, M., 67
Pinnock, C., 5, 67, 77
Plantinga, A., 84–90, 95–103, 103–5, 107–15, 116–20, 122–24, 125–26, 128–32, 192–95

Index of Names

Polkinghorne, J. C., 57
Pritchard, D., 113

Quarles, C. L., 41
Quinn, P. L., 113, 131

Radcliffe, D., 131
Rowe, W. L., 29, 67
Rushdoony, R. J., 139

Salmon, W. C., 181
Schellenberg, J. L., 112
Schlesinger, G. N., 40, 57
Schreiner, T., 195
Sennett, J. F., 128, 132
Sobel, J. H., 76
Sorensen, R. A., 51
Sproul, R. C., 4, 65, 67, 69–71, 75, 78–79, 174, 198–99
Stonehouse, N., 5, 171
Strawson, P. F., 150
Strobel, L., 75
Sudduth, M., 120, 128–29, 132
Sundberg, W., 61
Swinburne, R., 7, 8–23, 24, 25, 27, 37, 39–40, 54, 56, 59, 65, 67, 68, 75, 122, 124, 128, 130

Tilley, T. W., 113
Tipton, L. G., 194
Tooley, M., 96, 131
Troeltsch, E., 61–64
Tucker, A., 46
Turner, D. L., 196

Van Til, C., 135–39, 142–46, 151, 155–58, 160–63, 164, 168–71, 172, 175–76, 179–80, 195–96, 200–201, 212

Waltke, B. K., 81
White, D., 130
White, J. E., 172
Wilkens, J., 20
Wilkerson, T. E., 148
Willard, J., 112, 195
Wolterstorff, N., 84–86, 88, 96, 109, 117, 118, 132
Wood, W. J., 85, 126–27
Woodbridge, J., 5
Woods, G. F., 57
Woolley, P., 5
Wright, N. T., 4, 7, 17, 18, 28, 31–37, 41, 45, 58, 68, 75

Yasukata, T., 61

Zeis, J., 105

www.ingramcontent.com/pod-product-compliance
Lightning Source LLC
Chambersburg PA
CBHW062021220426
43662CB00010B/1416